The R-

& Her Brilliant Adventures

Lucy Mason Jensen

Copyright © 2022 by Lucy Mason Jensen

All rights reserved.

THANKS!

To everyone who helped me put this together. To my family who tolerated what may have seen like never-ending writing bolts to the coast, to my friends who sent me quotes and memories and to everyone who loved Rosie and wanted to be a part of this book. I think she'd like it a lot, laugh like hell and immediately forgive all the imperfections along the way.

Lu

Table of Contents

SECTION 1 – SOMEWHERE AFTER THE BEGINNING 1
- The Very Beginning 2
- My Plaster Parcel - By Dad 8
- Introduction to 'Sometimes there is no more' 12
- Sometimes There Is No More 14
- August 19, 1991 19
- Introduction to the death of snail mail 21
- Email Chitter-Chatter From About 1999 to Around 2006 22

SECTION 2 – SOMEHOW ALL ABOUT ME FOR A WHILE ...100
- Introduction to Somehow 101
- it's now all about me ...(for a short while) 101
- Someone else's story...103
- The Bitter Sweets of Living... 112
- Holding your own hands 115
- Light through the luminaria 119
- Fall 2014 119

SECTION 3 – SOMEWHERE AROUND THE MIDDLE 124
- Introduction to 'Somewhere around the middle' 125
- It is what it is 128
- Chemo Is Good For Curls 133
- My wonderful vacation..137
- Making deals with the universe 141
- The snapshots of summer 144
- And the World stops again – a 2014 conversation............149

Postscript to My Plaster Parcel 153
Bud-isms 2016 155

SECTION 4 – THE SUMMER OF IBRANCE 157
Introduction to The Summer of Ibrance 158
Intro to The Lazy Blogger 160
A snapshot of the Lazy Blogger 163

SECTION 5 – SOMEWHERE TOWARDS THE END 243
Framing Moments 244
Framing more Moments 246
The heart project 271
Happy Dust – The Last Goodbyes 275
It does not define her 278
The end of Ramadan 280
The Last Gifts 282

SECTION 6 – AFTER THE END 309
The Grief Study 310
Messenger from another realm 313
Letter through the ether 317
Day 55 322
The Rosie Day 324
3 months on – a letter through the ether 326
Carpe the diem 328
Cleaning is good for grief 330
2018 Get the tattoo 332
A letter through the ether 335
A New Year 2018-2019 336
Magic 340
The spirits of Rosie and Winston 343

v

SECTION 7 – WELL AFTER THE END 346

- Celebrating The Bud's birthday 347
- Enjoy the Journey 349
- Everybody Grieves 353
- I shall not pass this way again 356
- Sisters 359
- The Fabrics of Memory 362
- My Water Song 365
- WORDS OF SADNESS, MEMORY, GRIEF, LOVE AND SOLACE 367

ABOUT THE AUTHOR

LUCY MASON JENSEN was born in Aldeburgh, Suffolk, England in 1963. She moved to the US in 1988 and to California in 1991. She worked at the 'Salinas Californian' from 1991-2003 and it was there that she began to write regular columns for the paper.

Her work has appeared in various California newspapers and magazines since 2003. Several of her stories from the South County Newspapers and the Salinas Valley Tribune appear in this book.

She is the author of *Window on the World, Winston Comes Home* and *the Animals Teach Us Everything & Other Short Tails*.

Lucy is the co-founder of South County Animal Rescue (SCAR) and remains passionate about animals and animal rescue. She lives with her family of rescues in the Gabilans of Soledad - including, to date, llamas, dogs, cats, chickens, turtles, birds, a pig, a goat and a horse.

Foreword

From Mary -

Lucy asked me months ago to write a foreword for this book about our sister, Rosie.

Who would have thought it would be so difficult to write about Rosie, who certainly was never short of something to say. However, what is so difficult is to write about what she meant to me as my little sister who ultimately I could not protect at her death.

How do you write about never seeing Rosie again, except in dreams, never hearing her speak, or say 'Hey Moo...', except perhaps a faded voice in dreams. I felt something explode out of me and leave me forever the last time I saw her, and that empty space remains.

But yet, when I first dreamt of her after she died, we are by water: she is lying in a rock pool, she turns her head to the side and smiles sadly at me. When I swim in the sea, when I turn my head from out of the water to breathe, when I look across the sea towards the horizon, I see a pair of birds skimming low across the water. I breathe in, and in that moment of absolute peace and solitude, Rosie returns to me, as we promised each other, my sister, forever part of me.

Grief and feelings of loss come and go as the tide, never fully receding, yet in those moments there is beauty, memories of pure joy, of Rosie, always with me. And so grief, intensely personal and also so unifying, affirms life. Live your own life well, Rosie did and this book is all about her.

Rosie 16.01.1970 – 25.07.2018
Teach us to care and not to care
Teach us to sit still

SECTION 1
SOMEWHERE AFTER THE BEGINNING

The Very Beginning

Mary, Mum, Bud and me in Bures

The first time I met my youngest sister was in my parents' bedroom after Dad had bought Mum and baby home from the Colchester hospital to our country home in Bures. Mum handed her to me – a large woolly, screaming bundle. I was allowed to hold her on the bed, as long as I kept her neck up. She was dark and long, skinny with a beaky nose. Rumor has it that Dad asked Mum if she was 'alright' the first time he saw her. I thought she looked like a little rat; but I loved her anyway. I sometimes called her 'Spuggly' to rhyme with Ugly or 'Baby Spuglet'; but her esteem was always enormous, so it mattered not. To many she was simply 'Bud' or 'Rosebud'. She even had a boat named after her.

Growing up she was a sickly thing. Born with a congenital hip that required two surgeries in a row when she was less than 2-years old and several procedures of being in traction, plaster et al. Sure enough, this 'plaster parcel,' as dad called her on more than one occasion, required extra special attention – or, if she didn't get enough, she would demand it. I recall so clearly her shrill voice shrieking in the middle of the night that, if someone – Mum or Dad – did not come and get her and put her in their bed, then she would fall out of her own. It worked like a charm, every time, and we never got the brother I craved. Funny that.

Mum and Dad in Baytree House, Bures with our younger, bratty sister, the Bud

From there, she went from strength to strength. Her early morning fights with our mother were legendary – a lot of swearing and very loud voices, sometimes enhanced by the odd projectile. Her

The Bud at Iken. Very determined, even then.

reputation of having a voice that could cut glass preceded her. One dinner, I also recall Mother plonking a bowl of ice-cream on her head. My other sister Mary and I would make ourselves very scarce during these battles. We would not ever dare go there. Then there was the time the young one came home drunk. She was all of 12 or 13. Mother was trying to sober her up with coffee, hissing at her not to make a noise and wake up her father; but she didn't care. She never cared. She would definitely have been expelled from the school at Sarum Hall in London, except that her older sister was the head girl and that, likely, saved her bacon. But she wouldn't have cared either way. Nowadays, she might have been diagnosed with attention deficit disorder or something of that ilk; she was so easily bored and constantly looking for the next sensation. And that lasted through her life. Looking back, she was just like her mother.

Lucy, Mary and Rosie in Aldeburgh

 These were some of the incidents from the early days and regardless of father's best efforts to have her 'cool it', she never really did. She ran to her own beat and created her own vibrant life, wherever she went. She was always after the quality of life, never expecting the quantity, even in the early days. As her older sister, I was horrified by her in her younger years; then terrified for her and those around her during teen-dom — and then, as time went by, the younger-older lines faded and we just became good mates and solid sisters, coaching each other along through life.

 I shall always cherish the 48 years of the life of Bud I got to witness and share. Here are some of her stories — the funny, the sad and the in between. Though the timelines of 'after the beginning' ...'towards the end' etc. exercise a certain amount of artistic liberty, I think Rosie herself would have enjoyed the looseness of time in the structure, since time was never that important to her in a structured format; as long as the time spent was about having fun and finding the joy, no matter what. Over a few short years, we weathered together the death of our mother, our shared cancer experience, her own cancer battle that went on for practically decades and finally her long goodbyes to the planet she resided on. Not surprisingly, she consistently defied the odds. So much so she would laugh that she was a big old cancer faker, because everyone kept expecting her to die when she wasn't quite ready. We were always having our last visit, our last dinner, our last holiday together.

I hope you will find this not a sad story of sorrow and loss, but more of a journey in grief, an expedition in seeking the joy every day, just as Rosie did. It's an effort to make some sense of the fleeting nature of our time on this planet earth and how we would most want to be remembered. Rosie was a popular and gregarious spirit, wherever she went; so I chose to include many voices in her story and lots of photos of loved ones. I shall always remember her with so much love; as do many, many others.

Rosie Emma Alexandra Mason Arican was born on January 16, 1970, in Colchester, England. She died exactly how she wanted and precisely where she wanted to be in Indircik, Turkey on July 25, 2018, surrounded by her beloveds - husband, Ali and daughter of her heart, Dilgesu - in their home in the mountains of Turkey she loved so much.

I am, as she would fondly call me, her 'big sis' and these are the patchworked pieces of her story.

The Rose Bud & Her Brilliant Adventures

My Plaster Parcel - By Dad

I took this photo of Rosie in the Church Hall at Aldeburgh during the wedding party of Marianne, our baby sitter, one of Mr. Carey's the butcher's daughters. And my story begins some months later when nervously carrying Rosie encased in plaster downstairs at Bures I first called her "my plaster parcel". She was by now perhaps nearly two-years old, but only recently found to have been born with a congenital dislocated hip. A defect that should have been spotted at birth when a double layer of nappies to hold the thighs apart is all that would have been required. Instead, Rosie had to have more than one operation to build her hip, followed by months in what is known as a Frog Plaster encasing her from waist to below her knees where a rod held them firmly apart, like in a frog position as though doing a breast stroke. She, for all this time, had to be on her stomach, unable to stand or walk. The plaster had suitable orifices.

Had Una not noticed Rosie was late walking and then with only a slight limp, things could have only got worse. She instead took her to see the village GP who dismissed Una's worry saying, "She's imitating her father's limp". Rosie probably even then was such a strong character can you imagine her imitating anyone? Una, not one easily to be fobbed off by a careless suggestion, consulted the district nurse who immediately diagnosed a dislocated hip.

(A brief digression: many years later Una had a similar experience with our GP in London who did nothing when she consulted him about a lump in her breast. This led to several vital months being lost before breast cancer was diagnosed.)

Although Rosie had months, possibly a year, of living horizontally, I can recall only once sheer anger and frustration at her situation really breaking through. This was after the first operation when she chucked a toy at us as we left, and howled on finding herself trapped in plaster on a bed in hospital.

It was summer by the time Una brought Rosie home from hospital in the back of her car. This little car, being a Mini Traveler that opened at the back with double doors like a shooting break, was in fact perfect for the job of safely transporting a precious fragile, and awkwardly shaped parcel.

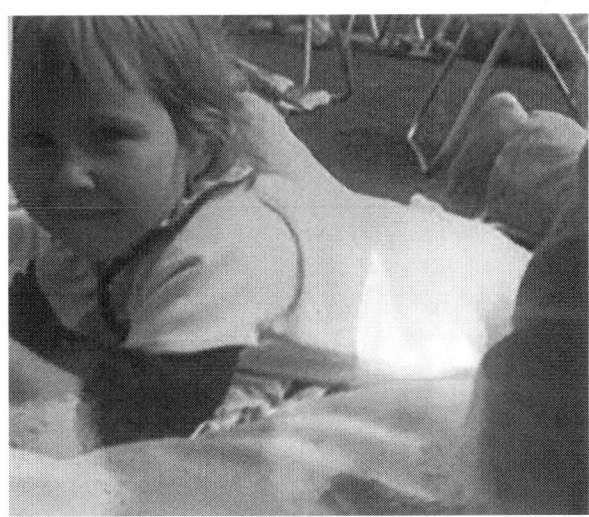

Bures

Rather than spend the summer at Bures the family went to Aldeburgh where we more easily could get out and about to be with friends — altogether a more lively and diverting scene for everyone, even for Rosie in her "Chariot".

"Discontent in Chariot", Una wrote
(Mary looks quizzical)

Rosie remained encased for a long time, going back to hospital several times for further operations, then emerging with a new plaster. Eventually, a degree of freedom began when she could stand upright for the first time and was "my plaster parcel" no longer.

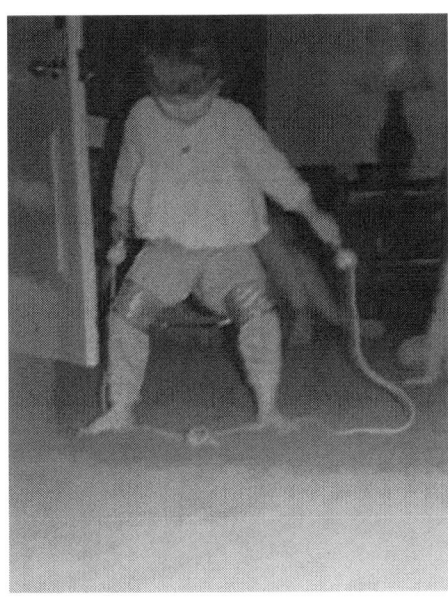

Even now she had to be carried up and down stairs. Several more years followed and we had moved to London before Rosie was totally free. This picture says it all.

Dad

Introduction to 'Sometimes there is no more' ...

As mentioned before, this patchwork quilt of our lives was sewn together by many strands, many colors and memories from over the years. Our family's adventures with cancer have been imperfectly pieced together from one point of view – my own- never discounting the voice of my sister Rosie from her blog and other places. Our mother Una would be the first one to say how imperfect she was, what a lazy brat and such a witch. All true. But she was also funny, spirited, talented, intelligent and charismatic. This is not really her story. However, I'm going to share an insight into her last days on the planet, as it fits into the puzzle that is our family rather appropriately.

This portion of the story begins as I am headed home from America to England to be with our mother before she dies from cancer (also osteoporosis, but that is a whole other subject). Yet, the thread between us, not just as members of the same family, branches of the same tree, is that Mother, Rosie and I all had breast cancer. Mother's cancer spread from the breast to the bone. Rosie being Rosie had to top that and have it, ultimately, all over her body. Since I was fortunate enough to have gained the wisdom in hindsight from my mother and my sister, I opted for a radical double mastectomy when I was diagnosed and have, thus far, managed to keep the cancer at bay; not something I take for granted.

This is a true story of a journey with cancer; but not just cancer; an illustration of how to live life with or without cancer. A quest to find the joy and sap every pleasurable sip out of your waking moments just like Rosie did.

where others bemoan their lot and say, 'why me?' when life stuff happens; Rosie would always say 'And why not me?"

I have touched on my own small journey into the cancer world, not to try and one-up Rosie's enormous adventure in any way; but to show how disease can color a family and, if you let it, take prisoners, suppress the joy. Our family elected to accept our lot and try to keep on keeping on; resolving to repair the fractures of each loss and carry on with life and living. Every family has something; our family happens to have cancer. Although we are all mindful of the disease and the distinct possibility that it might visit our family again, we are not defined by it. Nor do we dwell on everything that might happen and when. Live as if you are dying, which, of course, we all are.

November 2000-A race against time.
(Mum's last few days)

Sometimes There Is No More

I had already traveled back and forth across the width of the country and the Atlantic Ocean four times that year. I had become such a frequent flyer I didn't even get jet lag anymore. I could whoosh through the time zones like Superwoman, and it didn't faze me one bit. This specific trip I knew, innately, that if there were a Supersonic Concorde flight from San Francisco to London, I should be on it – there was no time to lose. The heavy tick tock of that grandmother clock in the hallway of her home was on countdown. The few days leading up to my departure from America were agony, the hours slow and weighty, crushing my shoulders with their somber load-like luggage I couldn't ever carry. Time was not my friend on this occasion. The hours were evaporating towards a finale of the inevitable end, leaving me riddled with anxiety. I had to get there in time. It was early November 2000, and it was to become quite the most memorable week of my life.

    Mothers and daughters – they are quite something, aren't they. At birth, you are attached. Her body developed my body and all of that becomes quite astounding later in life when you understand the biology behind it. We were born of the same skin. She carried my heart inside of her heart, literally and otherwise; to the point that we could often know what the other was thinking from continents away.

    From birth to around 3, my Mum was the best thing in the whole world; my all, my sanctuary, my life. I cannot imagine, during those early years, trying to function without Mum on any level and I never had to. I have warm memories of climbing into bed beside her, in the middle of the night, when I'd had a bad dream or heard a little noise; or maybe I just wanted to feel the security of her warm body next to mine. She always let me.

    At about 3, when I had really found my voice and often loud opinions to go along with the vocal cords, I would challenge my Mum, while still knowing she was ultimately the boss of me. She might have put me on a little time out when I'd really crossed the line – like the time I hid in the airing cupboard, listening to her not be able to find me in the house, or the time I raced my go-kart out into the street in front of the oncoming car; but the bad feelings didn't last long and soon I was back in cuddle mode again and feeling myself bathe in that sea of calm security once more. It is a mutual adoration society at that age and there's nothing like it.

At about 10 years old, it's sometimes I love you and sometimes I don't – funny how that happens. Sometimes you are annoying. You make up silly rules, you try to make me tidy my room, wash my hair, clean up my mess, but you still treat me like a baby as well. I get very confused about my feelings for you a lot of the time, because, when you are not around, I miss you and I look for you, if only casually in case someone were looking. When you are here, you make me clench up my fists and grind my teeth – a lot. At around thirteen, you are even more annoying. Don't come near me, don't even think about trying to read me a story at night, and would you please stay out of my room, if it's not too much to ask? I would like you to come and watch me play sports though, even if you are annoying, and can my friend come and sleep over after? She likes my home better than hers. Yes, you do need to go and pick her up, then take her home the next day. "What? Oh yeh! Thanks, Mum!"

At about fifteen, I can't wait to leave home and get away from you annoying people. Could anyone be more annoying? Why do I have to sit and eat with you people – you make such terrible, disgusting noises? What is the deal about *"how was my day and how was school?"* Who really cares? I certainly do not. Why can't we sit in silence with our food in front of the TV, like normal people?

Sixteen and I can almost taste how cool it would be to have my own place. My own front door, my own key to lock and unlock as much as I want to; it has to be just around the corner in my destiny. And trust me; you are never going to walk through that door, unless I ask you to watch the dog or something. I will visit with my friends and watch scary movies turned up really loud until super late. We'll have crazy parties and the freedom I'll feel will be out of this world.

I'm 21 and now I have my own small studio and my own front door and key, finally! I hate to say it, but it's not as great as I thought it was going to be. Strange that. I never knew how much you have to pay to just keep the lights on – that stuff is crazy! Food costs a lot too, and especially if you are lazy like me and just want to eat out and not have to do dishes. It's rough having to use the Laundromat also, because I can't afford the washer and dryer yet for my place. I'd ask you to let me use yours, but then I'd have to answer all those stupid, annoying questions again, and I'm not ready for that. Maybe I can let a pair of jeans last two days now I have my own place. I didn't realize how cool it was having your own washer, like when I lived at home. No one picks up after me at my place. If everything is torn up, it just stays that way. Not sure if that is cool or not – lol!

My child is going to be born soon and all I want is my Mum right there. I am afraid, I am young again; I can't believe I managed all those years without her right by my side. Come to think of it, I didn't manage so well, if I'm really honest; but she was always right there close by, watching me grow up and out as I should. I did not thrive exactly, but I got through it. She was always there if I really needed her and if I let her be there. She was there when I had my baby and I had so many questions for her; it was just as if I had been reborn myself.

Now I am 37 and racing to get home from across the world and be at my mother's side. I know it is nearing the end of her life and I'm terrified for all of us. I have never felt like such a child in all my living memory. We are always too young to lose our mother. My mother is dying. She is fragile and tender, like a child herself. She can't hold herself up. She is physically fading and mentally shutting down from the world outside. I hold her up and the roles are reversed; just as she held me up for all those years before.

She leaves me and I find myself still expecting more from her; another visit, another talk, another call on the phone; even arising from the dead would be acceptable at this point. There is the life before this loss and the life after, with a seismic chasm in between, when I thought I might be dying myself, or at least drowning in my own tears.

Eventually, as you cascade through your grieving period and almost out the other side — you never really get there, do you - you come to realize that, sometimes, there simply isn't any more. Sometimes, life stops, and you have to accept the fact that you have had everything you are going to get. There is no use regretting the years she annoyed you so much you could spit and the times you avoided her, the times you didn't travel to Italy or Greece with her, though you were invited and you chose to hang out with your friends at home instead, the times you should have made the time to go and visit and spend a little more time together, not knowing that time is a cruel and measured entity. All those things you didn't do. What you had just has to be enough. There will be no more.

In the afterlife, if you are very lucky and open to the idea, you will get a glimpse of her free spirit once in a while, on the wind or in the body of something beautiful before your very eyes. Sometimes a whoosh will go through you in the form of mother or, perhaps, just Mother Time herself. You will be reminded of all you had in that large, immeasurable package over the years, and you'll be so glad you let regret fly away on the breeze when you did, just as your daughter will need to do for you and, most likely, her daughter thereafter.

Our mother Una Bagnall Theodora Benedicta Mason died on November 9, 2000 at 9am. Time was kind enough to let me be with her at her end, no matter what came before, and this will always be one of my most cherished memories.

Rosie, Mum and Mary

And now you've had the flavor of our family and the short story version of the end of our Mum's life, it's back to the Bud. It was always back to the Bud - a family joke that has never faded with time.

Also, the dawn of a wonderful new form of communication called EMAIL!

August 19, 1991

Darling Lucia,

We are now into our final week here at Camp America and the counselors are exhausted! I'm sitting down by the waterfront to get some peace.

I don't envy you being there at home, but soon you will be back over here, and I'm determined to see you. I told dad that, at some stage, I would probably leave the others and either fly or Greyhound from wherever to see you and he had kinda an eppy (?) I shall be pretty sad to leave here, but Jac, Simon, Brad and I are getting really excited about our trip - being free, cruising around at a gentle pace. Our only deadline is being back in NY on October 3. I'll give dad an approx. route of our trip and dates, but obviously we won't stick to it. Charl drove up here for Saturday night - she looks brilliant, still cuddly and radiant, very much in love. She's going off to work for 9 months in Colorado - I think on a ski resort - also she's pretty excited. Plans have already changed. I'm going to go with Simon and stay with a friend from camp at his home in Woodstock for a few days, then go with Sims to New York.

The future seems quite exciting, one year at college and then hopefully take off for a few years. I think I'm becoming a bit of a hippy - my hair's getting really long and have taken to tie-dying sheets, wearing braided bracelets and god knows what. It's all a bit worrying. We are so waiting to leave on our great adventure. We have a road trip motto 'What a Burger or Bust Tour'. Apparently, 'What a Burger' is a southern chain and by the time we leave, we have to have tried one - probably in Texas, if we make it that far!

Anyway, my darling. I shall keep in close contact with you, so I know when you will be where.

All my love, miss you lots.
Baby Spuglet
xx

Introduction to the death of snail mail

There was the classic time when we still relied on land lines, as they are archaically called. My sister Rosie was working at Camp America on the East Coast of the US. 1991, I had just arrived in Monterey, California where we planned to settle after traveling cross country from Louisiana, having collected our dog and car and a few possessions from our former home there. This was pre-mobile phones in our world. We used our father in London as our base camp for communications in order to be able to meet up at a specific time and place. (I can only imagine his phone bill during this time, since it is likely we both called collect, or reversed the charges, as they say in England!) Rosie and I ultimately managed to meet up in Monterey and there is photographic evidence to prove it. We were both surprised and delighted by the maneuver. Things moved swiftly forward from there to the dawn of mobile phones for all and email and instant everythings in the world.

    In my collection, somehow, I still have dusty envelopes with time stamps on the outside and wonderfully preserved letters folded within from a different time. I also have copies of emails I, for some reason printed out and kept, and then of course, the gaps in-between when I wasn't able to collect anything. That is why this is a patchwork quilt of a memoir and I know Rosie would completely understand. She and I were travelers and wanderers in life and to think that we were able to copy any communications and preserve them for posterity is a little bit amazing. I thank everyone who helped fill in some gaps and make the memoir a little less patchy.

    You might notice that all Rosie's men in the story are called Ali – just seemed easier that way. Of course, the final Ali, her Ali, the real Ali, her beloved husband was the only one that really counted in the end.

    The following dialogues from those times date from around 1999 to about 2006.

Email chitter-chatter
From About 1999 to Around 2006

Subj: Re: Lust, fondness ...
Date: 11/11/1999
From Rorabud
To: Lumajen

Dearest Lucia,

Lovely morning call, so much better than alarm clock. Lots of mail to reply to before I go swimming! I like to be there waiting with the nun and the very fat lady to nab my pool lane.

Did you not realize, this is much more than summer love? I have no idea where we go from here, and we do not ask each other or discuss it, but this is really just the beginning of something, not the end. He is the first man I have met in 5 years who I could really contemplate having a relationship with, obviously this is complicated by the fact that he lives in Turkey and I live in London, but really I do not crave a full time man on my sofa sharing domestic bliss with. Ali is the only man I have come across who feels the same way, who believes that you can smother things very quickly, get stale, dull, routine. I always said if Sacha and I could have afforded it, there was no way we would have lived together.

Ali understands me very well, he's got a brain the like of which I have never come across before ... funny, kind, generous, serious, stressed, loving ... get the picture?

Love,
R

The Rose Bud & Her Brilliant Adventures

Subj: Re: Sunday and time to clean
Date: 1/8/2000
From: Rorabud
To: lumajen

Dearest Lucia,

Wow, you are right, it has been quite a week and I think the next few will be also equally interesting, the process of selling the flat begins next week. Demand outstrips supply in this area and flats are being sold as soon as they go on the market. I am hoping I am going to be able to cash in big time on this and sell it in no time at all, that is the plan anyways, so I must clean it!

I am having a fairly low-key celebration of my 30th birthday. It was going to be at the Turkish restaurant in Church Street, but right next door is a fab place which serves Thai and downstairs there is a jazz club, so I think that will be a bit more lively....

Bud, Lu and Charl

Loved to party ...

Subj: CALL HIM!
Date: 1/9/2000
From: lumajen
To: rorabud

Now that was quite a chat, wasn't it. Sod the email thing, call him! You have his cell number, you know he cares about you, don't play mind games, give him a ring. If nothing else, it will change the sick feeling you have in your tummy to one of butterflies. If he says 'Rosie, who?' at least you will know!

It will become clear what you need to do with your life situation, just don't make any impulsive choices. One thing I try to do, now I'm a tad more 'mature', is not to allow overnight whims to become plans. Only if they grow over the course of time, do I believe they are perhaps good choices and could become real. But, in some respects, you still need to 'carpe diem'. That's all I'm going to say about that. Call him.

All love,
Lucia

Subj: Re: Thanks for the message
Date: 1/9/2000
From: rorabud
To: lumajen

Dearest Lucia,

Say a big thanks to FrouFrou for the message and of course to you. I couldn't quite decipher what she said, but the sentiment was there! Have just had the ever-faithful Morts over for a bowl of my very good soup, lentil tonight with a hint of chili. She gave me the same pep talk you did. "Just call him!" and after a few glasses of wine and loads of fags, I did. He seemed very pleased to hear from me, his life sounds hectic, but he mentioned unprompted the possibility of him coming over here for a while. I don't think it will be for several months, but it would be wonderful for him to get a taste of London life and see how I live here. Just hope he gets to see it before I am back at Eton Ave. That would be strange. Rosie, 40-year old boyfriend and parents! Things are moving on apace, the only thing left undone now is to talk to the European MA course organizer and then make the decision.

Looking at it, the flat should sell in no time. I may find myself at Eton Ave before I really know what has hit me!

Time for bed. I feel exhausted, too much stuff whizzing round in the brain, time to put it to sleep.

Bud xx

Subj: Re: Resigned
Date: 1/10/2000
From: rorabud
To: lumajen

Dearest Lucia,

Your Monday does not sound like a thing of beauty and neither was mine. Excellent levels of abuse and violence throughout the day. So, the deed is done, they know I am going and now we have to figure out when best to tell the staff! I am feeling very upbeat about things, the agents told me my flat could probably sell at the 140K mark, which means I will have made about 150€ over the last 5 years! In the light of the huge amount of money I could get I may buy a studio flat with no mortgage, as that's a good place to put my money.

So now I am beginning to turn my mind to where and what I will do come April. I think I'd like to do some aimless traveling, walking is a growing idea. I want to be outside and go where it will be warm. Turkey fits the bill and I think Ali could do a little aimless stuff himself. Once it gets hot, I will install myself by the beach and stay there until the boredom sets in. The MA doesn't start til October so roll on long, long indulgent break! Bloody fantastic!

Love,
Bud
xx

Subj: RE: NO MORNING MAIL!
Date: 1/11/2000
From: rorabud
To: lumajen

Dearest Lucia,

You must be mightily busy to miss our night/morning mail thang! Tuesday was a breeze. It's my afternoon to make home visits for the school. One of the lil buggers I went to see was so uncooperative that I left after 30 mins and found myself free at 2.30, decided not to go back to work. I bought the papers, did the snooze thing and waited for the agent to come by. Had a great night with Charl, we did the mid-week bottle and half of wine, talking men, life, money-making schemes ...

Forever friends - bud, Mo, Lu Lo, Charl

I think there is a real 20/30 something crisis going on with all my lot. Almost everyone seems to be in some state of potential radical change. It's quite reassuring that I am simply doing what so many other people want to do. I had the idea of approaching all the weekend papers to see if they would like an anti-lifestyle, lifestyle column. I thought teacher jacking all in, selling flat, travelling, bit of working and return as a student could be quite entertaining, esp peppered up with tales of drunkenness and debauchery. Wouldn't you want to read something like that over your coffee on the weekend? Charl, in her state of drunkenness, last night told me of the Ali plan you two had been cooking up. It would have been bloody amazing if he had popped up! Perhaps, however, it has sewed the seed and he will surprise me some other time!

Hope all is well.

Love,
Bud

Subj: Re: Blisssssssssssssssssssss
Date: 2/27/2000
From: rorabud
To: lumajen

Dearest Lucia,

We just got back to London and I took him to the airport by way of Selfridges for a quick shop. We had an amazing time, going to Aldeburgh was the perfect thing to do. We had peace, space and just a few interruptions. We were the perfect holiday companions for each other. I introduced him to the delights of Suffolk cider and Adnams Ale. We went to Snape, Iken, Orford, Southwold. I didn't mention the fact that I have a job in Istanbul confirmed, but I am excited by the possibility of living in a crazy half-European/half-Asian city for a year anyway. I will probably go out there at the end of this term. What can I say, I have a big smile on my face! The meeting with the parentals was good, they were both well-behaved, Mum was typical "I saw a horrible film about Istanbul .. I never want to go there!" Ali simply told her not to believe everything you see in the movies. I think, on the brief meeting, they thought he was an interesting man, you know he is 40 and grey, with a buddha style belly, so he is not the usual sort of man I take home, but I had told them that in advance!

Have accepted an offer on the flat and now can plan Romania properly. Things are exciting, who knows where it will all end!
Lots of love,
Bud

Subj: Re: To live with or not to live with
Date: 2/28/2000
From: rorabud
To: lumajen

Dearest Lucia,

I think the not wanting to live with business stems from years ago. When Sacha and I came back from France, the only reason why we lived with each other was because we couldn't afford to live apart. I think the idea of being with someone and seeing them when you choose sounds like heaven. I am basically your classic commitment phobe, so even considering living in the same city as a man is a big breakthrough. This all seems a little premature. The school is in the Asian side of the city - it's right down by the edge of the sea, fantastic!

Ali, wonderful Man, rang me last night to ask me how would he manage without me. And I think to check that I would be sleeping alone! He arrived back to chaos, things wrong at work, mobile stolen ... welcome to Turkey! It's still very much a developing country.

Love V. HAPPY

Rosie
xx

Youngish Bud

Subj: Re: WHEN DO YOU TELL HIM?
Date: 2/29/2000
From: lumajen
To: rorabud

So, how long are you going to wait to tell him that you are going to be working in Istanbul? Does he still have a flat there? It will be most interesting to see how the 'living apart' thing works out for you. What about the MA? Forgive all my questions and nosiness; you see, I used to be the bohemian one. Now I'm married with 3 kids, I've been in the same job for 9 years ... but somewhere inside me, the bohemian thing lives on, so I'm going to have to exercise it precariously through my baby swuss .... Okay, so he misses you. Good! Happy days, my lil love bird.

L

xx

Subj: Re: Great Curry
Date: 3/8/2000
From: rorabud
To: lumajen

Dearest Lucia,

Flat is definite! The survey is being done on Friday! Goody, goody, will soon be free. Had great dins with the parentals, they are on good form. Mum is more upbeat and dad very chirpy about the publication going on. I told them I'm deferring the MA and will be spending the next year in Turkey, so in light of that I may rethink some of my summer travel plans. I really fancy doing some inter-railing for a month. Places to go, see, do!

Love always,

Bud

♡

Subj: Re: Friday, yippy!
Date: 3/9/2000
From: rorabud
To: lumajen

I am really looking forward to weekend of fun and frollicks with the girls! Don't drink too much is like saying don't eat chocolate, somethings just have to be done. By 7 tonight should be in glam hotel bar supping some good Chardonnay and smoking and generally unwinding big style.

Dad is a little concerned that some of his girls seem to be attracted to earthquake zones. What is it, do we really want to know that badly when the earth moves? Had mail from Ali, they have had a couple of small ones in the past few days, and they are thinking the big one is on it's waaay! Best not to dwell on such. Mail Sunday night.

Love,

Bud

x

PS I am optimistic that I will be heading off in May for a couple of months. Now that I will be doing a job in September, I am in favour of cruising around Turkey, Syria, then Northern Cypress and back through Greece, Italy ... in time for charl's 30th and then back to Turkey end July for a month lying on the beach in Adrasan. God, it sounds bloody marvelous. For now, all dreams, but damned good ones! R

Subj: Re: Body overhaul
Date: 3/14/2000
From: rorabud
To: lumajen

Dearest Lucia,

You are not wrong! The whole body overhaul thing will be done! Does this mean your gums are playing up again, what a bugger!

Being a part-timer now, have made plan for me and Lucy L in Islington for a bottle of wine and late lunch tomorrow at 4.30. Doesn't that sound damn civilized?

Ali is becoming a fantastically moochy mailer and regular caller! Haven't told him still what I am up to, and I am becoming a little stressed by that. He is meant to be a friend; someone I care about and yet he's the only one I have not told! I create my own problems, as someone said last night. He is not you and just because you would run a mile if he said he was coming to live in London, it's unlikely he will react in the same way.

Had top night last night with all and sundry dropping in at various points.

Bud
x

Subj: Re: Wonderful weekend
Date: 3/15/2000
From: rorabud
To: lumajen

Dearest Lucia,

Am I right in thinking you and Mike will have a wild night to yourselves? Do the dinner, movie, stroll, home thing or what? How bloody wonderful. You must hang out for moments like those and really anticipate them with such pleasure.

You are all so right about the telling of Ali about the whole Istanbul thing. He is so overwhelmingly positive about me coming over in the spring, I find it hard to believe he won't be equally pleased with the rest of my plans. He refers to me as his 'life partner,' so I don't think he is dabbling and I know I am not. Think of me today with Lucy L, bottle of wine, cigs and gossip at 4.30. We certainly don't have the sun, but it will do!

Love,
R

Subj: Re: BLT with mayo
Date: 3/22/2000
From: rorabud
To: lumajen

Dearest Lucia,

Think candle is being burnt too readily at both ends. Struggling up this morning, starving hungry, haven't eaten since yesterday lunch, car is still parked outside pub in Islington and Penny (The Head Teacher) is still comatose in my bed. Bit of a night. Sometimes it just happens against everyone's better judgement. Priority is to track down some food, have none in the flat. Am drinking sweet tea; always worrying.

I will tell Ali soon. Feel much more relaxed about telling him now for some reason. Just happy for me anyway. Generally enjoying life, ballet and dins with girls tonight, tomorrow dins with Myrt. All wonderful stuff. I know now it won't stop until I leave, so I am just going to enjoy it.

Bud xx

Subj: Re: Morning
Date: 3/29/2000
From: rorabud
To: lumajen

Dearest Lucia,

For some reason, I am having soup for breakfast. It must be so hard for you to be so far away when things like this happen. They are in such good hands. Parbou, the nurses, good GP - it could not be better. Who knows at this stage what they will find, but the knowing is better than not knowing! This will also help dad to plan properly for the future. For a long time, he has toyed with the notion of selling the house - now he will be able to take a clearer view as to what will be best.

R
xx

Sub: Sister Mail
Date: 4/27/2000
From: rorabud
To: lumajen

Dearest Lucia,

Ali will be back in Istanbul by the time I arrive, which is a shame, but he will be back down in a few weeks. Anyway, it's my chosen place to be right now, relaxing and among friends, so it will be a good way to start my travels. Today I sold the car, bought a mobile phone, sold the flat ... two more nights out on the town and then a finally curry take-away at Eton Ave. Tomorrow big session with the girls including staying at the Park Lane Hotel, lunch at the Mirabelle, one of London's top restaurants, and then a night trawling the bards. If that doesn't finish me off, I don't know what will.

OK sweets, hope all is well with you.

Love and kisses,

Bud
♀

Bud at the bar

Subj: Group mail
Date 4/25/00
From: rorabud (Actually Dad on Bud's email)
To: lumajen1

Now top floor of 22 Eton Ave, you are the first entry on my learning curve. Will advise my call sign. Mum in better spirits.

Date: April 26, 2000
From: rorabud
To: lumajen1

(Actually from dad!)

Thanks yours. Good wishes to the new Formula One Team. Rosie completing tomorrow: we celebrating in Soho with investment in a new teapot and sushi lunch — with take away from Mama.

Love to all,

Dad

NB THIS IS ABOUT MY MAX LENGTH OF MESSAGE

Subj: Group mail
Date: 6/7/2000
From: rorabud
To: lumajen

Dearest En Famille (Lucia please forward!)

Am in the armpit of Turkey with weather to match, grey and sweaty and not very savory to smell! It must also be the sweet capital as every other shop has cakes and Turkish delight in the windows! The only thing going for Syvas is the fact that there is an internet café opposite my horrible hotel. Have stayed in a few pits recently, but this is the worst! By 6 tonight, I had been on about 4 different buses and this was a way of saving my bones from any more shaking. Tomorrow I will be in a very pretty old town divided by a river and a nice pension. My Rough Guide to Turkey has been a life saver! I am now heading rapidly north. I was down near the Syrian border in Sanhurfa for a couple of days and that was an epperience. I had to go to the bazaar to buy myself a shapeless shirt to cover up anything that suggested I might be female! The influence there was very Arabic, women covered from head to toe and tattooed faces, tiny streets running with filth and an incredible bazaar. I didn't feel very comfortable there, though people were friendly and helpful. From there I headed up into the mountains to Nemrut Dagy, on the top of which is Nemrut's tomb and huge carved heads, dinner by the Attaturk Dam. I am certainly seeing the country, but am feeling a little land-locked and hope to be up on the Black Sea coast within a couple days. My original plan of going from Trabazon by boat to Istanbul is not possible, as I have missed the day.

Am meeting up with Ali on Sunday in Istanbul. He has finished a big job and will be at my disposal, which sounds good to me. I will visit the school and then take off. He has all my summer clothes, so I am looking forward to putting on a skimpy summer dress, washing my clothes and feeling civilized again. This traveling business is very grueling and the further east you go, the worse the buses, roads and pensions get. The next time I go this way, I will do it by car!

Thinking of facing the flea pit over the road and seeing what surprises the shower has in store for me. Often freezing cold water! The Cappadocya showers were so small you had to sit on the loo to wash! You never know - this could be a high point of this town - a big, hot shower!!

Lots of love,

Bud

♡

Subj: Re: no boobs on show here
Date: 6/9/00
From: rorabud@hotmail.com
To: lumajen1

Sweet thing – didn't you know that boobs is not a done thing in a good Muslim country where the men drink litres of raki, chase girls and the women stay at home? I have taken your advice and am now at the sea, it really was a very welcome sight and I am at an old fishing port with wonderful fortifications. I am hoping that today will bring me a superb dinner with good hotel, last night stayed in a grim hotel where you had to ask for the key if you wanted to shower. I mean, what is the world coming to. Also taking your advice where Ali is concerned. We were concocting a very complex plan which would have involved him getting the ferry from Istanbul, picking me up en route and us making a sea trip of the Black Sea, but I suddenly realized that term finishes here next week and if I don't get myself to Istanbul pretty pronto, I will not get to see the school!

So, will be doing 12-hour bus journey tomorrow, but really want to see Ali, do the clothes washing thing and feel clean, am really beginning to feel scruffy, smelly and dirty.

So, love thing, please pass on my congrats to Frou on her big swimming adventure, this is very good news. Will be back in London in 2 weeks, will only be there for a few weeks and then will come back to Turkey, thinking of doing intensive language course in Antalya for a couple of weeks. Plans change all the time, so we shall see! Speak soon, sis.

Subj: Re: Istanbul
Date: 6/12/00
From: rorabud
To: lumajen

Dearest Lucia,

Have rapidly found myself back in civilization after 12 hours on the bus yesterday and getting into the wrong bus terminal on the other side of Istanbul! Today have washed clothes and wandered around the area which is also where the school is and where my apartment will be. Pretty bloody wonderful, 2 mins away is the Sea of Marmara and this area is like a modern version of Hampstead. South of France style apartments with balconies and shutters against the sun and wonderful shops and cafes. It is hard to imagine this is the same country I was in just a few days ago. On Saturday I finally found a decent hotel - no key for the shower - and beach. Only weird thing was that I was the only tourist there, but I am getting used to that, everywhere I have gone, I have been the sole representative of international relations. Here is very cosmo, lots of posing with phones, convertible cars and the rest. Ali is working but will be back early so we can have a good dins together. In fact, we will have lots of time over the next year and I am a happy bee doing my own thing. In a few days' time, we will take off together to explore the Adriatic coast for about a week so there will be plenty of quality time together. Am visiting the school tomorrow, my only stress is what to wear, I don't think it's the kind of place which will appreciate the grunge traveler look. Sounds like you are ready for hols, teenage boys do sound like a real handful, but I am convinced it will get better. Let's face it, we all turned out ok and we were all pretty awful.

So, my sweet, one day I am going to get you here, I am going to be very happy here and can easily see the girls here for shopping gossip trips.

Lots of love,
R.

Subject: RE: BLOODY WET LONDON!
Date: 7/10/00
From: rorabud
To: lumajen, mjoconeman

Dearests,

Sorry, haven't really got back into the regular swing of this email business, but here goes./ London is wet, grey and cold. Am wearing winter-style clothing and they only managed just to scrape through Wimbledon a day late. Mum is very frail, but there seems to be no end to her social engagements. Imogen one day, Myrt the next!

That launch party sounded like a corker! What is this about the police coming and telling you to turn the sound down? Did you do a few shorts of tequila that night? I have finally realized that it is the drink of the devil. It was Charl's birthday on Saturday night, held in fab bar in Picadilly and they were dishing up 2 margheritas for the price of one. Everyone was off their faces, but you know the effect alcohol has on me. I really don't know how I would have got home if it were not for Lucy L who escorted me back; this included indicating to the taxi driver good spots on route for me to have a quick up-chuck outside the taxi. Ugh, horrible! Then had to face huge Sunday lunch with roast everything, but of course by that point was feeling starving hungry and managed to do justice to it.

So am now really excited about going back to Turkey. Am going to have a few days in Istanbul before going south. Turkish men are rather lovely and there are always more than you have time for. Whoops! Must try to behave myself or will mess up. So, life is fun. It will be quite a kick in the teeth finally having to face up to work and getting up in the morning.

Ok, sweets, am off to Mo's for dinner. Making Thai fish soup, sounds very exotic and delish.

Love,
R

Date: 7/25/00
From: rorabud
To: lumajen

Dearest,

Well, have finally tracked down email and am at present sweltering in a small office in a very pretty hotel on the beach. I am having a thoroughly fun time and as a result have decided that I must become t-total for a while. Really, they are a bunch of party animals here and even by my standards they make me feel tired. The best suggestion of the other night was to go to Olympos at 4am. I had actually had enough by then and went to bed. I am going off on a gullet (big boat) for a couple of days. I really do want just to chill out and have the opportunity to do some reading and sleeping. When I come back from the boat, I will be going and staying with Erol and Ursula, up the hill and away from the crazy beach action.
xx

Subj: Re: Turkish accents
Date: 8/7/2000
From: rorabud
To: lumajen

Dearest,

Good to have mail and be back in communication with the world! Ali left this morning and we always went to bed so late, so I am a little worse for wear. Am in horrible tourist resort with my mate who is the rep for the holiday company. Still enjoying lounging around but am ready to start using the old grey matter again.

Did you know that here you can sweat alcohol out of your system so quickly that you never get sick and can go on drinking for hours? Had a very funky night, involving going to Olympos, the ancient city where back packers go and hang out staying in the tree houses.

Date: 8/31/00
From: rorabud
To: lumajen

Dearest,

Well tonight is the last night here for a while and have gone out in style, or rather out to Marine Ices with Myrt and the ever-faithful Charl. Had crazy weekend in Derbyshire with the girls and a lunatic friend of Lucy's. We spent most of the weekend in Lucy's private indoor pool while the rain poured outside and we drank loads of wine, floated around the pool on all sorts of odd inflatable objects and sang songs from musicals, mainly the 'Sound of Music'. Top time! Parentals have been well-behaved. Dad likes to whisper in corners about Mum, but then she always knows when he is talking about her and yells from upstairs.

Have packed well, including winter clothes and endless pairs of black shoes. Had a stress dream - it was my first day of school and I looked in my ruck sack for something suitable to wear and found only a sarong and bikinis ...

Will mail all the news once have got pc sorted at school.

Love,
R

Subj: Re: Parental update- doing well
Date: 6/13/2001
From: rorabud
To: lumajen, Moo

Just spoke to father down south. He's sounding very relaxed. No tetch. He's out and about, had dinner at my mate's newly opened bar/restaurant, has walked down the other end of the bay to the river and tonight will be having a BBQ at the hotel. He already had a glass of wine in his hand and sounded well and looked after. Friday, he's going on the boat to Olympos and will be back about the same time as I arrive. My mates think he is a star on a stick and have taken him to heart, calling him father, ha ha. I wonder how dad takes to all this immediate bonding in Turkey!

Off to have my bits waxed, then an evening of toe painting, packing and plucking. Had to blow off the carpet guy and his mates tonight. Was meant to go over for dinner, but not up to it. Of course, got straight home from school and went to bed with a packet of cheesy Doritos and a bar of choc. Now feeling much better after sleep and artificial colouring and flavourings. Am planning to be good student tonight and revise the present continuous tense in Turkish. My fave word at the moment is 'pis' which means dirty! How sensible, of course it does.

OK, sweet things, until my next burst of inspiration, this is enough! Budx

The Rose Bud & Her Brilliant Adventures

Date: 10/16/01
From: rorabud
To: lumajen

Alright, sweet stuff, it's only taken me a month to reply to your email, but at least you now know why sometimes I am a crap communicator! I am now the proud owner of a gorgeous red car, I described to Mary as cold war, Russian style. Its called a Sahin, this means falcon and the make is Tofas. It will run forever. I did put it to the test and drove the other day with Charla, Mo, Lu Lo and big John in the car, up and down mountains to Adrasan and it ran pretty well. If it can carry that lot, it can do anything.

Had a lovely time with them. I drove to Kalkan where they were staying, a beautiful up-market resort 2.5 hours from Adrasan. The road is one of those very scary, very narrow ones with blind corners and no barriers. I had a wonderful time doing the drive alone, music blaring until the speakers exploded and the stereo came apart in my hands. I managed to lower the general tone of the resort very quickly. A couple of my mates from Adrasan came over for a night, we got drunk and went to a nargile bar, (big hubba bubba pipe bar) smoked and continued drinking, knocked over one of those big pipe things and began a small smoldering fire on a priceless bit of old kelim. Oh, what fun we had. Then we returned to Adrasan and spent 2 days on a friend's gullet, one of the big boats with 6 cabins, showers and naturally a few romances blossomed, what with the stars, moon, skinny-dipping and alcohol.

I have decided that Adrasan will always be a big part of my life; it is my favourite place and I want to have my own space there. I will be looking at land when I get back and have decided to have a very small and simple house built there, the whole thing will be very reasonable. The most important thing is that I am feeling that, once again, I need a place which is my home, where I can shut the door, or have friends in, or do the washing up naked. I am sure you know exactly what I mean!

pp

Date: 10/23/01
From: rorabud
To: lumajen

Girls on fab form last night. We drank champers, regaled sordid tales which the whole restaurant enjoyed and then I crashed round at Mo's place. Just had my bikini line waxed. I did say to the girl, if I get any more intimate with you, I will have to call you my midwife! If you get the picture. So now, lovely and hairless. Better dash and put cheese in bag. Very illegal, but must have stilton and cheddar.

γγ

Subject: Re: you waked hussy you ...
Date: 11/1/01
From: rorabud
To: lumajen

Dearest sis,

New living arrangements are bloody perfect, great room tv with CNN, the run of the hotel, pools, jacuzzi, hamam, nightly cinemas, so am a lucky so and so. I was smiling to myself and feeling very pleased that I had decided to leave Istanbul, when I was sitting on the terrace this morning having breakfast in the sun, looking at the sea and pools and any number of scantily clad Germans and Russians. Some not so lovely to look at. I will be giving the hotel 10 hours of my time over the week and the rest is mine – will have to find other contracts. I will be spending about 3 days a week in Adrasan, that is my real home. It is fine enjoying the nice side of living in a 5-star hotel, but you still want mountains and mates and nights sitting around the fire chatting and boozing.

Will be moving into Sue and Cenan's when I go back this weekend, they are making a room ready for me. I feel really that that is my home.

OK, sweets, more later.
yy

Subject: Re: Just call me Bridget Jones
From: rorabud
To: lumajen, Moo, Dad, Lu Lo, Charlawala

Well, this is a very overdue mail to update you on the joys of my 32nd birthday! Thank you all for your very kind bday thoughts. I was feeling pretty gloomy about the whole 32 thang. I had my first surprise party, my wonderful class in the hotel, which includes a fantastic cake chef had organized cake, coffee and candles. Arrived at Ali's apartment in Antalya to find smaller cake and candles. We couldn't do justice to it after cake number one, so we went to the local fruit and veg market where there are great fish restaurants. We got stuck into the rakıy, oh what a good idea that was. Not content to demolish a bottle together, we then decided to hit the bars in the old harbour. I was on the verge of getting up to sing a Turkish karaoke number when the world suddenly shifted somewhere to the right and I was still to the left, if you know what I mean. Staggered home and managed a small slice of cake in order to settle the stomach.

Being around on a Friday meant that I could do fun things like go to Kumluca with my mate Sue on market day and introduce her to the delights of Aybe's hairdressers where they do leg waxing. She was a little put off by the whole thing when she witnessed the bikini line bit, but went ahead anyways. The real excitement of the weekend was of course the birth of Birgit's baby, of course a boy!

Having good time here, sun shining and warm, tights under trousers to come off soon. XX

Subject: Re: Just call me Bridget Jones
Date: 1/23/2002
From: rorabud
To: lumajen

Dearest Lucia,

What can I say - a most wonderful bob full of treats. I now smell gorg, am wearing my new earrings, have eaten loads of wonderful choc and will soon go to bed with my new book. I am very lucky and happy. Please give Frou a big kiss and thank her for pressies. Now have photos of her in my room and my lovely card she made me.

xx

Date: 1/14/2002
Subject: Re: morning
From: rorabud
To: lumajen

Dearest,

Yes, sun is shining in my world in lots of ways. Just had another fantastic meeting with a hotel group, they have 2 hotels in Belek and are opening airport hotel in Antalya and are very interested in my plans. So, still at waiting stage. Have 3 hotels interested, but as yet no definite news!

Went on 6-hour walk on Saturday, over the mountains to Olympos through snow. Saw an eagle, picked wild mushrooms which we cooked and ate on the top of the mountain and then finally upon arriving at Olympos had to wade through river and got bloody wet, but loved it.

Last night all the girls got together and watched Bridget Jones Diary, have you seen it? Wonderful chick flick.

xx

Date: March 7, 2002
From rorabud
To: lumajen

Dearest!

I am moving into my own 3-bedroom apartment in Antalya as of Monday! I am feeling good, as my big lucky star is shining brightly. The apartment is owned by one of the schools I work for and, as my new policy is to ask everyone I meet for the things I need and want, it works. So that is going to be wonderful, to have the best of city life alone and with mates and then to have the beauty of Adrasan at the weekend. The weather is wonderful, spring is in the air, everyone is looking at each other again now that layers of clothing are being removed, I have parties to go to, new friends to invite round for dinner to my pad and lots of work. What more could a girl ask for?

xx

Subject: Sun is Shining
Date 12/12/2003
From: rorabud
To: lumajen

Well, boob is all unbandaged now, had wonderful bath yesterday, first time ever in Turkey because culturally they do not bath and you can never find a bath plug anywhere, but using combination of plaster and masking tape managed to seal up the plug! Also boob not as scary as I initially thought, kind of like a squinting eye, sorta leans to one side and a bit misshapen. I am really hoping that I will have the first bout of chemo in the next couple of weeks and then come over here for a week or so, depending on how I feel. From States - crunchy Reeses pieces please! As you can see, not off my food, eating 3 meals. Ok sweets, time to squeeze orange juice for breakfast.

Have lovely day ♥♥♥

Subject: Sun is shining
Date: 12/12/2003
From: rorabud
To: lumajen

Dearest,

Well woke up today feeling really good, slept very strangely included nightmares about wrong diagnosis and babies falling off a cliff.....but think now have got all the shit out of the brain. Also have decided now not to wait for this stupid visa to arrive and will leave Turkey on Thursday and pay the fine, so am planning to be in London Wednesday 17th, so will be there to meet and greet you, Lu!

We are going to the hospital for the last time today and then they will remove all remaining dressings.

I hope Lucy Lo will arrive on Monday and we will have a couple nights here and then go back to London together. So, all is rolling on.

xx

Subj: RE: thanks
Date: 12/12/2003
From: rorabud
To: lumajen

OK, love, the meeting and greeting party will be out in full force. I am flying back with Lucy Lo on Wednesday evening and so will be installed already in Eton Ave by the time you guys arrive. The only problem is that I may be rushing around, as I now have a very busy 'social diary' this of course includes doctors, hospital... you know!

But feeling very relaxed now that I know when the whole thing will begin and that I want to get it underway as soon as possible.

So, love, see you on Thursday.

xx

Various stages of bald

Subject: THANKS!
Date: 1/9/2004
From: rorabud
To: lumajen

Dearest,

Thanks for the info, have just been looking at the web site and certainly makes for interesting reading. Will ask the onc about it. I was back in the Royal Free today discussing the trials. I told them that I didn't there was a particular benefit for me, and they agreed, so I will have the standard chemo beginning on Wednesday. Moo is coming over on Tues to hold my hand through the first session. So far, I have been very impressed by the Royal Free team: they have referred me to every available service, physio for breast, orthopedics for hip, fertility for discussion (although confirmed that I am menopausal and that my eggs are finished). Today had bone density scan because they are now worried with menopausal status that I will be at risk of oesteop ... wonderful news. Now I am off the pill am also experiencing menopausal symptoms and they have told me to take sage leaf pills, begun today, Also, going to have the chop, hair is coming off. If I stand any chance of keeping my hair, it will work better if hair is short, and if it falls out, then easier to deal with. So Charl's Mum Di is going to cut it off for me.

I feel a bit overloaded with information and in the last 2 days have read that recovery and prevention book, as a result am trying to convert dad to organic foods, have decided to almost give up meat and start eating a lot more fish, soya ... sounding more and more like mother, but the truth is that there was a lot of benefit for her from the diet she had.

Promise will still scoff chocs, but I think for time being coffee and booze off the list! So, after all that went and met Joel after work today and then promptly went into Claridges for glass of wine and catchup. Tomorrow meeting Lucy Lo for film and fish dinner and dad going to Tate's for night.

Lots love,
xx

Subject: Treatment
Date: 1/15/2004
From rorabud
To: lumajen

Dearest,

Well day two after chemo and feeling less lovely than yesterday. They did warn me that the negative effects can take 48 hours to surface and they have just arrived ... sick, but only once so far and they give drugs to combat effect! The actual chemo itself really wasn't too bad. I am lucky because I didn't have a strong reaction to the drugs, some people react the moment they begin to put them in. It is done by a nurse with 5 huge syringes into the drip in your hand and she puts them in manually very slowly so that they can slow or stop if you have a bad reaction.

I had my hair cut. They told me to get it shorter so that they can freeze the hair follicles during chemo and stop the hair falling out, but I tried the frozen cap and couldn't take it, so expect hair to start coming out in 3-4 weeks. They offer wigs on the NHS, so may get one, good for interviews and formal situations. Even Myrtle may notice lack of hair, although for time being have decided not to say anything to her. I felt so good, actually walked home from this hospital and this morning Moo and I went up to Hampstead and I bought a pair of pink shoes! Just feeling sick now but have eaten something and feeling a little better. Main prob has been that I have just not been sleeping, so am exhausted.

I slept all afternoon and am planning early night, cancelled all bday celebrations this weekend. Sat nite I will veg out with Charl and Lu. I have such fantastic friends here, I want for nothing.

Lots of love, so far so good!
xx

Subj: THANKS, LOVE ALL!
Date: 1/23/2004
From: rorabud
To: lumajen

Dearest,

Thanks for fab pressies, I love all of them ... have not yet eaten all the Reeses pieces, will hide some from myself. The pants and top are lovely and the colours together a dream, photos gorg. In fact, Lucy Lo gave me a photo album and will put them in, but the one of Frou and I and umbrella on show for all to see.

Well, have been having dreamy time; adored having Ali over and how wonderful that he came without warning, only problem was no time to wax hairy bits (had been waiting for it all to fall out) Did so much great London stuff, ate sushi (he had never had it before) and went to classic English Restaurant, the oldest in London, and ate amazing food including rabbit and pheasant, he loved, loved loved it!

He left on Wednesday, but I felt okay because have booked my ticket to Turkey. Now I know how I will feel after chemo, I can make plans for coming months. Went in for blood test and platelets and everything good, that is why I feel so good. Also so far have not lost any hair, although they said be prepared, may wake up and find it on the pillow any day now. That will be a shock, but hey I will wear one of my lovely hats. Today thought a lot about Frou. I went to the art café, (drove myself for the first time, like falling off a bike) and painted the most beautiful teapot for Charla. I am really proud of myself. But more exciting is that I have started to make enquiries about setting up a franchise in Istanbul. I spoke to Ali about it, and he thinks it is a wonderful idea. Isn't life grand! I should by rights be feeling ill, but not at all, very happy and making lots of plans for the future. I know that I will make my life in Istanbul and that I want to work to make a real life and home for myself there, no more shit jobs.....how exciting it all is. Even enjoying time in London, have started yoga, but plan to do more. So far just once a week with Martin (Mum's old teacher) - he runs a session at Cancerkin. He remembered her well and of course Bala.

OK am now rabbiting ... lots of love ... xxx

Subj: Re: jammies
Date: 2/3/2004
From: rorabud
To: lumajen

Dear Lucia,

Thanks for fab jammies, they are perfect, very comfy and pretty too! So, what's this I hear about Frou, she is excelling at school. You must all be really happy about it all.

Well returned yesterday from IOM, had a lovely time with Moo, although there was a huge amount of rain. Today off to Charl's for dins, she will russle up a little something lovely, I am sure. Tomorrow chemo again! Ugh, but I now know that it is really okay. Tomorrow will be a long day, first blood test, then meet oncologist, finally chemo and then wig lady. Now have stylish bald head, well not totally bald, grade 1 all over and then the bald patches.

Will try and chat to you this week before I go to Turkey, not coming back until 22nd Feb, yippee!

Please send my love to Frou and tell her how proud I am of her, bloody brilliant ☺))

yy

Charla and Bud on the Isle of Man

Subj: Re: Here it is!
Date: 2/27/2004
From: rorabud
To: lumajen

Here! yes, I know, was feeling a little guilty about mail to Frou and not you, but am finding get very tired all of a sudden and have to go lie down. In fact, chemo is every insomniac's answer, as I am now on 12 hours a night plus afternoon snoozes. Well, not too bad, had a bit of sick stuff 24 hours after, but ok now, just tired. However, managed to make to Cancerkin yesterday for support group, not sure if will go again.

Well Turkey was fab, despite power cuts, storms, rain and snow. It was so hard to leave and began sobbing day before I left. I will go back out there after next chemo though. And it looks as though there will be a break between end of chemo and start of radiotherapy, so will go out there again then. The whole thing will take longer than I thought.

More tomorrow, will go snooze now.

xx

Subj: RE: PRIVATE for FROLIE!
Date: 2/27/2004
From: rorabud
To: lumajen

Throw the cat at her!! She told me she just printed the mail, she didn't say she read it, ok, you have my permission to 'whip her butt', as you would say in California and say it is from me.

Congrats on getting your award for student of the month and say hi to Carl, who is he??? Does Mike know about this???

OK love for now — Rowie ♥♥♥♥

Subject: Re: Genetic testing
Date: 3/12/2004
From: rorabud
To: lumajen

Dearest,

Well, yes, went to meet genetics team yesterday. Good bunch of people working with shitty budget, but have offered me test, although even if my cancer is result of genes, may not identify it and results will probably take about 6-8 months. But will go ahead anyway as they do it by simply taking blood. Have to do that every 3 wednesdays, so when I go for chemo next week, they will do it then. After that, tried to cheer myself up with spot of retail therapy, bought white things, I guess one day sun will shine again and Ali assures me that weather is getting good in Turkey. Have booked flight, phew, feeling rather claustrophobic here and wondering what the hell I am doing ... blab blab bla. Anyway, off to ceramic café today to try out different techniques and glazes, so that is bound to cheer me up. Love to the husband and child ... xx

Date: 4/8/2004
From: rorabud
To: lumajen

Dearest,

Well am back in UK and first of all thanks for book, scarf and of course Reeses! The book is very good for dipping into and makes a good general read about a lot of things. Well, am having a very funny old time of things at the moment, left Turkey on Tuesday and at point of departure, passport control was told that there is now a ban on me re-entering the country. This order has come from the Governor of Antalya! There is no reason we can think of for this, but when I worked in that religious school in Kumluca, I had a problem with the head, he threatened me and told me that if I did not finish my contract with the school, he would prevent me from working and living in Turkey for 5 years. Well, that was about 8 months ago, but what has happened recently is that a new government and political change has taken place and now this man probably has the kind of contacts to actually have done this, I can't think of a single other reason why this has happened. So, I had to leave Turkey and Ali not knowing when I will be able to return, and also not really knowing the reason why. Well thank god for Ali, he is following the matter there and trying to find out what is up. So, the reason for leaving on the Tuesday was because I had chemo yesterday. Lucy L had booked the day off work to come with me., Had the blood test, but my blood counts were too low so couldn't have the chemo. Will have to wait a week and then after the next chemo will have to have an injection every day for a week to boost bone marrow or will end up very ill! In fact, I feel fine, have been taking it easy and this is very normal towards the end of chemo, body begins to wind down and take longer to recover. Instead, Lucy and I had a great day, lunch, shopping and saw a great movie 'The Station Agent'. Then when leaving the cinema fell into shoe shop to die for with wonderful people, they are making shoes in the basement to order and ready to wear range ... anyway we bought next season's stock at wholesale price, so have bought my perfect boots for winter! Will be heading off to Aldeburgh tonight with Lucy Lo for the weekend. So now in real limbo, had planned to get over chemo and then have trip to Turkey, but looks like that won't be possible for a while and we have to resolve this problem. Trying to be positive and cheerful, but very worried. Turkish bureaucracy is a nightmare! Looking forward to weekend and being with nice people, walks and Easter choc. Will mail next week. Love to the guys, very pleased to hear Mike doing so well. And Frou, the sportswoman .... PP

Sub: Re: chemo 5 done
Date: 4/14/2004
From: rorabud
To: lumajen

Dearest,

Well, something is going right, have just had chemo number 5, so blood is behaving well. On the scary visa front, Ali is going to have a meeting on Friday with the guy who issued the ban and see what he can do and at the same time, I will go to the embassy here to see what I can do from this end. Ali seems to believe we can fairly easily solve this problem, and if we can't, he will suggest to the governor that his lawyer will be following the matter, so if they don't want to have to prove my wrongdoing (of course there is none) they will, we hope, be favourable to my case. Well, had good weekend in Aldeburgh, the sun shone a bit, we ate lots and spent time sitting outside on wall. Spent time with Lizzie, what a nice person. So great to catch up with her. Can't believe how huge her boys are! Have lovely weekend plans for the girls - Charl and I are going on Friday evening to health spa hotel, we will swim, have massage ... then on Saturday, Lucy and Mo will join us and big John, so it should be wonderful. I feel like a good pampering session!

So, things are not so bad, and London is looking lovely, flowers and blossom everything and sun beginning to shine. Met a very nice girl today in the chemo room. She is Colombian, only 30 and with breast cancer. The nurses asked me to speak to her, because she is worried about losing her hair, she seemed to like my bald head. Even Ali said he will miss it when the hair grows again. I am going to meet up with her next week and go to a yoga class with her. Her mum has just arrived from Columbia. It is good to meet someone nearer my age and good for her too. Ali is planning his trip over for my next chemo and he will get to meet Moo, as she will be here in London for a couple days on her wayback from Brazil. I have just had lovely chat with Bala and will probably take myself over to see her, she has been praying for me at the temple, how lovely! Send love to your crowd, you sound busy and happy. PPP

Date: 7/11/2004
From: lumajen
To: rorabud

Sooooo happy for you that you'll be headed home so very soon. It's been a long haul, but I do have to point out how your sense of humour is still totally intact, even with all the crap you've had to deal with. All will be well with you.

Anyway, have a fab time this week and do the best of London.

Bises,

Lucia

xx

Subj: Re: women!
Date: 7/13/2004
From: rorabud
To: lumajen

Have had lovely London day ... Waterstones, Fortnums, Selfridges and Sushi! Was blasted twice today, so last go tomorrow. Hard to believe, but one day away from over. I am off to the Isle of Man on Thurs for a weekend with Moo and then back Sunday for lots of last dinners and lunches with girls. Will be relieved to be back in Turkey in order to get away from all this rich living. Had stupendous lunch out yesterday with Lucy Lo and Big John. We went to very old established fish restaurant and I had fruits de mer ... huge platter of seafood, including cockles, whelks, clams, oysters .... Nearly exploded. Had to have very serious digestive lie down after lunch. Today's sushi was a little light affair in comparison. After tomorrow I have Monday at fertility clinic and Tuesday seeing Parhboo. No scan. That will happen later because they need to let effects of radiotherapy settle before they can say anything, but I am not worried about any of it. Just wanting to get on with living full life again. Future will tell all. Exhausted now. Reading good book, think need another lie down. xx

Subj: RE: Rosie
Subj: RE: another lovely day!
Date: 7/29/2004
From: rorabud
To: lumajen

Settling back into Adrasan life of course, this means adjusting to weather (hot and humid after Istanbul sunny and cool) and catching up with mates and making life here in construction site habitable. In fact, Ali has made our room here lovely with a big worktable and internet set up, so quite civilized upstairs, but downstairs now populated by lots of loud Kurdish workers, singing all day, quite lovely actually.

I traveled overnight by bus and arrived on Thursday morning. I have to follow what is happening here. Erol takes no interest and spends all his time out on boat trips and drinking with tourists, so I have been negotiating with the crew here how to do the stonework (very interesting indeed, I think they got the drift eventually) and organizing getting the jeep repaired, which is used to transport their working materials up and down the still unusable road to the site. So, settling in well and having a lovely time. Danish Birgit has now moved into Kybele. She has been here for 6 weeks and is very brown. Last night with had a lovely evening in Golden River with Ali, Birgit, Sue and Elif. Ate great grilled fish and fed the ducks. Today up and about early as sun comes in room and starts to get hot! Also, will go with Birgit to market day in Kumluca. I have to say it is just wonderful being here, really feels like a kind of homecoming. Everywhere I go, I am greeted and kissed and cuddled, a lot of 'Mahsallahs' being said (my god) and hair stroking going on. It is lovely to be so known and liked, always good for the ego. And, of course, being in the sea ... in fact I don't think this year has been tooooo hot, as the sea is still reasonably refreshing and not like bath water. Everyone here seems and well and happy.

I did love being in Istanbul. Bought myself a set of ok-ish water colours and I can say the paintings are rather good. I am developing my system using small sketch pad and pencils outside and then coming home and making larger paintings. Also, rather interesting self-portrait. Feel very inspired to paint here.

Hope all well in sunny CA ... what is Frou up to, horse camp finished? Get her to send me mail. Have been taking photos with digital camera here, but having trouble sending them. Will get Ali to help.

pp

Bud and Sue in Adrasan at the Street Cafe

Date: 8/9/2004
From: rorabud
To: lumajen

So, I guess you have had the funeral by now. Woke up and thought of you all today for some reason and felt very remiss about not mailing - how are Shirley and Mike? Pleased though that he died in such a way that everyone had a chance to talk to him and see him first.

Here am feeling lazy from heat and a big night out, but in fact been very busy in Chateau Kybele. Despite all those months in England, haven't really lost my Turkish, in fact in some ways it has improved. It seems to be in a different part of my brain now and is more automatic.

Keri, Bud, Ella and Danish Birgit

We had one group of builders leave here in the middle of the night, so suddenly a building site with no workers ... lots of problems, but we seem to be solving them. So, between trying to clean out Kybele and run after workmen, of course am having lots of fun. Friday night went over the mountains to Olympos and danced 'til dawn, literally. I have to say it totally wiped me out, but I loved it. Weather is perfect and even night sweats are less. My small apartment here is lovely. I have my fridge and small cooker in my studio and so even if it is full of noise, dust and builders downstairs, it is peaceful and civilized up here. I have a fantastic easle for my painting and have been doing small water colours of the mountains, not very successful as yet, but getting there.

I am really well and loving being here, seem to amaze the people here. Most people know why I have such short funny hair, but am still occasionally bumping into people who don't know and I have to explain. It really does now feel like rather like a dream and even the problems with being banned from Turkey are a long way away. Anyway, hair is good, growing and thick, dark but not black, just long enough so when I wake up in the morning, I look like a chick with fluffy hair all over the place. Spent lovely afternoon catching up with all the gossip in the bay, including my imminent marriage and Sue's pregnancy, of course neither of which are true .. ppp

Subj: Re: paid the bill
Date: 8/17/2004
From: rorabud
To: lumajen

Dearest,

Sorry for delay in replying but managed to pay wrong phone bill and cut myself off! Gosh, you know the brain level is still rather low, and still doing dizzy and silly things, like going to the beach yesterday with shower attachment which meant to only take as far as downstairs in order to descale. Ok, nothing too serious. Well noise has begun already of stone being cut. I am currently living with 2 Turkish stone men and 3 Kurds. If someone is not watching the work level, it rather falls off and they end up drinking a lot of tea and gossiping, but as soon as they see me, they are up and running. I am loving being site foreman here and enjoy following all the work. Gradually the building which is white and not that attractive is being clad in stone with arches and being transformed into something quite

Sue, Birgie and Bud

lovely. Had a lovely fish dinner up in Ulupinar with Sue and Birgit, great to get them away from husbands and kids!

I consider myself to be the happiest and most positive person I know. I love being here and feel fantastic waking up to this weather and these views.

Hope you guys are getting to do some nice things together, even if it is very quiet stuff. PP

Subj: Re: The roof!!
Date: 8/20/2004
From: rorabud
To: lumajen, dad, Moo, Charlawala, Lu Lo

Well, life is most exciting and unpredictable in the world of construction! We had our first accident yesterday, fortunately nobody was hurt but the roof did come crashing down. It would have come down at some point, but yeah .. the bigger problem than the roof on a daily basis has been the question of bread. Bread is the most important food product here, each person can eat up to about 5 breads a day and I had been going to get the bread daily or even twice daily from the bakers up the road (old stone cooking method). I decided to order the bread so that it was delivered fresh at 7 in time for the guys' breakfast, and yet day after day they forgot to bring it. Finally, after me going up to the bakers each day and very politely reminding them about the bread, I went yesterday and was less polite and today they have remembered. Amazing how good my Turkish is getting, although a bit concerned about accent, slang as around workmen all day, 3 of them speaking Arabic. Now know words for brick, concrete, steel, mallet, nail, flat tire, bread and, of course, roof.

The swimming pool foundations are in and the whole of the patio will be covered with huge slabs of stone. We have a team of 3 stone specialists here. Last night they were laying outside, Turkish workers seem to be rather philosophical and romantic, looking at the view and dreaming up ideas of waterfalls cascading from the mountain side into a pool and then the water being recycled again in a continuous stream. Not what you would expect from a labourer in England. These guys are all very skinny, so also no unpleasant builder bottoms on display.

Seem to have inherited a cat, it appears every night and comes in for a bit of nosh and a chat. I have named it Boncuk, which means lucky charm. Today going to the beach for a few hours and then will go back to inspect work, quantity done versus amount of tea drunk and see whether the two tally.

Very well, really feeling good and strong, swimming, running around generally and outside all day. RB

Bud at Kybele

Subj: Re: plans
Date: 8/26/2004
From: rorabud
To: lumajen

Dearest,

Well seems that I have now got a hotel to run! Am rather excited at the prospect of being hotelier. I had really come to the conclusion in the last few weeks that as Kybele really feels like my home and I am loving being involved in the construction, that I would also rather like to run it when it opens. And so, I waited until Ali came and then he actually suggested it. So, I will rent it from him as a business agreement which will get me all my legal status here and we will do it with proper legal contract ... very exciting! There will be 8 rooms and 2 small studio apartments. There will also be a bar and restaurant, so I will have to find a good chef, will not be slaving away in kitchen myself. It is really taking shape now, the scaffolding is coming down and the beautiful stone walls are being finished. Now onto the pool ....

xx

Subj: Re: father's arrival
Date: 8/31/2004
From: rorabud
To: lumajen, mary

Dearest sisters,

Well just trying to get myself organized before father's arrival tomorrow evening. Thinking about all the possible problems and pitfalls of having an aged parent around, like the distressingly poor quality of the pavements in Antalya, potential broken bones at every step, also of course the possibility that, if we do get him up to Kybele in the Jeep, there are then 100 wires lying around he could trip over, or simply be electrocuted by! And the question of whether or not we should go out on a boat, or not, the rickety jetty ... this is stress! In fact, we will have a lovely time, I will chaperone him well, and in fact he can't really get up to too much mischief in the Antalya hotel where they are very OAP friendly. I will have to leave him alone by the pool on Friday while I go to buy stone from a town a few hours away, my god, that means potential grade 3 burns as he will be unable to apply his factor 50 suntan lotion to his back, or his 'donkey jacket,' as someone once called it. I will bribe a member of staff to look after him. So, as you can see, I am feeling very relaxed about it all.

Well, must get up and go to bloody Kumluca to bank, buy 50 liters of petrol for the jeep, food for the workers and of course, get my bikini line waxed ..

Subj: RE: November
Date: 8/8/2005
From: rorabud
To: lumajen

Dearest,

Well, weeks are flying by and suddenly the crazy hot summer seems to be cooling down a little. Today have been picking figs and made fig jam with the help of Birgul (translated as First Rose) she is one of my village women mates and her husband is the local electrician. She came and brought her kids, they swam and we made jam. I love this village life. Tomorrow am going to go and learn how to make butter ... the village is certainly taking the city out of me!

xx

Subject: November
Date: 8/6/2005
From lumajen
To: rorabud

Hi lovie,

Hope things doing a little better with you – let me know. It was nice to catch up – I haven't seen you in a million years. Mary and I talked about Dana and I going over and seeing her while we are on our whirlwind week in November, (going to the island on Nov 14 and spending 2 nights). Any chance you might come along? I know you are supposed to be in the UK sometime around Nov, so wonder if there could be any crossover. If not, I probs won't see you until early summer 2006 when we come and stay in your hotel and that is a very long time away.

Let me know, sweetness.

All love,

Lucia

xx

Subj: Re: Rosie
From: lumajen
To: Carey
Date: 4/12/2006

Dearest,

Sorry to burden you more than you already are weighted down ... Rosie is off to the oncologist again tomorrow — they have found 'something' in the same place as before on her scans. We are all sick with worry. She is being marvelous, of course. Mary is with her. Mum is not happy at all and keeps jabbing at me.....indispersed with sending me magical birds I can't find in the books and hovering angel hawks through every window.

Sending fairy dust across the planet to you, dearest.

Bises,

Lucia

xx

Subj: Rosie
Date: 4/12/2006
From: Carey
To: lumajen

Dear Lucy,

Just picked up your mail and couldn't believe Rosie is having to deal with uncertainty again. Because, at the moment, that's what it is and nothing's confirmed for good or bad. The not knowing is always a shaky time, and the worry veil falls and automatically tends to make one think the worst. I can imagine Rosie keeping a brave face and I think it would bolster her for everyone to be as positive as they can. If there is something, it may be benign; first thing. If there is something which needs dealing with then things can be dealt with and successfully. Rosie's done the battle before. She is a very life-affirming person and she has a great life and that, psychologically, is a big strong plus for her, as I do truly believe that a positive state of mind has an important effect. It's good to hear that Mary is with her and Rosie has a strong set of friends too. Let me know things go and if there's anything at all I can do.

With all my love,

Carey

xx

Subj: Re: yoghurt
Date: 4/19/2006
From: rorabud (in Kybele!)
To: lumajen

Dearest,

Back in the Bull and very happy! Having a quiet, domestic time with Ali in Istanbul before going down to Adrasan for what I hope will be a busy summer. Have lots of new projects and plans. We are planning to begin making our own cheese and smoking foods there. Very scientific processes, but Ali will automate them, so nitwit like me can do it! I had ordered loads of books on the subject and am now ploughing through them trying to suss out the processes needed. Can even make stilton with the right bacteria, very exciting. If we don't poison the punters, may actually be able to sell some in Istanbul to good cheese shops or in markets. Yesterday made yoghurt, very easy and delish, had for breakfast with strawberries, so expect to be eating well when you come! Husniye is a wonderful cook, so you will enjoy the best food you can find anywhere when you come with some eccentric mason additions. You never know, may get you in the kitchen and you can learn how to make stuffed vine leaves, easy as pie! Had great day yesterday. Istanbul, city of wonderful markets, so bought summer wardrobe, found espadrilly things for about 2 quid, cheap as chips, new bikini. Today another market — need to buy cheesecloth as want to drain the yoghurt to make something more like Greek stuff, richer and creamier. Am actually becoming Felicity Kendal from the

Good Life, it is surely only a matter of time before I have my own goat or two.

So, sweet stuff, will be fun to have Ann and Caroline with us during your stay. Hope you excited too. Remember to bring sea-sick pills just in case.

Bud
x

Subj: Re: Hols
Date: 6/12/2006
From rorabud@kybele
To: lumajen

My god, it really is happening, believe you will be with me by afternoon of 20th. I am really looking forward to it and we will have a hotel full of nice people. I'm having a bit of a breather from Adrasan life; been in Istanbul since Friday and am going back tomorrow night. Kybele is gorg. Don't buy any suntan lotion. I have loads! Also have hats for boiled brains and the rest. Hope Frou won't get too bored with us old farts. Hope we will have a night of live music and Turkish dancing up at the hotel. Off to watch footie ... xx

And there the collection of emails stopped and, I believe,

And that is where the collecting of emails stopped. I believe we had all moved along our chit-chats to primarily instant messages, texting and social-media-ing like crazy at this point.

The Internet had come a long way since 2000 when these email communications began. Even in Turkey.

The Bud in her happy place. Always loved this picture of her.

SECTION 2

SOMEHOW ALL ABOUT ME FOR A WHILE

Introduction to Somehow

it's now all about me ...(for a short while)

That was one of Rosie's lines. "IT'S ALL ABOUT MEEEEE!" because, frankly, when you have someone in your family who is constantly ill, it is always all about them. But, actually, in the spring of 2010, Bud was already through her next stage of treatment when I was diagnosed with breast cancer. I think that about blew everyone's minds.

I was nothing like the Chemo Champ she was and struggled through my infections and treatments like a real lame ass the summer of 2010 and through to the winter – in and out of hospital like a complete loser. In August 2010, Bud and Dad came over to see me. I still had treatments to go and my memories from that time are all a bit of a blur; but serve to say, there are some superb photos still in existence that say it all.

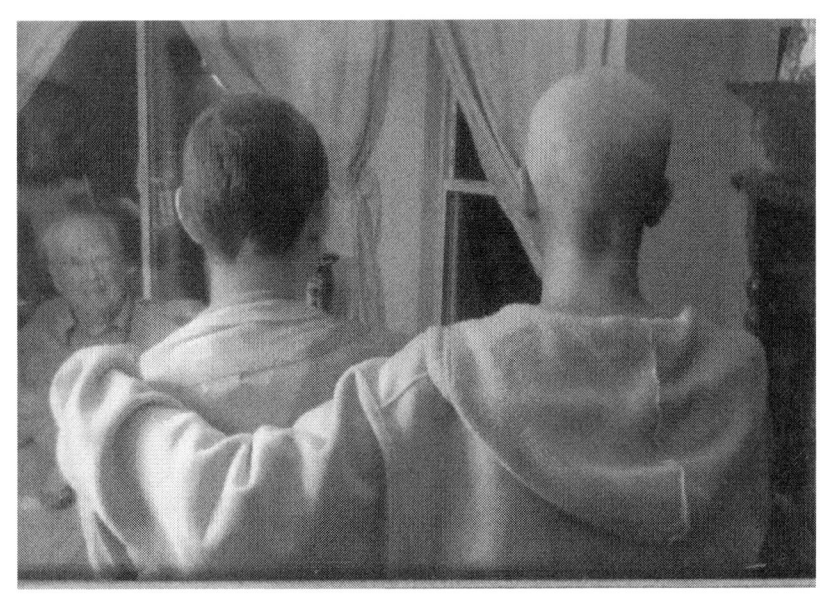

Beautiful bald heads ... Dad, Bud and Lu – August 2010 in California

Rosie's classic comment, when I told her I would be losing my hair, resounds in the memory, however. "Oh sis, let's just hope your bald head is as beautiful as mine!" (It nearly was). And also … "I really love being bald. It suits me so well."

And that was the essence of my sister; always making the best of a situation and expecting others to do likewise. This stunning attitude served her well through her illness and onto the day she died.

Someone else's story
Published in South County Newspapers in 2010

Some stories are easier to tell than others. It is much easier to talk about other people and their struggles, to sympathize with others over loss or illness, to offer condolences and empathetic counsel to anyone outside of your own self. It is quite another thing to go face to face with your own disease and mortality.

This journey started out many years ago. My mother was about 55 years old at the time and she stopped me, as I was leaving out of the garden gate of our London home. Some moments in time are simply frozen that way. "I am going to have an operation tomorrow," she told me blandly. "I have cancer and they are going to take it off." Right. I later learned that no one else knew of this. Even my father had thought that she just had a cyst which needed to be removed. Not a mention of the big 'C' had been made. My mother found health items completely boring and therefore not worth general discussion with anyone.

Mum went on to have a simple mastectomy of the one breast with removal of lymph glands in addition, and she'd never even had a mammogram in her whole life. She refused chemo, but accepted radiation. She lived for a good ten years plus after the surgery and then, with the onset of a rather cruel case of osteoporosis, the cancer came back in the spine and took her away. She was, thankfully, not to witness the 'gift' that was passed along. I can only imagine it would have broken her heart.

A few years later, and my baby sister is stricken with breast cancer in the same breast as our mother. Don't tell me breast cancer can't be passed along; even without a genetic marker in sight. Three women from one family, really?

Obviously, when you have this much breast cancer in your family, you take it rather seriously. 'High risk' folks such as me are very diligent about our testing. I first had my mammogram at 35 years young, which was several years ago if you are counting. 'Early detection is the key', they tout. "Make sure you go for your yearly mammogram!' Every year I have hoo-rahed about my clear test result. That is until I didn't get one.

    I went for my yearly check up with my doctor and we talked frankly about my baby sister and the scary fact that her cancer had now come back in the bone. Our whole family has been thinking about little else for several months now. "I think you should have an MRI of the breast," my doctor suggested. At the time, I thought this a little radical since there were no obvious lumps and bumps on the horizon. My mammogram was clear, wasn't it? I also wondered about what the cost of such a large-sounding procedure might be. But she was my medical advisor and I always played by the rules where that was concerned, so we would have the MRI, we would pay the large bill and we would walk out triumphantly, still touting a wonderfully clear result. That was until we didn't.

    I went away on vacation and had a totally super time. So much so that I completely forgot about all the nasty doctor visits I had lined up for my return. 'What is all this garbage?" I said to just myself, as I eyed the calendar on my return. I suppose that is what vacations are all about — you go away to be away from yourself and your real life. We came back home, and they were all still there. We had the additional mammogram, the ultrasound — of breast and ovary — plus that expensive Super-Giant, the MRI, all lined up in a neat little row. We had the whole menu of possible breast-plus options to keep the health insurance providers happy and the doctor confident that all bases had been covered.

    "They found something on the MRI," my doctor tells me. Oh. "We need you to come in for an ultrasound." It was probably just dust on the film or something. Hocus pocus. These medical folks just want to keep you coming and coming back. It's called job security. The ultrasound showed two lumps—we will just call them Nigel and Neville. Nigel was bigger than Neville, but they were obviously brothers, because they were very close together. "We need you to come in for a biopsy," the nice medical lady told me. A biopsy? The MRI had cost me about $1500 plus and now we had to pay for another high dollar procedure, all in the same week? Thank god for plastic money, however we berate it in our normal lives. I still figured there must be dust on the film. (Gosh, they really do need to do a better job of cleaning this high-tech machinery!)

The day of the biopsy comes around and I am required to save my valuable valium pill – just the one–that I had to get in advance from the pharmacy, until the nice lady at the biopsy place tells me it's safe to take it. Golly, it must be either a super-special or stunningly-strong pill! I was almost looking forward to trying it! The prep work for the biopsy was a big old build up to nothing, frankly, since the super-sized valium pill served to make sure I didn't give a damn about anything and, besides the fact that I thought the nice doctor was taking a large staple gun to my breast area, which was bizarre at best, the whole thing passed without incident. The valium buzz also lasted a nice long while and, thankfully, I had to promise not to work on any heavy machinery for the rest of the day, with good reason I might add. Yes, and I thought that that adventure would be that. Not.

I was told I would have my clean results back anywhere between 24 and 48 hours. On the 49th hour, I was losing my mind. Not only was I checking and rechecking my life insurance, but I had written my obituary ten times over. How long does it really take these qualified folks to check the results of a biopsy? Can't they see that some one's life is in a holding pattern for all those days that they cannot find the time to make the diagnosis? I felt like a plane circling Heathrow Airport. I was waiting, I was waiting. I was getting a little sick, but I was still waiting and watching the ground below me going round and round and going nowhere. It was similar to a game of Russian roulette. This shot good, the next one maybe not so good. Two choices, only. Good or bad. Bad or good. Which will it be? How can you properly function when you are dealing with those kinds of odds?

Really close to quitting time on a late Friday afternoon, I finally got the call back. It was the bad shot. Breast cancer. "Ok, so now I know. When can I have them removed?" I enquired politely. I can be a very practical person under duress.

"Sorry, madam, everyone has left for the day. You'll have to call back on Monday," the nice lady told me. And so, it is. It is not their life, or their body; it is their job, so they really don't care, though they are paid to sound as if they do. You, on the other hand, are wandering the lonely plain of disease, completely alone with your diagnosis. It has a name – the home of Nigel and Neville – it is called Ductal Carcinoma – and that is not a name I'd give to anyone or anything remotely pleasant – but that is its vile-self and it needs to be exterminated. I immediately call my lovely lady doctor and she takes my call at stupid o'clock on a Friday afternoon and lets me bawl, helpfully, down the phone. She tells me we will make our plan on Monday and assures me the cancer is small. You call up your folks, your friends – anyone that has been waiting for you to get your test results the way you have – and they are shocked and sad, the way you are, which does help you a little. They tell you they are there for you and you feel a bit better. They take you out of your lonely plain and into their warm home; but it still feels lonely because it's your body and not theirs, your cancer and not theirs and they are most certainly glad for that.

I couldn't wait to talk to Rosie, my baby sister, my guidance counselor in this cancer journey. She lived with the damn thing; she could help me live with mine. I have more folks living in my house than I even knew. Nigel and Neville have been here for who knows how long, and I didn't even know it! Words from the now wiser woman – mammograms do not tell the full story. Ask the 'N's' – they've been flying under the radar for who knows how long. They have been hiding quietly in what the professionals call 'deep tissue' and no one knew it, not even the owner of the body. Nothing hurt, nothing ached, nothing oozed, and the body continues to feel incredibly well, despite what it saw on the MRI and the ultrasound.

    Over the preceding several years, I have had a mammogram every year on the dot without fail. All had clean results. I had three clear mammograms in the space of one short week. I have a letter from the mammography experts stating that my mammogram was fine, and yet, I have breast cancer.

I opted to have a double mastectomy that finally occurred in early June 2010, about 6 weeks after diagnosis. Those 6 weeks were some of the most difficult of my life. It was near impossible to convince the surgeons – and the insurance company – to remove the healthy breast; but I was eventually successful. They installed implants during the same surgery: a mistake.

My beautiful implants that didn't work

Fortunately, the cancer had not spread to the lymph, but the pathology showed an aggressive triple negative tumor. My lovely oncologist advised, in light of my family history, to still have the chemotherapy treatments, which I duly did. Chemo is not for wimps. I ultimately went through a series of infections and hospitalizations with my body rejecting the implants and not having the immune system to fight the infections.

Even more beautiful bald heads

Rosie and Dad came to visit us in California, August 2010, after she had finished her treatment. She was glad to see that my bald head was nearly as beautiful as hers.

I was in the middle of chemotherapy, so my memories are a little blurry, but I do remember going out for a lovely steak dinner at the Braga Ranch one evening and snapping a shot of everyone's bald heads.

Dad, Rosie and Mike at the Braga Ranch

Dad, Bud and Lu

In November, I had the implants removed and have since lived as a near-flat chested scarred mess; but I'm alive. In the past few years, I have been 'NED'. In the biz, that's the lingo for 'no evidence of disease. I graduated Dr. Aziz's class of 2010 in 2020. I had mixed feelings about not going to 'class' every 6 months; plus, he was such a lovely and clever man, I shed a tear when we said goodbye.

(PS I can tell you that, after I lost my sister to the disease, survivor guilt is a real thing. I may be 'NED', but I will always have cancer.)

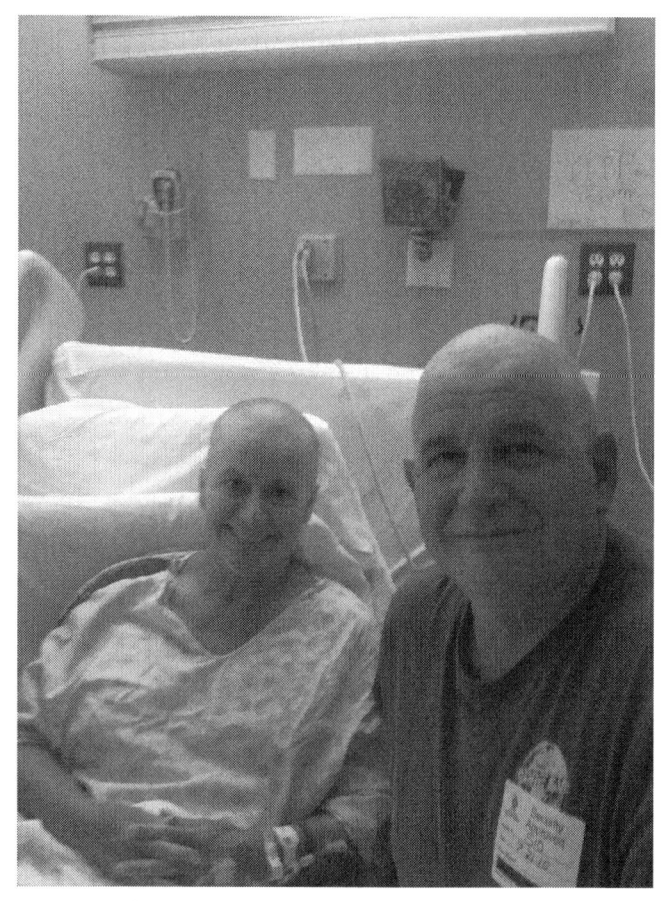

Back in Salinas Valley Memorial with an infection, summer of 2010.

Mike shaved his head when I lost my hair. Everyone said he looked like Shrek, bless him. I thought he looked rather more like the FBI.

Love is

The Bitter Sweets of Living
Somehow it's all about me-
Published in the South County Newspapers –

It has often seemed to me that with the passing of one soul comes along the unexpected arrival of a new one; and that is the way of the earth as we have come to know it. I recently had the opportunity to breathe in the sweetness of a newborn and watch his fresh, new eyes watching me, as if we'd met before. I also had the honor to be present at the celebration of the completion of a long full life and the heralding of a passing soul, cherished by many. Both the arrival of the new soul and the departure of the older one were surprises to us all. The newborn was a surprise, since he needed a home and my friend had been waiting to give him one; she just didn't know when he'd be arriving. The older soul had certainly not known he was ready to be called home, as quickly as he was; but he left us full of the life and humor he had always possessed and that life-full picture of him will be immortalized with us for always.

In light of my own latest 'surprises', I have been trying to extract the sweet from the bitter recently, in order to be able to live with myself and my 'new reality' over the coming months; not to mention attempting to lift a little of the inevitable burden from my friends and family. So, in light of all of that, here is my bitter-sweet pledge in black and white, with the best of intentions, from the heart:-

1. I must try to pass along some of the kindness I have recently received to others who might need some of that for themselves. Whether it be in the form of a nice card, a friendly phone call, or just a flower from the garden to lift their day. I must step outside of myself and remember that I am not the only one with life challenges. That is part of life.

Recently, someone who had just lost their life partner and is currently immersed in helping their daughter battle the same disease as me, stopped by to give me a basket of flowers, a card and a hug. They did just that. They stepped outside their own realm of suffering and into mine for just a few minutes. I think we both felt a little better for that. I know it lifted me up and made me resolve to try and be a better person and find compassion in my heart for others who are also suffering. Another friend took time out of her day to talk to me about her own struggle with the illness and cheer me into believing I can and will get over it, the way she did. She also assured me that life, just around the corner, will again taste sweet. I needed that. Another friend made sure we had delicious dinners cooked for us every night; the fortitude of the body being just as important as the conviction of the mind. And that helped enormously too. Another friend sensed my anxieties and would somehow call me when she felt I was at my lowest ebb and sitting alone with my diagnosis. She would talk me through it and out the other side. She would wait patiently, the international minutes ticking away, as I blabbed and sniffed my way through my own selfish agonies. I must remember all these compassionate gestures when I am up again and on the top of my game. I must remember to pass them along, packaged in the same way that so many gave them to me.

2. When I come out the other side, I must also remember to thank everyone who helped get me there. From my friends at the newspapers to my family and friends from all over, to neighbors, colleagues — and not least my husband, sons and daughter and animals — it will be a group effort to get me up and going again and back into the driving seat of my bossy self. I am not one that sits well and can tolerate any kind of physical challenge before me which will stop me getting up as usual and going to work. It will take a village to convince me that I will need to stop and heal and take the time out that my body will most likely require. I am thanking everyone in advance, because I know you'll be there to help me help myself. Contrary to how I currently feel; I'm sure the world will not stop operating, because I am not in it for a few days.

3. I must remember to document my experiences. What is an experience if not something that can assist someone else who will, for sure, be in the same situation somewhere down the line? It is a lesson to be absorbed. Even when I am low and down and ugly with myself, I must relate the journey in the raw language of

someone who is tasting the tougher side of life; and I must share it as a donation to humanity. If those who have gone before me were not sharing now the most intimate details of their disease, I would not feel the comfort that I do that I, too, can come through the other side and back to a wholesome life they promise me will still exist when I return.

    4. I must stay true to my hero – my baby sister Rosie Emma Alexandra Mason–who has been battling with this same life challenge for some years now. She is a professional to the core and has let me lean on her heavily through these tortuous early days of my diagnosis, even though she is still going through chemo herself and currently getting herself geared up for 6 weeks of radiation back-to-back. She has taught me a lot about how to be, though I am supposed to be the older sister. She has managed to cheer me up when she is herself not feeling so good and made me laugh, 'til I could cry, about the darndest things. If she wasn't busy being a teacher, I've decided she could certainly be a comedian. Her grace and humor, throughout this life ordeal she has been dealt, have made her rise to the top of people I enjoy being around. I need to be more like her and less like the vision I've seen in the mirror recently of this rather sad and wrinkly individual, who is feeling a bit sorry for herself and the deck of cards she's been dealt. I need to quickly shed that skin and become more like Rosie.

    With all that said, I will work hard on all the above while I am away. They say that if you write it down, you make it so; and herein you have my pledge. I will be cheerful, I will be kind, I will not be self-indulgent – please, call me out on all these things if you witness them–and then, I will be back.

    Enormous thanks to so many of you in this wonderful community I call home, for lifting me up during what would have otherwise been very grim and dark days. Thanks too for helping me see that the spring flowers are, indeed, still gorgeous, the hills are still green, there are humming- birds waving to me outside my window, my dogs kisses are endless and divine; and you – all of you – are what can make up a very, very sweet life I plan on returning to soon, very soon.

Love,
Lucy

Holding your own hands

Looking back at old photos, I did this a lot. Any time I was in an awkward position at grade school, anytime the teacher called on me to – oh, no you can't be serious – read out loud in front of the entire class; anytime I was not quite, what you would call, comfortable in my own skin, I would hold my own hands. There is photographic proof of this throughout my life. And here, several decades down the road into middle age; I find myself doing it again, as if it were the most comforting thing on earth, or at least my last resort, as a forty-something woman faced with a nasty disease and my own mortality. I saw an accused man in the dock on the local news the other night. He was doing the same thing, holding his own hands. He and I were a little similar, I thought. He was accused of a bad crime; I was accused of cancer – both of us were at the last frontier of a 'free' life and felt the need to hang on tight to the lives we thought we had through the warmth of our own flesh.

    I wake up at least three or four times a night these days, as the power of the Tylenol is on the wane and the niggling reminder comes back to haunt me. "Yes, you are sick, you ache, you hurt. It's time to feed the pain monster that is currently ruling your life!" As I come back to my world and am reminded that, yes, this is my real life these days, and I am not dreaming of some unfortunate other; I realize that I am holding my own hands above my head like some kind of an elegant ballerina, or perhaps just a sick person in physical therapy who has been instructed to do exactly that stretch, as I have. It's all part of my bizarre new world. I've taken to holding my own hands most of the time, each and every day.

    On April 30 2010, for those of you who have been wondering where the eccentric Brit has been hanging her soon-to-be-ever-present hat, I was diagnosed with invasive breast cancer. The MRI doc called me with the diagnosis late that Friday and then left for the weekend. Ever since then, I have been wondering what happened to my former life. Since I am now the third female in my immediate family to be gifted with these medical findings, such breaking news struck me as either the makings of a bad movie, or a thoroughly sick joke. Ironically enough, I had thought the odds were so much stacked in my favor, it had not crossed my mind that the lump which had showed up on my MRI could turn out to be such a cruel one.

So, then, the results are in and you quit crying about it, make a plan with your wonderfully qualified doctors and get into the 'beat it' zone. You discover that the human quest for survival is more powerful than you ever knew. You get back to the core basics in life; love, family, health, and you trim all the other dross from around the edges. You come to realize that so much of what we are concerned about has no actual relevance in the world of living and surviving, and that is all we truly value when the rest of it is stripped away. The simple things give you so much pleasure; the sun, the moon, the smile of your dogs and the kindness of your neighbor. At the end of it all, your work doesn't matter, the fact that the milk is sour is irrelevant, the issue of your daughter's unmade bed just makes you close her door; the only thing you are really interested in is beating the monster, achieving your goals and being able to proudly proclaim to the world, or anyone out there who still cares. "I'm back!" The sun, the stars, the immeasurable kindness of others and the doggy smiles will still be there to greet you and shine on your parade when you return.

And while we are talking about the journey that more people take than I even knew; let me tell you how amazing some of the gifts are that you receive along what can also be called the path of wretchedness. This can also be the pathway of amazing grace. You receive gifts, cards, books, letters, drawings, dinners, flowers, prayers, towels, calls, candy, fruit, bandages, bras, crackers, jams, rides, emails, texts, plants, soft toys, painted nails, Tylenol, vitamins, more dinners and calls. You get all that and more, not to mention the freely given words of encouragement. You even receive international visits from your friends and all kinds of unforeseen aid packages which help you back onto the saddle of living and coach you on towards a better day. You receive love galore and kindness without bounds; the purest of human emotions that serve to fill you up and help you ride high on the wave of solace to recovery.

I have never felt more loved than during my journey through this illness and out the other side. Even when I was sore and stubborn and refused to properly do my prescribed exercises, my friends would forgive me and make me a cup of tea, let me lie down lazy and willful with my bolshie self and then let me whine on just a little bit more; as they patiently allowed me to pick myself up and slowly get myself back to the land of the living, while they did my dishes. When I was bleeding and messy and unable to pick up my own bandages, I had friends and family to pick everything up around me. I was fed, carried, clothed, dealt with. The true meaning of when you cannot carry yourself, others will step in to carry you in your place; now that is humanity at its best. And that is what you really yearn to do when you are dealing with cancer this, cancer that — let's have another doctor's appointment shall we — and please, oh please, I don't have enough bruises, could somebody please stick me with another needle. You just want to be able to carry yourself again. Once you start the healing process in earnest, you want to get back to regular, independent life as you knew it. You want to drive yourself to work, you want to go to the grocery store. Heck, you'd like to be able to back the car out of the garage without feeling that stiff neck thing again. You'd like to be able to pick up a gallon of milk without shooting pains across your chest, and you'd love to be able to deal with a full day at the office, as you used to, because it would remind you of the old you and the life you used to have.

    Now I have the lovely chemo lady to deal with right around the corner, and she is to be my angel and the icing on my cake. My sister has told me so and she is qualified. I am to embrace my angel and love every bit of scientific wisdom and particles she'd like to instill into me, during the brief three hours we shall be together every three weeks for a while to come. I shall love her, and she will love me back and maybe we shall part on good terms and miss each other a little when we leave? (Who knows — I might make some really good friends in the infusion room!) I will not think of her in negative form nor with fear. So much of this journey is mental, even the experts concede that; and in order to be able to receive the highest gifts, we had better make sure we are at the top of our mental game and ready to import all that we need from the journey to be able to step out from the adventure a bit stronger, a bit wiser, a bit more healthy and maybe even a bit kinder, which has to be one of the greatest gifts of all.

We may walk out holding our own hands; but not at the dock of our own existence; it will be in triumph that we are still alive. We may even be cured.

(P.S. So many thanks got out to the many wonderful people who rescued me when I was at my lowest, picked me up from the floor of my diagnosis and gave me hope that I could and would get through this and be able to, one day, boast myself a proud survivor: one of many in our wonderful valley and wide-open world.)

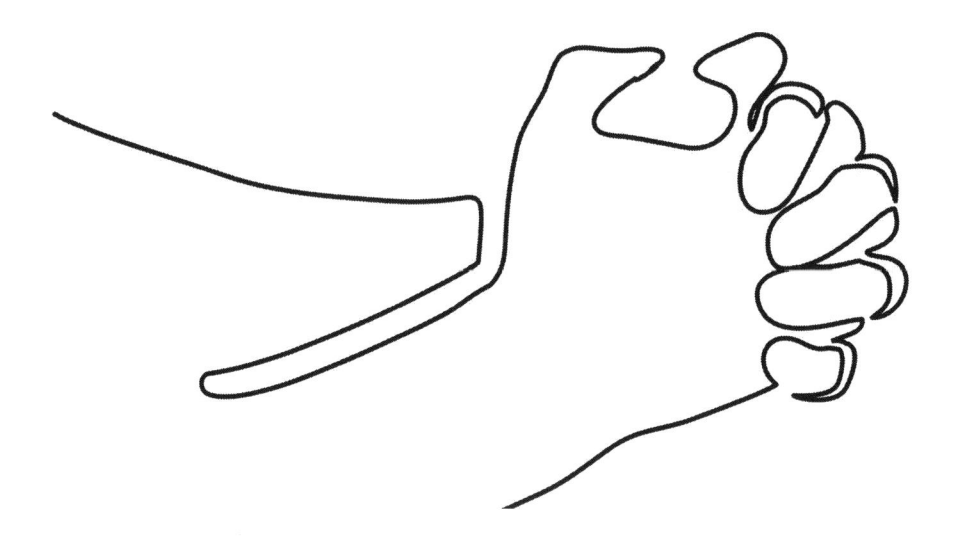

Light through the luminaria

Fall 2014

It was a special Relay for Life in King City this year. It is special every year, truth be told, but this year it had an indescribable intimacy among the survivors, their partners and families and thoughtful community members present, that made me positively buoyant with hope. We are all members of a large club for sure. None of us voted to join this club; but since that was the hand we were dealt, I think I can say for the group that it makes you feel less lonely knowing that there are so many people out there in your shoes, wearing your shirt and sometimes sporting less hair than the baldest man in the world – so many people, that you feel raised up by them.

I was strangely proud to walk alongside super-survivors such as Dr. David Phillips and Debbie King. If they are still here, against the odds, then why not me, why not you, why not my baby sis? Their spirit and longevity made me feel light on my feet and hugely optimistic about the future. I hope the rest of you in that village, that night, felt the same way. You rocked the house, yet again, King City. If you invite me, I'll be back.

A friend of mine couldn't make the "Luminaria ceremony" that I was honored to open this year – gosh how stunning that was– and so I hope my humble speech bears repeating, since she was one of the many players in my recovery, always supporting me with a loving heart and putting out a helping hand to lift me up when I couldn't get up myself. Sheryl, my darling friend, for a long time and forever. This one's for you.

"It has been 4 years since my first chemo. The American Cancer Society talks a lot about celebrating birthdays and, though I don't think that you are ever cured from cancer in the mind, time does heal a lot of things. It heals the shock and the denial of your diagnosis, it heals the 'why me' syndrome, the tunnel of self pity and the all-consuming fear that your life will never belong to you ever again; the long range forecast stipulating that your life will always belong to 'It'.

A lot of things can happen in 4 years. My friend – also a survivor – and I don't use that word lightly – told me that I will get to the stage post cancer where I feel my life is better than it was pre cancer. I didn't believe her at the time. What kind of a hogwash could that be? But I'm crawling towards the light, I can tell you, and life is looking pretty delicious on the outside.

Fortunately, I think, I am mostly too busy to think about cancer and the possibility of recurrence. I did everything I could think to do to keep it away. I removed every part of me I could, at the time, to give myself the best odds, batted a fighting chance at getting it gone and keeping it gone. Now I just have to get back to the act of busy living and it feels pretty good to be there. I try not to think about anything coming back to bite me, any rogue cells reappearing and gnawing on my new life, chewing on my family with their all-consuming bite. There is just no point in challenging the unknown. You learn that quickly when your life has been changed by disease.

I read my diary from 4 years ago. "My first chemo in my whole life. The fear is probably worse than the actual experience. The nurses at the chemo lab were so nice. It is a strange feeling though, willingly infusing poison into your body. My system didn't react so well when the infusion started. I started sneezing as if I was never going to stop. My face flushed bright red, my body heat was intense and the nurse had to stop the infusion. Will I really be able to handle four to six of these?" I asked myself. Fortunately, at the time, I did not realize the full impact of my cocktail of Taxotere and Cytoxin. I didn't know that I would not be able to sleep at night because of the steroids, exhausted though I was and craving slumber. Equally, I had no idea that I could ever sleep for 21 hours, that my body would keep taking me under and away to planets unvisited in order to escape my awful reality. I would have taken better measures to protect my digestive system, had I known how intensely I would be impacted by the onslaught of the chemicals and how painful constipation can be. I would have also been more solicitous of my teeth and gums – a common victim of chemo's powers. Had I known that, by day 4 after chemo, I would be in another zone, I would be in a tunnel I can barely remember – I would have probably never agreed to do it in the first place, so, in that case, ignorance is possibly the better option. Someone famous once said, "When you're in hell, keep on going" and that pretty fairly represents the chemo experience. Days 1-2 you are in a weird spot, waiting for something really bad to happen and feeling 'chemically enhanced'. Day 3-4, you are in a terrible dark place and you think you are definitely dying. You know you are. If so, at the time, you welcome it. Days 5-6, you don't really remember. By day 7-8, the sun is a little brighter and life a little more, thankfully, ordinary. By day 9-10, you might even be back to work.

4 years ago, I had my chest removed. I was the 3rd female in my family to get breast cancer, so I wanted to give myself a fighting chance. I was certainly going to lose my hair. What else would I lose apart from my vanity? I was recovering from surgery and, simultaneously, battling not to lose myself to the strongest potion you can ever imagine. When they say that in chemotherapy they take you to the verge of death without actually killing you and then bring you back; they are not kidding. I remember those months of multi-surgeries and chemotherapy patchily; a fact that still frightens me, as if the poison took away a portion of my brain as well. My lost life, my days of turmoil and confusion – I remember some of those. But, with that, and, by contrast, the light outside the tunnel is so much brighter, the days sweeter, now I have crawled out the other side. I cannot believe how I taste and experience and see things differently now. No cliché; life is good, life is better, after all, than before.

Life is not always fair, is it? The hands you are dealt are often tough and everyone has their own issues they carry in those hands; but now, on the whole, my life post disease is really good. My gauge is simple nowadays – is it disease, is it death? No? Then it is nothing. I feed the birds and watch them bathe, I play with my dogs, laugh at my goats–a lot–love on my horses–all the time– watch patterns of clouds in the sky, smell the flowers, pick the flowers, call my friends, read interesting things, make fabulous plans, hug my daughter, tell people I love them. I do all kinds of life enhancing things, some of which I used to do 4 plus years ago, but certainly not with the same abundance. If I receive a tough call I'd rather not deal with, I say 'phooey to that'—or words to that effect—and go for a walk or a swim. The tough call can wait, life can't.

    Not that I would recommend anyone develop a life-changing disease in order to really sample the essence of life; but I am here to say that my friend was right. Life is different on the other side and its flavors are enhanced. I never wanted the disease in the first place, who would. I wouldn't wish it on anyone. But since it came to me and hopefully, left me, at least in the physical sense, I can now look back and say that we were well met in life. I emerged from the experience a little different from when I went in, (and I'm not even talking about the hair or the chest.) It is easy to go through life and not be appreciative for all the wonders around us. Put yourself in the chemo chair for a minute and imagine where that might take you.

Today and tonight and tomorrow, I am walking for many friends and family. I am walking for my dear Mother Una who I lost on November 9, 2000 at 9am to bone cancer. I am walking for many dear friends and family, some who are happily still with us and some in spirit only. Some who can't walk real well at all at the moment, like my sister. I am walking for her, especially Rosie, my baby sister, who is undergoing treatment for her 3rd bout with cancer — this time a tumor in the spine — and I am walking for all of you. Let's honor the light tonight of those who are here in spirit and those who are here in body. The fight goes on."

    And with that, we lit the luminaria illuminating the word 'HOPE' and we walked the track in silence, as the luminaria were lit, as we passed them by and, in the stunning silence, I was able to take in the enormity of the starry sky and the possibilities that lay beyond. I spoke to Rosie when I got home that evening and told her about the event and how we walked for her. She seemed to like it, she loved the luminaria we decorated for her and she had had a good and uneventful second dose of chemo in two weeks, so it had been a really good day. We have to take it one step, one day at a time and use hope as our crutch to trust that the medicine will do its magic, the doctors will practice their craft and the universe will make some resounding wrongs right once again.

Thanks for listening.

Love,

Lucy

2 hats at a volleyball game

SECTION 3
SOMEWHERE AROUND THE MIDDLE

Introduction to 'Somewhere around the middle' ...

I warned you, in advance, that this was a patchwork quilt of a memoir. The timelines are tipsy, the recollections patchy and the coherency, frankly, way off. But, however you might best piece together some one's colorful life in the best way possible; the only way I can do justice to my sister's is by giving it a rather loose, artistic framework – she'd like that – add some photos – always good – and then make a huge apology for any enormous mishaps along the way – she'd understand completely and laugh at me for it. (In the manner of, 'Sister! You suck!')

'Somewhere around the middle' means that she is not still in nappies, trying to crawl around the place being a complete brat; but equally, she is not yet on the downward spiral of her life that eventually took her off to other realms. This is the colorful middle part, where she was still and always a brat, but a bit more mobile and well ... brattish. This is the bit where she properly moves to Turkey and, not surprisingly, shakes things up there. The bit where she had another bout with cancer; but didn't let that slow her down. The bit where she really accepted her vocation as a teacher, founded a school in Kumluca, enjoyed life with her friends, met Ali and Dilgesu and really enjoyed the very best part of her life, never mind how short it was in time measure. It was also the time that sisters became cancer sisters as well. Some of my fave pictures of us are when we were both bald.

The early days

The middle part, Rosie told me, was the most brilliant part of her entire life. It is where she truly found love and it found her. Around the 'middle part', she found her family with Ali and Dilgesu and she was finally content. She had stopped looking for love in all the wrong places. 'The middle' took her to the very pinnacle of her existence. It was this portion of her life where she honestly embraced the quality of her life and worried not where it went from there. She had arrived and planned on staying where she was for as long as humanly possible.

Without a doubt, the happiest time of her life. With Dilgesu and her beloved Ali, the last and best Ali.

It is what it is ...

My baby sister has been one of the walking wounded most of her life, as mentioned before. She was born with a congenital hip and limped her way through the early days, almost as soon as she could put one foot in front of the other; and that was, most of the time, with a swagger. Everyone thought, at the time, that she was imitating our father with his pronounced limp from a boyhood accident, when he had been run over by a bus. Baby sis was always quite the comedian, and, at the time, this had been a most possible theory; but the doctors suspected otherwise and, from then on, she was in surgery to try and fix this most debilitating condition. I remember her, one hot summer, entirely cast in plaster from her stomach down to her knees with just a small open area for her nether regions that seemed to continually have a urine stain around the edge. Funny what your brain chooses to remember. Our father called her his "plaster parcel," since she required carrying around in her frozen state. She had already been forced to undergo two surgeries and a period in plaster and traction well before she was even two years old. For sure, those were the days for long, drawn out procedures. She made it through, however, without ever losing her quite spectacular sense of humor and unbelievable naughtiness; though she did claim the prize of the 'spoilt brat' in our family, being the one who always got all the attention. This was an award she never lost.

Bud was married at the age of 44 in Turkey to a wonderful man she had loved for quite some time. She had wanted to get married; they had wanted to get married and the time soon became ripe to do so and seal the deal. Sadly, for those of us who live a long way away, the happy couple had not given us quite enough time to be able to get our act together and plan the long trip over there to make it to the church on time, as it were. I was one of those who couldn't make it and I was sorely sad when I realized that I could only be there in spirit.

I spoke to her prior to her wedding, and she asked me about sciatica, which was not a very romantic subject, beings she was about to get wed. "Oh yes," I told her, "I get it quite a lot, especially when I am the weekend warrior and try to be all athletic when my body is actually not." She laughed. "Yes, I definitely have sciatica," she joked. "I danced too much at my bachelorette party, I think, and I have shooting pains all over the place!" We both laughed about that. She has always loved to dance and party.

"I think I have really done something to myself," she confided in me a bit later. "I'm in a lot of pain!"

"When did this start?" I asked her.

"I slipped and fell when we went hiking a few weeks ago. I think I jarred something in my back." Oh yes; that would be it. She fell on her back and had done something silly. Too bad it would come back to haunt her around the time of her wedding; how unlucky is that. A small fracture of the vertebrae or something? They had friends arriving from all over the place; they had rented a beautiful place on the Mediterranean for their wedding and party. It had to all be wonderful and perfect. It was going to be that way.

Her friend sent me pictures of the wedding prep, the bride preparing for her make up, the bride getting dressed in her gorgeous white dress. The bride looked tired, I noticed. The smiles on the bride's face were not quite the open faced, supreme gleams of your average newly-wed. She was not wearing shoes and she was drinking a glass of water. Something inside me twinged just a little. I'm not her older sister for nothing.

She called me on 'FaceTime." It was late. I wondered why a newly-wed would not be full on honeymoon mode and rich with sleep. "I'm in a lot of pain, sis." She tells me. "Something is going on." The plates were shifting, and I felt my internal equilibrium alter and start to slide on a downward kilt.

"What's going on?" I ask in a whisper, as if there are people out there who shouldn't be hearing us talking. Maybe if we spoke of it softly enough, it would make it go away. It came to light that she had been in excruciating pain for several days and that the only way she made it to her wedding ceremony was through large injections of steroids and pain pills to numb the unreasonable pain. A cool chill went through me from archived times in the past, but never too far from the here and now. No, surely not. That would be too cruel. It couldn't be; it had better not be.

And so, the Monday after the wedding that she had looked forward to for so long, when she should have been on her honeymoon, baby sis was back in the waiting room of her life. She was back at the hospital having the MRI's, the blood tests, the scans. She was prepping herself to face what she already knew was going to be something not that great. And she wasn't going to be surprised. The shadow on the spine on the MRI turned from a concern to a nightmare. The cancer had returned as a tumor in the base of her spine. The agony she was experiencing became no surprise at all. It was back.

"It is what it is," she told me when we 'FaceTimed' again, as she lay on her back in Antalya after another bout of tests and enough drugs so that she could function even just a bit. "I can't feel sorry for myself and wonder why me. Why not me, sis? I just have to get on with it. It is what it is." And there she had it. It was beyond her control. She had no control over what was happening to her, only her reaction to what was happening, which communicated itself with her usual grace and humor.

"Oh, I'm so glad your friend is coming this weekend," she tells me. "Then you will have someone to cheer you up!" As if she knew that I would now be sad and crying for days; as is truthfully the case. "Wait! Your hair is growing, sis. I like it! Let me see the pony-tail!" Already she was changing the subject and the mood and cheering me up all over again.

So, she is on the game again; back to the radiation lab and the chemo chair and the never-ending cycle of tests and checks and drugs and tests again. It is what it is for our family, so afflicted by this disease and its never-ending assault on our peace of mind and our lives. It is what it is, as it has been for a long time now. But it will never take her courage, nor ours, and it will never take her humor, nor ours, I hope; those will remain intact for always.

And as Rosie, my baby sister, embarked on her third bout of radiation and chemotherapy with the great attitude that she has always had, I ask you to dig deep inside yourselves and remind yourselves to never sweat the small stuff; don't complain about paltry inconveniences and tedious common day annoyances that plague us all. There are many, many warriors out there in the chemo chairs and radiation wards, the world over, fighting for their lives against tremendous odds and with heavy burdens to bear.

I asked, selfishly at the time, for the universe to hold up my baby sis, Rosie Emma Alexandra Mason Arican, and lift her in a united strength and courage so that she could overcome her latest obstacles in the same clean and magical way she overcame all the others.

This story is dedicated to her.

The Engagement Party

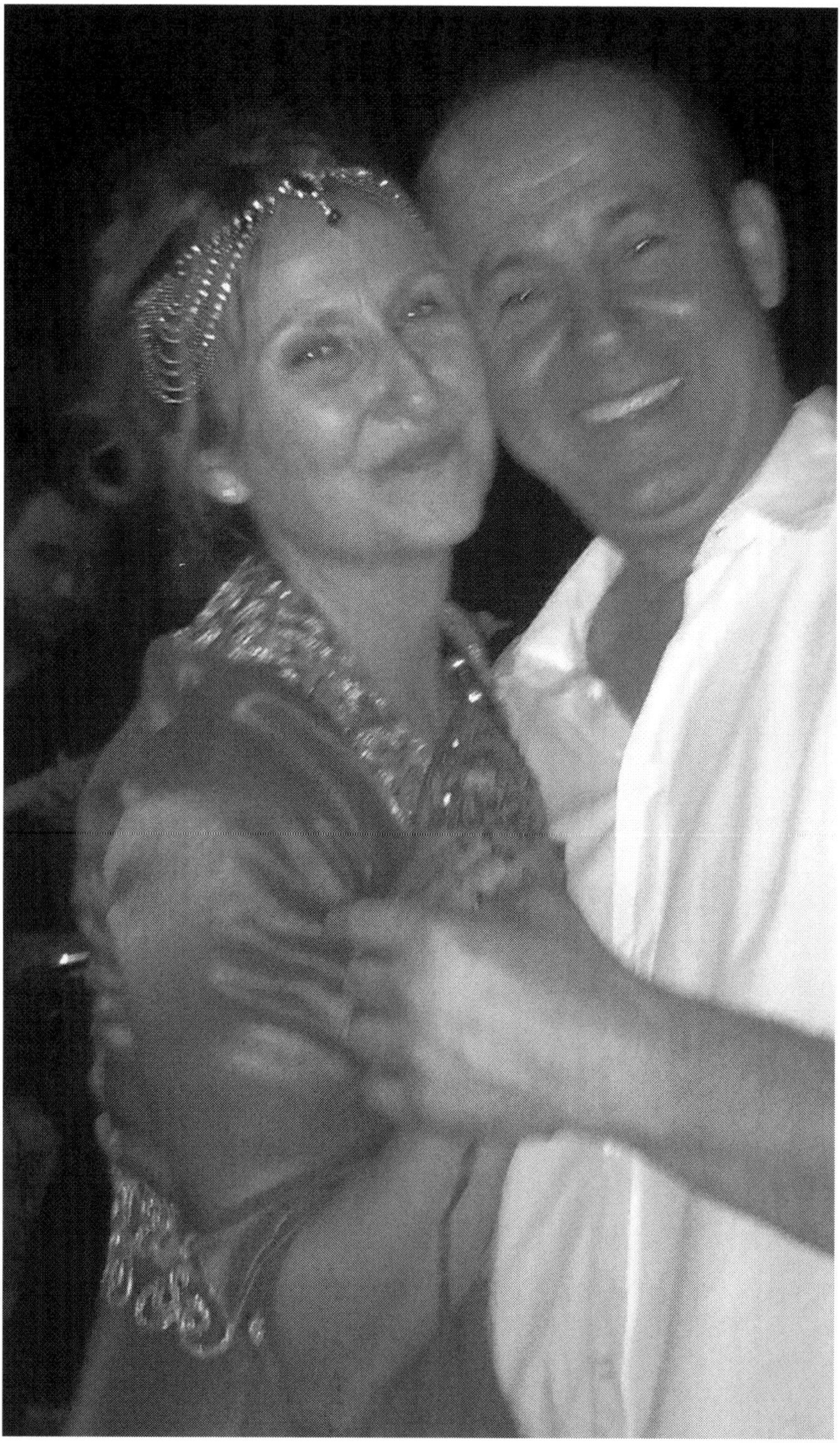

Chemo Is Good For Curls

When my baby sister was going through chemotherapy for breast cancer, she got really tired of her hair dropping out in clumps. ("The chemo is worse than the cancer!" she'd comment, only slightly tongue in cheek.) She hated waking up with a pillow full of loose hair in the morning and then finding the remains of her head's bounty in the bottom of the shower. She briefly contemplated buying a wig to soften the visual blow for her Granny who might not handle the stark curse of her chemo very well; but then, realizing Granny was no fool, opted for the bold coming out party and shaved it all off. Granny naturally handled it very well.

"Send me wild hats!" sister told me. "I'm going to need them. Plus, you might not know that it's really cold when you don't have hair! You forget that's what your hair is for!" There would be no wigs for her. In company, she would whip off one of her wild hats and show off her beautiful bald head. "Don't you think my head is really pretty?" she'd ask whoever was gathered around. We'd laugh, of course, as you do. "I guess I am really lucky to have such a lovely-shaped head and you'd just never have known that before! Take a pic, Lu," she'd coax. And that was simply the kind of stunning attitude she carried with her, as she dealt with that cursed illness that had taken away our mother a few short years before. My sister laughed and she made us laugh. She talked about the tough hand that she had been dealt, as if it wasn't tough at all; just one of those annoying things you have to deal with like a headache or a toothache that we all suffer, but is best dealt with in as cheerful a fashion as possible. She didn't carry with her an ounce of self-pity. Once, when I went with her to radiation, she was joking with the tech who administered the radiation, that they should try and fix the "sunburnt" look that the radiation created on her chest and at least give her a decent tan. When her hair grew back after the chemo, she would show off her long, luscious curls with a self-impressed stroke of her new 'do'. "Look at this amazing hair!" she'd laugh, running her hands through her newly divine tresses. Having had very thin hair before, it had now grown back, like the gift she'd earned, as a luxurious deep chestnut brown mane with delightful thick curls that cascaded down her back. "It's almost worth going through chemo for!" she chortled. And we'd laugh again. No matter what – there was humor there throughout and there still is. Always will be, I'm sure. That is her eternal gift she carries around with her; and ours, too, from her.

A few years down the road and we thought she was in the clear. You read a lot about cancer when you have cancer in your family. Like it or not, it is the plague that always gets your attention. You always try and lean towards the positive stuff, the amazing stories of survival against the odds and more and you, naturally, avoid the less happy outcomes; but, whatever you read, where cancer is concerned, five years has pretty much been heralded across the board as the salute to the clean bill of health.

Well, our family is here to tell you it doesn't always work out that way. After an absence of nearly five years, it's back. The bad stuff is back in our family like a cough that just won't quit; a reminder of what can happen when you relax for a minute and, unthinkingly, sigh with relief that it's all over; you hope.

My baby sis–a month shy of her 40th birthday – calls me up all breezy like from her home in Turkey. "Hi love! Just wanted to let you know that I have a tumor!" She pauses to give me a chance to breathe. "I know – a pain in the butt – but anyway, I'm not worried about it. Super bad timing with all I have going on right now, Christmas and all; but oh well. Can't worry! What would be the point of that?" The very next day she was headed in for a biopsy and decision as to the immediate course of action. "At least I will be out of it and won't feel a thing!" she commented. And so, she tripped on in her inimitable way, working hard to make me feel better about her lot, as she laughed and joked her way through an explanation of what she had found and what was likely to be done with the wretched thing.

And then the sing-song voice hung up and she was gone. I hadn't wanted to let her go, but there was no choice. All of a sudden, the rock hit me and I had to sit down. I was in the mall finishing up my shopping at the time. I no longer wanted to Christmas shop. I didn't want to hear nostalgic Christmas carols or think sentimentally about years past. I now wanted to be on a mission. I wanted to donate blood, marrow, money – whatever I could – and head over there on 'Operation Rescue Rose' and fix all her problems in one foul swoop. I wanted to rip that darn thing out of her, burn it on the stake and stand guard so that it couldn't ever come back. She's my baby sister – of course you feel that way – when your clan is threatened again and the second time around comes across as just a bit much. You feel so helpless you could spit, cry, scream. So what do you do? You call up your father and your other sister, who you know are feeling much the same way, and you make each other feel better by recounting the amazing spirit the young one finds every time to lift all of us up with her. You hang tight to the knowledge that she is such a fighter, this is just another one of her squabbles along the path of the rich and interesting life she has created for herself. She'll canter her way through it as she has in the past; and she'll make lots of jokes along the way. You have to know that.

As I turn on my Christmas music again and light my candles – just carrying on with the festive season, as she would want for us all to do – I lift my glass to all those who are suffering enormous trials in their lives and wish for them not only the courage they are certainly going to need, but also a huge infusion of humor into their lot. I stand back in amazement still at the funny stuff my sister spits out, when life is spitting back at her in such a different way; and I have to feel confident that attitude is all in the larger scheme of things. Without a sense of humor, we will never really have any gift worth holding onto.

Always funny, often shocking. In cirali

My wonderful vacation

"You always have something to say!" Those were the famous words of my oldest son, recited some years ago when we were sparring about something that he should not have done, but did anyway, with the ensuing result that I had something to say about it and its consequences. The words have since spun back around on occasion, when I have found myself saying too much about all and about everything, as sometimes I am wont to do. So, normally, I have to say that the oldest boy would be correct.

But, at the end of one of my most favorite trips away in pastures formerly trod and some untrod, I find myself unusually tongue-tied. I am, strangely, serene and calm. I keep being drawn back to my photos and my thoughts from the past couple of weeks. Words are failing me, where, in 'normal' life, previously, I could usually find myself with too many.

'How so?' I ask myself as I ponder this unprecedented state of affairs in my living memory of my newly reticent self. How is it that I am not effusing about where I have been, what I saw and what I want to do next; now that I am all energized and ready to plan the next outing full to the brim with Kodak moments from where I have just been? Possibly I am silenced, because the gifts I encountered along the way were very rare and precious ones; ones that perhaps are easier to photograph or capture in a moment than to describe on paper, in word doc format or, truthfully, in any easy way that comes to mind.

I made the trip to Turkey this time and I made it right. There, you have it. This was the one that I should have made three plus years ago when I was diagnosed with cancer. This was the one I had to cancel, the one that made me sore and anxious about the wiles of the world and the way that chips can fall, sometimes catching you unawares. That all might sound a little simplistic. Okay, so you planned to go a while back, you had to reschedule and now you are going? Well, yes and no. When I planned to go back then, my sister had been re-diagnosed with cancer and was going through chemotherapy. Ironically enough, when I was supposed to go and see her in her place through the times and trials she was enduring, I myself was undergoing cancer surgery and chemotherapy. Sounds like something out of a bad film; but it was all, sadly, a very true and present event in our family's world at the time.

I would be lying if it did not occur to me this time that I could be slighted at the post a second time in my quest to go and see my baby sister in her home over yonder, when we were both doing seemingly so well. I stepped on the plane at London a little tentatively, I hoped that all would be well with our flight and nothing untoward would befall the occupants of the flight EZ 48 from London Gatwick to Antalya, Turkey that late afternoon. I would also be not entirely truthful if I did not mention that I was more than a little humbled when the plane touched safely down on Turkish soil, and we were still all in one piece, and I was poised and ready for the next portion of my adventure. To be honest, I almost kissed the ground.

I knew, at the time, that these were rare and glorious days that I needed to bottle ahead for the less than perfect ones that we always experience in life. Here I found my sister well and settled, looking healthy and happy in her life with her divine partner and daughter, her solid life and granite foundation that she has constructed for a wonderful future; however long that might be. We ate lovely meals together in her gorgeous home with achingly picturesque views from the mountain to the fields and over to the bay. We swam in azure seas, sat on empty beaches, visited beautiful places together – the ruins of Olympus and more – and we laughed a lot at all kinds of things, not least at ourselves. Our slice of time together made up for the memorably awful times that we had previously endured, when we were both bald, and both scared and scarred for the future and what our lot might be in the months ahead. Do we look over our shoulder and wonder what is chasing us? Yes, we both do that. Do we hope that life might deign to throw us an easy curveball, for the heck of it, and allow us to still do a lot of things and go a lot of places in the world? Of course – we would not be human if we did not wish and hope for these things.

"I do look over my shoulder a lot," my sister tells me. "When I was diagnosed with bone cancer, I asked the universe for three good years. Now we are at the three-year mark, I am asking for a few good more."

Bud on her magic beach in Cirali

I wish the same for her and the same for me, and our family as a unit; because what happens to one of us happens to us all. And that is the nature of the beast, is it not. We are always looking, always hoping, always having something to say about a lot of things, and, in some cases, trying to make deals with a universe that has, perhaps, run out of cards in our favor; or not.

But in our case, my sister and I, we will keep asking, always we will keep asking. We will also keep looking forward and we will keep expecting that the universe will deal the rightful hand back to us and grant us just a few more days, months, even years in the sun with our people and our lives as we know them. If the wrong hand gets dealt, then we will keep fighting like the warrior women that we are and expecting – with glass half full – that things will right themselves in due course and we will get to take another vacation in another beautiful place with rich, sun and light drenched days, with the appropriate witnesses in place. For my part, I expect and hope for no less.

Making deals with the universe

These days I find myself making more and more deals with the universe. I'm not sure if I am alone in my random spiritual communications with the ether and I'm sure one of you will tell me if I'm not; but it's an ongoing thing. Truthfully, it's been running for years. If I were a religious person, I would spend most parts of most days on my knees in some institution somewhere, hoping that a significant super-power would hear me; but, fortunately, in my belief structure, you can be out there on the ranch, neck deep in horse manure, and still be working on your spiritual endeavors.

There's a ladybug, flapping and helpless in the water trough – I fish her out and right-side her. "UNIVERSE! DID YOU SEE THAT? I DIDN'T HAVE TO DO IT, BUT I DID!" (Lucy speak for 'please find a miracle for my baby sis ...') Today there was a pincher bug belly up in the dog's water. I really don't like pincher bugs – they fall out of roses unannounced and creep their itchy way through my apple orchard with gluttonous abandon; but they are creatures of our universe no less and I was in a position of power to save–or not. I rescued the little itchy booger and right-sided him. He was last seen scampering towards my Golden Delicious and I didn't even try to stop him. "SEE UNIVERSE! I RESCUED THE PINCHER BUG AND I DON'T EVEN LIKE THEM!" (Lucy speak for 'please make the chemo work on my baby sister's liver.')

The dove died in the valley. I didn't want the dogs to tear her up or the cats to eat her. I took her to the Secret Garden and laid her gently to rest in the redwood tree where she could be safe; where the only sound would be the occasional splash of the turtle into the pond and the wind in the apple tree. I said a small poem for her sweet spirit. I asked the universe to let her soul fly once more, free of fear, and find that place where anything is possible, the place where magic could be found, and miracles performed. I'm reaching here, I know; but you will go to some pretty strange places when you are desperate, and things are completely out of your control. The hummingbird flutters by and lands on the feeder

I had just filled. Then another comes and then another. "Yes, universe! See that! I filled their feeder and they all came to visit, those beautiful, magical birds!" (Lucy speak for ... 'Surely that has to count for something, hello? Anybody out there?')

"How are you sis?" I ask her, cautiously, because she always tells me she's fine. Stage 4 cancer all over the body and she's pretty much always fine. Then she will ask me how I am, how we are, what's the kid up to and what is going on that is a sight more interesting to her than whether the chemo she is on is going to smash those liver tumors or not. She is on the chemo of last resort — I read that somewhere about this experimental treatment — chemo for stage 4 metastasized cancer -and it seemed apt for all the different treatments she has used over the years. And now this one, fresh from the US. It has been sitting in her fridge in Turkey, expectantly waiting until the other chemo stopped performing in all the places it needed to, and, here we are. The side effects of this drug proudly list 'neuropathy' as one. "Who cares about that?" she says. "I already have neuropathy." I look at her half smile and unusually less-than-sparkly eyes and feel that she is close to having had enough. She is close to wanting the port out of her vein, the drugs out of her body and everything to just go as it's going to go. I believe I see that in her face as she tells me that she's so glad I'm going to come and see her, but she's sorry that we won't be able to have all the fun she'd like. "I'll be under some days, most likely," she ventured. "Probably won't even be able to drink any champagne," as if that were the be all of our time together. When she tells me she will be 'under', that is a memory that never fades, though I was 'under' now 6 years ago. The lost hours of sleep when your body endeavors to figure out what the heck is going on and why it is needing to work so hard. The oblivion to life and all around you. The time travel you go through when you go to 'under, the dry mouth, the craving for carbs, the strange, drug-induced journey you are on for months. It's not a memory I want to lose, lest life hold any less value for me than it has these past few years. I wish I could take on a treatment or two, so that she doesn't have to. Infuse it into me, so she can have a break, I can handle it. Let me take it on for a while. But the universe doesn't work that way. Guilt comes and goes sometimes, that I am still here, and she is leaving. She scoffs at my admittance of those feelings, but they are real and likely to become more so as time goes on.

"Look universe! I just rescued another animal! Surely that counts for something, doesn't it? Not just a pincher bug either. A dog! Wait, universe. I have rescued lots of dogs and cats if you would care to take a look! Not to mention llamas, goats, horses, birds, turtles. Universe? Universe, are you tallying up the total points earned here? Need a little pay back. A favor?" Gosh I'd like to believe it all makes a difference. Our family could really use the help right about now.

Playing Scrabble on the beach in Cirali.

One of her very fave things to do. She was an aggressive player to the very end.

The snapshots of summer

Nowadays, photos are taken by and stored in phones. If the phone is lost, they are lost. Invariably, they are lost anyway, as they sit in some folder or other inside some one's computer and then soon die a cyber death, once the machine is traded up or out. We don't do much with our snap shots these days, let alone put them in an album, as we used to do, for later viewing and sharing, or make a photo collage for the wall, which is always my preferred thing to do with my very favorites.

When my baby was born, I took at least a roll of film a month with my stupendous Minolta 35 mm. (I particularly loved the black and white photos processed in color, which created the sepia tone.) "She is the world's most photographed baby!" my mother announced more than once; and only slightly tongue in cheek. The baby, she was that; and I look back at all those albums I have in my shelves and know that one day, we will all enjoy the heck out of them and thank our lucky stars for the snap shots that mean so much more now than they did then.

These days I take far fewer photos, especially of my daughter, who no longer allows it very often; but I do try and print out the good ones, when I can, if only for them to gather dust for that magic wet week in November when I have nothing better to do than to put together my photo collages and hang them on my memory walls, where I will proceed to enjoy them every time I stroll past. As we speak, I am almost a year behind in my photo projects, but the piles are there and growing and the intent is good.

My baby sister is getting married this week in Turkey and I cannot make the wedding. It would involve a 24-hour journey approximately and a $2000 ticket and I just can't do it. Not only do I feel like a secondary citizen, because who does not attend their baby sister's wedding; but also, she has made both of mine, so I currently feel like less than pond scum. In addition to that hefty hamper of guilt I'm carrying on my back, there is the added fear that, since I won't be in attendance, there will be little to none recording of the actual event. I am the family photographer; that is just what I am, so I get pretty frightened when I know I am not going to be there to document the event. People expect me to show up and take photos and then share them with the rest of the clan who are too lazy to bother to take their own – or at least that is my marginal take on things. It is a monumental and somewhat thankless task, except when you capture a real jewel and then it is like a home run. However, mostly it runs something like this:

"Didn't you get one of so and so? Oh, what a pity!"

"Can you please forward that one to so and so? It is quite good."

"Gosh, I wish you hadn't taken that one of me; please burn it, it is horrendous!" And so, the back n' forth banter can go, when you are the chief family photographer, without the least modicum of appreciation for any of the work or effort it took on your part to freeze frame that special second in our family's history and then share it with the rest of the non-photogs. It is a big job and very unpaid.

In the recent creation and editing of my father's special photo album from his birthday party, the job jumped into my lap and stayed there until it was finished. The real photographer on the job thanked me for my participation in a project that might never have been completed. I had already put together Dad's birthday scrap book and he seemed to really love it. Then I had to go through and edit his official photo album and I was glad to do it. Snapshots from his long and wonderful life; moments in time forever captured. And that is how I see it. I am not a video gal. It is just not my thing, but I feel strongly that, without the precious moments frozen in time, we are all families without a documented history and that is a crying shame.

This time, on the happy event of my sister's marriage to Ali, I am sorely absent and horribly guilt-ridden. I should be there; I should be snapping and documenting. But I am not; I could not make it, and I hope the regret does not weigh me down too much and that I am able to forgive myself in time. Thank goodness a dear old friend of my sister's was able to show up and to document, almost by the minute. I felt as if I were almost there.

I was proud of my 85-year old father recently. He published a fine work of memories, photographs and "Letters to my children" about his early life that he presented to us girls on his birthday. I think that we should all be required to do that before we pass on. I had known this man a long time and thought I knew him quite well, but his short book shared all kinds of insights and moments that I would never otherwise have chanced upon. Other tales made the light go on and make me realize why certain things were as they were. I immediately asked him for part 2. (The life of a writer is that the ink is still fresh on the page, and everyone is already asking you what you are going to do next!)

I shall do that one day myself, whether or not I think my children or grandchildren will actually ever read it. They might when I am gone, perhaps; but I think that is hardly the point. At least the published snapshots from my life will have a position on the page and a stake in our family's history for when I turn to dust and there are only, perhaps, piles of last year's photos lying on a table and begging for someone to do something with them. I shall do it for the sake of history, for fun and then for all of them left behind who, I hope, will still be taking lots of snapshots of their own in their own way, probably through their finger- nail or something by then. In the meantime, my IPHONE snaps a great photo that I can edit, pass along or, equally, kill. Things have really moved on since my old 35 mm.

On the beach for Dad's 85th birthday in Aldeburgh.

Lucy Mason Jensen

Another picture I didn't take.

And the world stops again – a 2014 conversation

From: Lucy
To Kate and Carey

July 7, 2014

My dear friends,

Shit of a thing. My poor sis is back in the waiting room. She has been in excruciating pain for the past week and only got through her wedding on enormous shots of cortisone into the spine. The MRI shows a mass on the spine. We don't know what or why yet, but it's probably not great news.

I just had to tell you. Life is so fleeting, and happiness can run through your fingers and away like water. I cannot believe that she has to deal with this again after 4 years of recovery. I am so sad for her, for them, for all of us.

I am back in the waiting room with her and wish I could take on some of her pain. We shall know more by the end of the week, as her team of oncologists get to examine the MRI etc. Sadly, she is in no shape for any tests tomorrow because she is so full of medication and her system is too toxic. Also, Ali's daughter Dilgesu has to have surgery on her leg tomorrow, so it's all systems go for them on their honeymoon.

Thanks for shouldering some of my burdens.

Love you both,

xxx

From: Carey
To: Lucy
CC: Kate

July 8, 2014

Honey,

Rosie is amazing, strong, spirited. It is hard for those around her to see her assaulted yet again with pain, and the uncertainty that brings. What a beautiful carefree bride in that picture you sent. She has learnt to live in the moment, as should we all. Who knows what the next day brings for any of us? Let's learn from her and stay positive and strong. I remember how my sister looked to me for strength, and how hard it is to find. Rosie has strength in abundance and part of that comes from knowing how much love she has in her life. Stay in that moment, Lu. Focus on hope. Put on your fighting gloves and punch out dark thoughts. You have all our love and support.

Carey

xx

"Look to this day,
For yesterday is but a dream,
And tomorrow is only a vision,
But today, well lived,
Makes every yesterday a dream of happiness,
And every tomorrow a vision of hope.
Look well, therefore, to this day."

July 8, 2014

From: Lucy
To: Carey, Kate

Yes, yes and yes. She is an amazing warrior. I just got off the phone with her and she said that it is 95% likely cancer of the spine. The PET scan will confirm tomorrow. Today she sounded a lot more perky, since Ali's daughter came through her surgery just fine, so that was one good thing, and her pain was more under control. She says she will do whatever she needs to. I cannot believe it. I am sick and angry and reeling. I woke up at 2am this morning and started barking in my own mind to my mother who did not seem to be with me. At 4am, I realized that she was with Rose.

Hey – ho. Living for the day. I need to cheerlead for her, so she can find the strength to keep fighting.

Love,

Lucia

xx

July 9, 2014

From: Carey
To: Lucy

Hi honey,

I hope you did not have a white night, despite everything that's going on. So important for you to be strong. Be angry too, and let all of it out, so you can make room for strength to grow. Rosie has faced this so many times now, and will take the best advice and move forward with it. I'll hope pain-wise it's localized at least, though god knows that might be horrendous enough. We have to hope that the tumour is somewhere within the spine where it can be removed; it can be done. And chemotherapy remains an option for treatment if location is difficult; in short — there are ways to deal with this both surgically and via chemo. Let me know as soon as you have any news re outcome of the scan. Thinking of you. With you. Love you. Carey XX

Postscript to My Plaster Parcel

Once all Rosie's frustrations of life at the horizontal were over she soon amply demonstrated to her surgeon that his building of her hip, where little before had existed, was a complete success.

Croquet chez Lomas, Greenwich

Rosie for years after was able to walk without a limp, she loved to party and dance too, even more to dive and to swim using her powerful crawl. After a night out she would dive into the pool at Kybele to swim, I don't remember how many, certainly a challenge of lengths. Also, at Adrasan she swam the width of the bay, a distance of several miles.

The day came however when after niggles in her hip over many years Rosie found the arthritis had reached the point where she could neither stay on her feet all day teaching, nor walk with Ali over the hills as they loved to do together. By then the cancer had returned but for Rosie it was quality of life that mattered most, so against the advice of her excellent doctors she went ahead to have her hip replaced. She made the right call: I never heard her mention it again.

Dad

Bud-isms 2016

(Me ... The world is going to be very quiet without her)

July 9, 2016

Her: I can't take it on sis. If he dies of a broken heart, cos his youngest daughter dies, there are worse ways to go. Easier for you and Mare to plan a joint funeral ....

July 15, 2016
Her: I seem to be taking a very long time to die. I can't believe I'm still here! Let's go shopping for summer stuff. Oh, hmm. Maybe not.

September 20, 2016
Her: Well, there's shit going on in the back ...

December 30, 2016

Bud: What you think - I want everyone arriving to witness me croaking on my death bed? "

Me: Umm, hello. I'm not here to watch you croak, I'm here for New Year.

I ponder her every moment, watch her moves, shadow, reflection, as if to photograph and forever capture each last moment lost in time. She loves her home, her kitchen. It's warm and snuggly in there, fire in the stove. She has no interest in going outside. The voice is starting to go again — that incessant cough that makes me so worried.

Delicious food, turkey, music. Hilarious games and laughter. Stealing presents from the children was too much fun.

She is tired, tiny. She will die in the same house where Didem passed. I felt our mother in the kitchen, visiting and watching the serving of her famous red cabbage, bread sauce and sherry trifle. Typical of Mum to want to be around the kitchen, food and bustle of a special day, rich with lovely people, food, laughter.

The rough cough continues — she says it's allergies. Lots of tears this trip to Turkey. In bed, listening to the angry barrage of rain.

January 2017

Sicky, irritated. Plan for movie, no movie. Mentally prepping for tomorrow's chemo. I think she's done with it. Scan will be crossroads.

(Her: I'm not going to have it every week. Ruins the quality of life!)

Several lovely, snuggly days. I savor each one carefully like presents I want to save for later.

SECTION 4
THE SUMMER OF IBRANCE

Introduction to
The Summer of Ibrance

When Bud was lucky enough to secure that wondrous designer drug Ibrance, her 2017 summer world opened up in a most generous and marvelous way. She had several of her most brilliant adventures that summer; mostly because she felt so well. The photos from that period show a near chubby, healthy-looking creature with tanned skin and blond hair. (She told me she looked like 'a big ol' cancer faker!') Of course, we knew she wasn't. She had stage 4 cancer and, though we hoped for a miracle, we knew better, as did she. She had just been gifted the summer of Ibrance and she loved every second of it. Life is so precious; especially when time is running out. Ironically enough, the following summer she was dead.

Bud is constantly smiling in all the pictures that summer; doing her 'thang,' as she would say in her appalling American accent...whatever she wanted actually ... swimming, eating, relaxing, reading, playing Scrabble, visiting with friends, boating, swimming, eating, drinking ... She was able to do all her very favorite things without treatment or having to run back and forth to Antalya ("gawd sister ... all that treatment is like a full-time job!") It was her blessed last summer in her chosen home country with all her people and she didn't skip a beat, eating lots of breakfasts – her fave meal in the whole world– going on oodles of boat trips – another firm fave – and hanging out with her beloveds, Ali and Dilgesu, at their beautiful home in the mountains.

I was so happy to see her so happy that summer. I knew it couldn't last and I photographed the heck out of it and her. In fact, some of my very favorite photos of the Bud were taken during this period and I hope that they reproduce appropriately in her story. Her joyfulness and love of life shine through, regardless, and made me proud to be a small part of her last full summer on the planet.

Blissfully full of beautiful memories.

Big sis,
Lu

Joyous – the summer of Ibrance

Intro to
The Lazy Blogger

Bud was doing so well during the 'Summer of Ibrance', she took to writing a blog called 'The Lazy Blogger' about her breast cancer experiences. She and I were members of an online support group for breast cancer survivors, and she recognized how helpful it was to have a pro on board like her. And so, she began the blog. www.stage4and40.com.

She could not believe the response her blog received and was unusually humbled by her new fan club the world over. She also co-founded in Antalya, with her friend Almila, the first ever Breast Cancer support group in that city. There are marvelous photos of their parade through the streets of Antalya and what amazing exposure Rosie and Almila brought to this disease and the support they gave the ladies of Antalya, a movement that continues to this day.

In typical Rosie style, nothing ever lasted too long, because her attention span was always limited and there was so much other living to do elsewhere. By the fall of 2017, it was clear that Ibrance, the wonder drug, was wondering no more and it was back to less kind forms of treatment. As Rosie piped up in her usual peppy fashion ... 'well nothing lasts forever, does it ...' And, of course, she was right; nothing does last forever. Not even if you have her amazing attitude onboard.

So, a return to treatment meant that the blog was stopped. Sadly, it was also lost in cyber space with the unpaid blog bill. I rescued what I could and took a little bit of poetic license in my reconstruction. When I asked Bud, towards the end, whether I could get all her log-in stuff, she smiled at me very sweetly and told me she couldn't remember any of it; so, there we are. I stole what I could.

I was so glad to be able to retrieve at least some of her blog entries from headers on her Facebook profile page and her laptop that was rediscovered a year after her passing, thanks to her husband, Ali. For those of you who know the Bud, you will hear her voice loud and clear through these entries. I only made spelling and punctuation changes where absolutely necessary, and I can hear the Bud laughing at me as I do it.

Lucy Mason Jensen

REPORT CARD - SPRING 2017

Date: 05.07.2017
Report: 07.07.2017

Name: Rosie Mason
Doctor: Prof.Dr. Mustafa Kunt
Hip MR: Technique
Coronal T1 – mainly spin-eco
Axiel T1 – mainly spin-eco
Axiel T2 – mainly fast spin-eco (FSE)
Axiel fast – STIR

After Dotorem 10cc IV contrast injection the following was observed:
In both hips significant liquid was not visible. There was not obvious widening of the joints. Nothing unusual was visible at the head of the femur. Other visible soft tissue all normal.

- Right hip joint material relating to the hip replacement surgery is seen.
- The left iliac bone 45x12mm and left sacrum 50x45mm, right iliac 24x13mm in size several T1A hypo intense and T2A hypo intense masses were seen. It is thought to be bone metastasis in appearance.
- Right anterior iskium 14x11mm, left pubic bone iskium and on the asetebulum 12x8mm multiple T1a and T2A hypo-intence bone metastasis are visible.
- Furthermore the right femur intertrochanter proximal area several masses, one of 5x4mm and other millimetric masses to be seen. These are thought to be bone metastasis.
- The left hip joint has signs of degenerative changes
- The pelvic area has minimal signs of liquid
- The left iliac bone and its neighbouring soft muscle tissue shows T2A hyperintence changes
- Neither overy is visable

RADIOLOGY FINDINGS:

- Bone structure multiple metastasis lesions visible
- Right hip joint material related to hip replacement visible
- Pelvic area minimal liquid is visible
- In comparison to the MR abdomen report of 20/03/2017 the number and size of bone metastasis was noted.

A snapshot of the Lazy Blogger

STAGEHAND40.COM
The Bud blog

May 16, 2017

BALD IS BEAUTIFUL

I have been thinking about having terminal cancer and what that means. I'm also horrified by the almost total lack of support here in Turkey for anyone at any stage of their cancer journey. I've decided to get up and start doing something about it. So, I have started my blog. Bear with it and will post pics n some useful links n stuff going too. Also setting up a private group in Antalya ..

(From Zeynep on the Facebook blog ... "one of the bravest, the most loving and caring people I know so far ... inspirational to me and many in so many ways that she may have never been aware of. She is a friend, sister, family to me....")

May 17, 2017

About me - Rosie Mason

I was born in Colchester in 1970. As a family, we moved from Bures in Suffolk to London in 1976. Family folklore has it that my sister Mary no longer recognized Dad. He had got up early to take the train up to London every weekday and often came home after we were in bed ...

(From good mate Jan on the blog... "Please read my amazing friend Rosie Mason's blog. She is one of the most truly inspirational people I have ever known. I know this will be of help to so many going through the dreaded c.")

On the boat with the blondies. Bud, Jan, Carol and Jan

May 17, 2017

SPEECHLESS

Just a small word of thanks to everyone who has read, shared and taken the time to respond to my first blog entry. The word is SPEECHLESS! (Not something usually associated with me!)

I have been totally stunned by the response to my blog! The lovely comments on the site and also through FaceBook. It has been inspiring and given me so much energy, I'm literally buzzing.

May 18, 2017

DIAGNOSIS - WHAT'S IN A NAME?

So, friends, the journey goes on - today's entry is DIAGNOSIS Part 1. As ever, I have far too much to say. I'm still trying to learn that less is often more.

In 2003, at 33, I was living it up on the southern Turkish coastline, working as a teacher, tanned and blond, the centre of my own world ....

May 20, 2017

MEEEEEE!

Well, there have, of course, been a few important events and details along the way. Two lives, being reborn in Turkey, breast cancer at 33, stage 4 at 40, but still here at 47!

May 23, 2017

YOU'VE SUNK MY BATTLESHIP (OR DIAGNOSIS PART 2)

And here we are off again. Today scan results, a new treatment plan and we're back onboard for the next part of my cancer journey!

What are these? Battleship coordinates! And so it begins, but not on a games board, but in my back. My spine from the top at C5 to the very bottom ...

May 25, 2017

MASKS, STRAPS AND A WET JELLYFISH!

I wanted to share with you the steamier side of my hospital visits. Many of this week's experiences go down in a list of firsts...

May 27, 2017

IT'S ALL ABOUT ME!

This is actually my big sis Lucy's column which is published in her local newspaper ... as you'll realize, it's ALL ABOUT ME! I feel like I should introduce you to my big sis Lucy. She is also a member of the breast cancer club. In 2010, when I was getting over having a large section of my sternum removed and subsequent treatment, sis was diagnosed herself.

A different kind of sisterhood
(Bud has just finished treatment and Lu is going through treatment)

June 1, 2017

FRIENDSHIP AND LIFE CELEBRATION!

Bud and Charl in Monaco

I've been spending more time than I could have imagined with the people I love the most and sharing the mundane and the magnificent with them, winning at Monte Carlo and the helicopter ride back to Nice.

Forever friends - Bud, Mo, Lu Lo, Charl

June 5, 2017

CAROL KING HAS GOT A LOT TO ANSWER FOR!

The same girls have been with me from the beginning of my story and they're still here with me today. Despite not living in the same country ...

This post could also be entitled Stamford Hill Wives, 'The Soup Diaries' or perhaps it should simply be Girlfriends - They Rock! Despite not living in the same country for the last 17 years, our friendship has survived, ebbed and flowed, but we are all here for each other as ever.

These are the girls I have grown up with, bunked off with, slammed tequila shots with, vomited with, on one occasion even shared a boyfriend with, although I'm pleased to say not at the same time and, along the way, I've gone from being arty-farty Rosie at Central/St. Martins, to Right on Rose, the North London teacher, and then later, whilst carving out my new life in Turkey, they offered me nothing but support, until I finally became the person I am today.

Run a hotel? Great idea!

Grow a tasteless tropical fruit? Yes, why not (a lot less enthusiastic about this venture)

Sell swimming pools? No comment.

Open a school? Definitely!

 And the final question to run by them, Marry Ali? Resounding vote of support.
 Anyway, by my mid-twenties, I was living in Stoke Newington (North London), as I called it - but to all taxi drivers it was Stamford Hill/Tottenham border. I was newly single, and it just so happened that so were most of my mates, and we all bought in the same area. We spent almost all our free time together, and when we weren't we were using that brand new communication tool, email, to plan meeting, cooking and eating. Those emails have all been preserved and were long ago named 'The Soup Diaries' after our food obsession. We are still hoping that they will become the next 'Brigit Jones Diary' on the big screen - we've already worked out which movie star we would have playing each of us.
 Our special soup combos were immortalized in the diaries and the ordinary and extraordinary of our then lives. Even the men of the moment were named after favourite food products. I had a particularly pungent boyfriend I named Mr. Gorgonzola.

My two fellow Stamford Hill wives were Charla and Mo. Charl was working in sales for the Orient Express and Mo in the city. Crazy Lucy wasn't a permanent resident, but very much in and out and glamorously working in TV or dispatch riding. What a twenty-something dream we were living.

At that moment I was 'Right on Rose,' working in a pupil referral unit with some challenging students ….'Yesterday's theatre trip was pretty uneventful; heckling the actors, stealing ice-cream and ashtrays, all seemed fairly tame for our kids. Some of them actually watched the play.'

Looking back on those diaries today and the few photos from that time I'm aware that that was another life - we were living it up and had absolutely no idea what the future would throw at us.

Over the years, we have cemented our friendships by sharing absolutely everything. The support has been constant, often bonding over copious amounts of alcohol, tears and laughter. I'm not sure how or when but at some moment or other Carol King's 'You've got a friend' became our theme song and still is. It can instantly reduce us all to tears and take us back over everything that we've shared - good and bad - and all that's yet to come.

We've been shaped and changed by life. In our little group many of our experiences are universal and I put my breast cancer into that category. In each group of friends, surely there must be the one with the serious illness. Thanks to cancer, we have never taken our tomorrows for granted and every visit is the last. We have shared so many bonus days, as I've been living on borrowed time for a lifetime. Every extra day is a blessing and I've been able to spend quality time with these girls, much of it on FaceTime, but also with lots of trips over too. Many of those have coincided with a new stage in the cancer story; a new diagnosis, more spread, a new treatment here, extreme pain there. Each arrival has been like a lifeline at that moment for both Ali and I.

Mo arrived in just such a moment.

I've been blessed with mates who have sometimes been between jobs or courses and one of my many crises just so happened to coincide with Mo having some free time. She became my chauffeur, ferrying me to and from my hospital appointments, expert changer and protector of the blessed morphine plasters and demon 'Scrabbler'. Mo not only held us together during that time, but also sorted out buying herself a new home, put into place a move back into the city and having sorted out the first two within 18 months, she'd also met the man of her dreams. I like to take some credit for Mo getting her shit together; I know she certainly helped me get my ducks in a row.

Charla, the real cook amongst us, began selling sandwiches in the playground at school and this finally ended when she progressed to selling her tarts at organic farmer's markets in the pouring rain. Having met her husband – he was her first customer – she went back to the hotel business and stuck to cooking out of pure love, not necessity.

She pitched up here and filled the freezer with portion-controlled chemo friendly food, aka macaroni cheese, muffins and soup all in the correct colour. During one particularly vile chemo, which lasted for 30 hours a week for a relentless 8 weeks, I could only stomach food in shades of white and cream: toast, butter, cheese, pasta, carbs, the only acceptable thing of colour being strawberry jam. And Charl, bless her, made me food which got me through the icky days of each week.

Crazy Lucy, now a full-time mum to Gorgeous Grace, has managed to nip over and juggle home and care so that we can spend precious time together. And we've also had Grace here, tossing her first pancake and reminding us all how exciting life is at 3.

Lucy Mason Jensen

Bud & Gorgeous Grace

what a wonderful gift time is!

These girls have been there for me through thick and thin, from the first day to the last. They all came to Istanbul to celebrate 'The Weekend of Love,' Valentine's weekend 2016. We bellowed our hearts out on the Bosphorous to Carol King's 'You've got a friend' with tears, laughter and adding new memories to all that's been and all that's yet to come.

The weekend of lurv - Lu Lo, Bud, Mo and Charl

The Bull - Charl, Bud, Mo, Lu Lo and JP

June 7, 2017

HOW TO CALM YOUR PATIENTS

Today I've got my final radiotherapy session for now. I could be back here again any day ... it is never over, but let's just say it's the last one for the moment....

June 11, 2017

WHAT DO THE RADIOTHERAPY DEPARTMENT AND HOTEL CALIFORNIA HAVE IN COMMON?

At 12.55 on Wednesday, I was demob happy. By 12.58 I'd done a total u-turn and was back exactly where I started ...

Hotel California

I'd had a lovely morning, chatted to a nice English couple down in -2, the bowels of the hospital, the radiotherapy department. My new mate from our 'Breast Cancer Women's Group' was with me. She's a fellow stage 4er and, when I met her, I knew immediately that we would get on and of course we do. There's a lot which we have in common: same age, same year of diagnosis, metastasis. We sat and compared where it had gone to. But she wins that game hands down; she's had a brain tumour not once, not twice but three times! I can't tell you how inspirational that is for me ... she's a real fighter. If you met her, you wouldn't see any traces of her treatment unless you look closely, a scar here and there.

Anyway, she was due to be zapped too on number 3 brain tumour, so it seemed fitting that she should be there with me for my last session.

I'd said farewell to the techs, the secretaries, the guy who gets zapped after me, I'd been signed off by a new doctor, I'd smiled at all the people still sitting in the waiting room, the three old guys, and had actually managed to get past the glass doors and as far as the lift. I was about to get out of Hades and was heading for the exit, the ground floor, sunlight, the cafe, maybe even a celebratory tea when ... I heard my name being called. SHIT!

It was 12.58, I'd enjoyed three whole minutes of freedom before I was caught trying to escape. Just like Hotel California 'you can check out any time you like, but you can never leave,' and look at my prophetic words from my previous entry, I just hadn't thought it would be quite so soon: 'Today I've got my final radiotherapy session for now. I could be back here again any day ... it is never over but let's just say it's the last one for the moment.' That particular moment had lasted well, yes, three minutes.

Everyone was still sitting in the same place, although this time they were all looking at me and wondering why I'd been recalled. Faulty goods, I suppose.

This time however things were different. I was ushered directly into the Big Cheese's office, or better known as the Head of the Radiotherapy Department. Rather like god, everyone tells you he exists however no one's ever actually seen him. Well, getting into her office is a little like that. I felt honoured, privileged and absolutely terrified.

After I'd relaxed a bit, I realized what a very difficult job she has; she spends her life pouring over patient's films, reports and scans making millimetric calculations about where to, not to, which angle to, not to, previous radiation given, amount to be given, total amount. The Radiotherapy and the Nuclear medicine departments are the scientific heart of the hospital.

Her: Do you have any pain in your left hip?

Me: No, not really. Should I? (Almost instantly it began to throb)

Of course, when I think about it, I vaguely remember something on my last scan about hip and lesion. I suppose when they did that extra-long control zap the other day that they saw the lesion, fracture, tumour, whatever you want to call it and decided that it would benefit from a dose of radiation. Love the stuff and no mask required this time. So, without even getting as far as the front door I was back with new dates, a planning session, ten doses in all, ten more days of coming and going, the three-hour round trip ......but the benefits are clear.

So now that I'd got myself into the hallowed ground of the Big Cheese's office, I realized what a hugely daunting task she has and felt so grateful that, before I needed my stash of bottom drawer morphine, she was already on the case and looking after my best interests. But it isn't simply her and her department, but the entire hospital is working to give us stage 1-2-3 and 4ers the best treatment and quality of life possible.

As I go from the 12th floor chemo suite, more spa than hospital, with roof-top views of Antalya, live music and painting, to the 2nd and oncology, where I get to gossip and talk goats, dogs and swimming with the nurses, down to ground for the very-very cool sounding Nuclear medicine department where they scan and create the imaging which so much of our treatment is based on, taking a quick breather before heading back down to -2 and the capping department, I know that there's an integrated system here working for me.

I almost never feel despondent when I enter the hospital. That's largely due to the people who work here: from the secretaries, to the chemo nurses, doctors, professors, the hospital psychologist, they all treat me as an individual and the program is tailor made to suit my needs.

I'm always greeted by name; the same lovely nurse does my bloods each week. If I don't have chemo and I'm not using my port (an entry point on my chest where they can take blood and give drugs,) she knows exactly which veins on my hand to use. Last week I whats-apped my blood results to my oncologist who happened to be away at a conference in Chicago. I text to change appointments and can call and actually get through and speak to a doctor any day of the week.

This is Team Rosie; this hospital is working for me.

So, I decided to take advantage of the warm glow which had entered the Big Cheese's Office since I'd thanked her, her team and the hospital. I plucked up the courage and asked the million-dollar question:

Me: Can I have my mask please? (Terrified)

She immediately picked up the telephone and ordered a stay of execution!

Her: DO NOT MELT THE MASK DOWN!

June 12, 2017

PRIZE GIVING DAY
or the Which Guide to Cancer treatments!

As you might have noticed, I like it so much I'll be back there next week in the treatment lab, excluding the mask, but ready to receive my prizes.

I've trawled my way through numerous cancer treatments especially for you, and here is my personal 'Which Guide' to some of the best and the worst.

IN FIRST POSITION IS RADIOTHERAPY — As you might have noticed, I like it so much I'll be back there next week, excluding the mask. I have already spoken at length about its benefits, so won't bore you with any more of that here.

IN SECOND POSITION IS S.I.R.T. (which stands for selective internal radiation therapy.) Last Friday, having finished my standard radiotherapy course on Wednesday, I was back in hospital for this little treatment. It's also known as radioembolisation.

In comparison to the average 5-10 minutes, which a normal radiotherapy session takes, this is a little longer. Anyone who's ever had an angiogram will be familiar with the procedure and this radiation is given in the same way, however here it's via the hepatic artery in your groin directly into your liver. You have to lie still without moving, after it's all over, for a full six hours with the high-tech aid of a sandbag on your thigh! But the actual treatment is state of the art and highly effective. It's a targeted therapy to the liver and, for me, this has been successful where numerous chemotherapies have failed ... it has magically shrunk and killed my liver tumours big and small and look at this, without sickness, hair loss or any other nasty side effects.

The worst thing I can say about SIRT is that you have to be nil by mouth for six hours prior to the procedure and, as you cannot move for six hours after, you end up both starving and desperate for a wee!

The best thing I can say is:
'Today's Sunday and just 2 days after SIRT and I'm back in the sea and haven't been off my food.' A silver medal winner!

I note that this treatment is not widely available in the UK on the NHS, particularly for breast cancer. If you need more advice or details about this treatment, then follow the link below. Link - cancerresearch.co.uk

IN THIRD POSITION IS CHEMOTHERAPY - Now I don't want to dis chemo, because it has performed an invaluable job for me and has kept the spread of cancer at bay for many, many years. However, chemo is a very broad term and there are some shockers out there. And, of course, each one varies widely according to how the individual reacts to it. However, there is one which stands out above the rest and to this I would like to award a special prize in a category all of its own:

THE CHEMOTHERAPY BOOBY PRIZE - goes to FOLFIRINOX, a delectable mix of not one, not two, not three, but four chemotherapy drugs. It can be given over 48 hours every two weeks; however, I was lucky enough to have it over 24 hours every week. It is primarily used as a treatment for pancreatic cancer; however, as I'd raced successfully through all known breast cancer treatments, this was untried. My oncologist decided it was time to call in the Big Bad Boys and see if this one could reach the parts where others had failed.

This chemo is so toxic that, on my first session, I had to stay in hospital overnight so they could observe and monitor me for allergic reactions. As I have the constitution of an ox, it didn't touch the sides. I believe that all those years spent drinking vodka must have stood me in good stead.

One of the things I particularly liked about this chemo was that I got a going home present each week. I was handed a small cloth pouch with a plastic hand grenade to pop in my pocket so that the lovely stuff could be given over a longer period of time, via my port, in the comfort of my own home. Actually, it looked like a colostomy bag, not most people's idea of a desirable fashion accessory. Apart from this, there was a list of side effects as long as my arm - all of the usual, plus a few more.

My favourite was the one which really caught me out. A few days after my first course of this little delight, I had begun to notice a twitch under one of my eyes, then it also spread to my lip and gradually I was beginning to lose the use of both thumbs. I assumed I had a brain tumour. Believe me, that's a perfectly natural and logical thing for a person in my position to do. I called my oncologist in the evening, long after his day was over, and, god love him, he answered! My fingers had become contorted into abnormal and odd shapes, my eye (only one) was twitching frantically and my mouth was stuck in a snarl. I looked like the Hooded Claw.

My oncologist wasn't overly worried, but told me to come in the next day and we'd do a brain scan. As he predicted, the results came back negative. However, there was one thing which he'd warned me about, which I'd paid no attention to whatsoever and that was THE COLD.

I started to follow the twitches, claws and, of course he was right, cold air, cold hands, feet, drinks in fact cold of any description and I literally froze inside and out. Cold and this Bad Boy are not a good combo. When that drug cocktail comes into contact with cold, all sorts of hell breaks loose.

It was hard to avoid the cold, as it was winter and a near record-breaking one at that. We kept warm in the village by keeping our wood-burners on the go non-stop and burnt two lorry loads of wood. I wore hats, gloves and socks, all cashmere and almost gave up going out for the next 7 weeks. It wasn't great for my social life, but we were hopeful that such an aggressive treatment would have some positive results and get on top of those tumours, especially the ones in the liver. And do you know what, after all that, it hadn't done a bloody thing ...

June 15, 2017

THE MASK

Sometimes an image is worth a thousand words!

(I did see it and it was very Hannibal Lector-ish ....L)

June 17, 2017

HAIR TODAY, GONE TOMORROW!

A little light weekend read to make you laugh and cry! I've always had a fairly easy-going relationship with my hair. I have never considered it to be my best asset ...

Lucy Mason Jensen

Hair today, gone tomorrow!

However, no matter how you look at it, hair is an essential part of us. I could try to convince you that it is overrated, but we are all surprisingly attached to our locks. Hair defines us as women in so many ways and externally is the first thing which people notice about us, without it we look strange, ill, odd and, because of that, it immediately changes how people we don't know treat us.

I have refused to be defined by whether I have hair or not. The simple truth is that I want to be loved, liked, admired, or even respected because of who I am, not what I am or what I look like. I've spent more time without it in the last three years than with it, but I haven't let that bother me.

I think I've been in training to be bald for most of my life. When we were young, my sisters had long locks they could sit on and I was the one blessed with 'the pudding bowl', a form of parental torture. I think Mum rightly assumed that washing, combing and plaiting my hair would just give me yet another excuse to have a tantrum and she was probably right, so kept things simple and the myth was born, 'Rosie looks good with short hair.'

So, I had to settle for doing my sister Mary's hair. Fortunately, this phase coincided with 'The Bo Derek,' a perfect do for Moo. It involved long blond hair, and beads plaited into it, and all done in time for 'No Uniform Day' at school. I was probably sporting a crew cut and half shorn head by then. Who knew that this style was simply a taste of things to come?

Of course, my sisters, friends and I romped through the usual series of terrifying hairstyles ...the new Romantics of the 1980's had a lot to answer for.

Rosie and Mary with their 80's hair

Back-combed, crimped, hair-sprayed, peroxide blond or shades of orange with bits of tatty lace and material tied here and there and the head of hair became a wishing tree rather than a do.

And then along came Jen (that's Jennifer Anniston to my father's generation) in the early 90s, with sleek, coloured and beautifully cut hair. She saved most of us from mullets and perms forever more. We threw away the crimpers, combs and spray and began to pay real money to hairdressers instead of doing it ourselves. Thank-you Jen! What would our barnets have been like without you?

And, of course, one of the most shocking things we have to face about Breast Cancer is that on top of having a mastectomy, or lumpectomy and being thrown into the menopause, but you also find that the one vestige of your womanliness is now also challenged, your hair. While there are many chemos which do not make your hair fall out, some of the most common first line treatments do. And so your hair sheds and drops further, adding insult to injury.

And hair is so much more than just the issue of hair on your head; eye-brows, lashes, under-arm, lady garden, under-carriage, et al. Even the hair you didn't know you had suddenly becomes no more and then you notice it, because you haven't got it. And yes, nasal hair does actually perform a useful function. Without anything to filter out dust and a chemo which dries up every mucus membrane in the body your nose becomes a sand filled desert, a huge vacuous wasteground to store what? Well, stuff, but mainly crumbs and crunchy bits. My advice, girls, is a little vaseline to keep it moist; it will do the job which your much maligned nasal hair did in the past.

There are many solutions to being folically challenged. A wig is an option, but it doesn't necessarily solve the problem either as, without eyebrows and lashes, even if you have 'hair,' the face is a blank. I only realized how much of facial expression is derived from the eyebrows once I'd lost mine. Most women I've come across during chemo struggle to get up, let alone deal with wig, false eyelashes and painted on brows. I certainly didn't bother.

I have generally loved being bald, it made me feel different in a good way and family, friends and Ali have always told me how much it "suits you," so fortunately I've never felt its loss. My ego was constantly shored up with comments of "lovely-shaped head," and Ali genuinely didn't seem to notice, but that could simply be a man thing.

Remember that I'm a person who mistook people's stares for admiring looks! I think, in this situation, delusion is a good thing. When Moo suggested that perhaps I might like to get my eyebrows tattooed on, or even just pencil them in, I simply replied that there was no need to "Gild the lily." Such is the degree of my confidence, or just a total lack of a physical perception of myself.

But, in general, the only thing which's more traumatic than losing your hair is when it starts to regrow. Post chemo hair is HORRIBLE. Ok after my first chemo in 2004 when my hair grew back it was very curly and brown, but now when it grows back it is more shit-brown and with a smattering of what I like to term 'Aunty Louie's pubes.' There's no going out uncovered with this pile on my head.

Bud with the 'Aunty Louie Pube' look .... At Indircik

And then when you begin to look more carefully, you realize that it is not just the hair on your head which needs attention. It's everywhere and often where you didn't have it before. THE BEARD! What's that about? Forget waxing the legs ladies, I actually waxed my face. This is not justice.

And do you know what everyone says, "After chemo your hair will grow back all thick and curly," and yes, they are right. All over the bloody place. You actually go from zero maintenance of the garden to having to get in a whole team of strimmers, pluckers and trimmers to deal with untamed hedgerows, shrubs, and bushes. You name it, it's back with a vengeance. Whatever money you'd saved during the six months of being bald, you now need to invest in the gardening business.

So, this time, I just couldn't go through the horror head again and have made the decision for the final time. I will never again have 'The Jen,' but neither will I have to deal with 'The Aunty Louie' either. Short, neat, strawberry blond (ginger) .... and the only thing is that when I look in the mirror, the thing which springs to mind is 'The Joker' from Batman.

A monk, or the Joker from Batman?

Bud and Birgie at the Street Café, Adrasan

June 19, 2017

RADIOTHERAPY AND NOUGHTS AND CROSSES

And back to the serious business of being a terminal breast cancer patient ...... Friday was day one of my new course of radiotherapy.

Noughts & crosses

June 20, 2017

X MARKS THE SPOT!

I had a little accident yesterday morning, when I was removing one of my surgical plasters protecting the bloody great X's and circles, the entire mark came off. Whoops! I imagined no end of trouble ...

June 22, 2017

THE BIG C

    Is the bane of all cancer sufferers' lives! Have you ever been unable to go for a day or two? That's nothing! We're talking 3-4 day cycles! But it's a subject that the med profession don't seem to take that seriously!

Get your shit together!

CONSTIPATION is the bane of all cancer sufferers' lives, however it is a subject which the medical profession doesn't seem to take seriously. And while I love my oncologist dearly, it's not a topic which seems to enter into our chats very often.

On occasion however, I have perked right up at the prospect of a chemo which may actually give me a really good dose of diarrhea, only to find of course that it too blocked, bunged and dried the passages, just like all the others.

I have often eaten unwashed fruit and semi-raw meat from the barbecue in the hope that a couple of bugs will get into my intestines and perform a thorough clearing out job, but so far, no joy. Most of the time, the problem of being constipated just affects my nearests, dearests and myself; however, the other day it became a source of embarrassment for me at the hospital.

Last week, when I was having my pre-treatment set-up scan in the radiotherapy department, I was a bit alarmed when my bowel movements or rather lack of them became an issue for the tech doing the scan. I was lying on the table in a vest and pants, already feeling a little self-conscious, when he came back into the room and ever so politely asked me 'I wonder if you've been having trouble going to the toilet recently? Could it be possible that you may be a little constipated?'

How embarrassing! Obviously, the build-up was inhibiting the clarity of the view of my left hip. I had a vision of a huge intestine serpent which of course the tech could see with perfect clarity.

I equally politely replied 'Of course I'm constipated, I'm a cancer patient and I've had almost constant chemotherapy for the last three years!' Every single treatment I've had and still have, directly affects the production of regular, normal bowel movements.

Following that informative little outburst, he then, politely, suggested that perhaps I should drink a couple of glasses of water and make more of an effort. He obviously had absolutely no idea just how difficult it is to 'drop the kids off,' as Crazy Lucy refers to this particular activity. And does he honestly think that a couple of glasses of water will make any difference? Laughable. Am I constipated because I am dehydrated?

Anyway, I agreed to try his suggestion and obediently went off to drink a few glasses of water and concentrate on the job in hand. I sat, tried, rocked, pushed, nothing! I drank a few more glasses of water and, in between, called a friend, Nikki, fellow breast cancer sufferer and constipation expert, and tried once more. No production!

To keep this most basic of bodily functions ticking over is no small achievement. Even the smallest of productions is met with a fanfare and full-scale announcement. It is nothing to be taken for granted.

Evidently, the technician had no idea who he was talking to. I was gutted that I was going to have to disappoint the ever so polite tech by less than politely telling him that 'NO, I cannot do a bloody SHIT!' That's like asking me to turn water to wine, bringing the dead back to life; it's nothing short of a miracle and to perform on demand is IMPOSSIBLE.

The tech had muttered something about failing to come back without the treasure, medication may be required bla-bla. I was horrified. I may actually have to come back another day, once I'd managed to expel the serpent. But fortunately, between drinking my first and second litre of water, he'd spoken to the Big cheese about my 'little blockage,' and it hadn't affected the image of the hip. Too right, let's not lose sight of the real issue here. It's not my bowel movements which are on trial here! It's my crumbly, cruddy bones.

So, eventually, we finished the scanning and drawing and I was free to go home and deal with my little embarrassment in the privacy of my own home.

Next, I'll be sharing my Top 10 constipation tips with you – with expert advice from Nikki Bregazzi. If you are a member of our club, you'll be grateful!

June 25, 2017

GET YOUR SHIT TOGETHER!

For anyone who missed the latest from the Lazy Blogger, check out Nikki and Rosie's top tips – all about the BIG C!

In order to ensure that you are never blocked, bunged up, excrementally challenged or fartipated, you may want to read on!

NIKKI AND ROSIE'S TOP 10 TIPS TO EASE THE BIG C
CONSTIPATION relief for cancer patients

The delicate subject of our habits whilst on the khazi, bog or the House of Lords are generally a deeply private and personal matter. That is until you become a cancer patient and are thrown into the spiral of chronic constipation caused by chemotherapy and opioid painkillers, if you're using them.

1. Drink 2-3 litres of water every day: of course for us, Chemo Queens, water is our champagne; most especially on days when we have treatment. It flushes those toxins from the system, your skin will be radiant, you'll wee copiously, but this alone will not promote evacuating your bowels. You will need more help.

2. Eat a high fruit and fibre diet: We all know that, under normal circumstances, this is the key to the production of healthy stools! However, these are no ordinary circumstances – to promote a smooth ripe banana type stool you would need to consume industrial quantities of fibre. Taking Fibrogel may help, however it will not be enough.
3. Probiotics: We all know that these promote good gut health and, believe me, you need that at the moment. They are available in many forms from your supermarket or health food stores and are also easy to consume as yoghurt, a tasty drink or in pill form, so, if you're on the chemo diet and baulk at the sight of anything which isn't white and toasted, you may be able to stomach this without too many problems. I think it is unlikely that these will shift the mass, but you will be promoting excellent intestinal health.
4. Olive oil: You're well hydrated, full of fruits and fibre, healthy, glowing and yet are still constipated and becoming increasingly uncomfortable, so try a couple of tablespoons of olive oil with the juice of half a lemon. Drink this first thing in the morning before having anything else. It may work, but no guarantees.
5. The Bi-carb cocktail: This is a favorite of mine and brings back fond memories of a dose of chronic constipation. My mate Mo and I were neck and neck in the constipation challenge race, however she was beating me in the daily Scrabble score; but this one was going to the wire. When we both got to day four, we decided we needed to find a solution to this pressing and increasingly unpleasant problem. So first thing on the morning of the fifth day, without any effective evacuations, we armed ourselves with

a bottle of mineral water, a packet of bicarbonate of soda and the juice of a lemon. We made this gaseous mixture into a frothy cocktail and downed it in one. Mo immediately felt sick. I think I belched, gurgled, bubbled, not entirely sure which end it may come out of and produced a couple of pellets. It was a semi-effective, crap inducing, stomach cramp making horror.

6. A coffee and a cigarette: desperate measures called for desperate solutions.

So, by now, even I'd realized it was time to call in the big guns.
From here on this list largely comprises Nikki's tried and tested top tips....
Guaranteed success within a couple of days at the most....
And within minutes if an emergency evacuation is required

7. Lactulose syrup: in order to avoid fetid flatulence, stomach aches with little or no 'follow through,' Nikki advises moving straight on to number 8.
8. Dulcolax tablets: These are a mild laxative to be taken in the evening. In an ideal world you'll have a production the following morning. If you have a no show then try again the following evening. You'll probably be sorted within 48 hours.
9. Glycerol suppositories: Nikki describes these as 'slippery little suckers' however she's had a 100% success rate with these and you'll have a movement within about 10 minutes. Nikki's other piece of invaluable advice is to remember to lock the bathroom door and, if possible, send partners and children out somewhere. A very impressive result.

10. DIY Enema Kit: This is Nikki's absolutely must-have piece of hardware which we should all arm ourselves with. It's available via mail order from Amazon. The whole process takes no more than an hour from beginning to end. She recommends the bicarbonate of soda enema recipe and stresses warm water, not cold. She did mention something about bathroom floor, relax, perfectly normal so prepare yourselves in advance by reading 'How to ...' top tips which you'll find online.

So here you have it! The truth is that.....
chemo = constipation
chemo + opioids = constipation
opioids = constipation

My enema bag is ordered and I, for one, will be following Nikki's advice.

Nikki and Rosie - fellow stage 4-ers

June 26, 2017

EVER WONDERED ...

What stage 4 breast cancer looks like? Today's life-affirming model - Nikki Bregazzi - showing us how to do terminal cancer in style!

There are some really good things about having cancer, believe it or not! And one of the best things to have happened in the last few years is that I met Nikki.

From day one, our conversations generally began with a list of possible chemo side effects;

'Got any hair loss, funny taste, bad feet, still constipated, of course ... oh that's great!'

We both laughed at the start of our current treatment, palbociclib (aka Ibrance) as they warned us that it could cause diarrhea! We both laughed that off as fiction and of course we were right, not a regular bowel movement in sight.

My sister Mary, the one who lives on the Isle of Man, as opposed to the one who lives in California, knew Nikki vaguely but had a feeling that we might get on. Mary was aware that like me Nikki was a stage 4er, breast cancer and similar age.

When we first started chatting on FaceTime, we were both on cepacitabine, an oral form of chemo. I was at home in my village in Turkey and she at home in the Isle of Man. For most of our chats I've always been the bald one and she's been the one with the very stylish, short blond hair. It's obvious to me that we would have been mates, if we'd have met under any circumstances, but I think as a cancer buddy she has become an indispensable part of my life.

Nikki's road to discovering that she had terminal cancer was very different from mine. I've had years to get used to it. By the time that she knew she had breast cancer, it had already metastized to her liver. Mine has now spread there too, so we can tumor brag, compare treatments, side effects, the continued bowel issue, and we even know what the other one is talking about with the internal buzzing thing. Does anyone else get that?

But most of all, we have provided a support system for each other that even our nearests and dearests, even our childhood friends, cannot do.

Nikki and I have both bought strongly into the living with cancer thing; we're not dying of cancer. When you look at Nikki you don't think.....

'Terminal cancer!'

She's got her kids, bottle fed lambs, a husband, a massive group of friends and when I call her, she's usually just back from a bike ride or about to go for a swim.

So yesterday when I asked Nikki whether she would mind about appearing in my blog, she said she didn't mind. But she did draw the line at putting in a photo of her amazing, reconstructed breast, tattoo. I didn't have a mastectomy. If I had I would have liked a tattoo like hers. But I'm a total coward and it must have bloody hurt. It's very, very cool.

I'm full of the utmost respect for her, as she also managed to do a whole course of chemo using the cold cap in order to hang on to her hair. I literally lasted 10 minutes. And what's more, she's even had her eyebrows tattooed, so that she never has that bland, bald chemo face. RESPECT!

When I finally met Nikki in the flesh for the first time she rocked up in a full mod-cons, luxury, converted transit van, complete with beds, sink, dining table and banquet chairs, a fridge and a few bottles of champagne. That was the only way Nikki could arrive. I believe in the past it may have been on a motor bike or even a horse.

It's quite clear that Nikki was always one of the wild ones, and although I wasn't there in person to witness it, I have seen her drumming in a band recently, her husband singing! who gets to do this stuff in normal life, let alone when you have terminal cancer! It's quite clear that cancer hasn't managed to tame her!

IT DOESN'T GET MUCH BETTER THAN THIS!

So is it any wonder that people don't believe either of us about the dying bit? When life's this good, what's the problem? But of course there is a problem; a lot of the time it's just over your shoulder and you only remember when it comes up and bites you. For all the laughs which Nikki and I share, the subject which has brought us together is deadly serious.

Through our friendship, we have nagged and bullied each other into getting the best treatment possible. At the moment, we are both on the movie star drug palbociclib. We have both got there through very different means, but give or take a tweak or two or a few grams here or there, it's almost identical. We also know that while one of us may stay stable for some time, the other's cancer may continue to grow. However it plays out, we will always be happy for each other, even if we are sad for ourselves. We are both giving ourselves the best possible chance to enjoy our lovely lives for just a little longer.

So tomorrow we have our first women with breast cancer group meeting in Antalya, Turkey. I really hope that some of the women there may find their Rosie or their Nikki — as good as a dose of chemo any day.

June 29, 2017

    Today's blog involves a little game of 'SPOT THE ODD ONE OUT'

    Without that chemo 'look' or the dead-giveaway baldness, can you identify which of us has cancer?

    It doesn't matter which, the point is not what we look like on the surface but what's going on inside. All our preconceptions of what it means to have terminal cancer generally involve images of bald, emaciated hospital patients at death's door. However, if you've looked at the photos which I've shared this week you'll notice that they all have a few things in common:

    a. Nobody's bald
    b. Nobody's emaciated
    c. Nobody's sitting around waiting to die

    In fact, when you look at these pictures it's hard or even impossible to know who is the one with the terminal illness.

    Meet Gill! Today she's looking after her two-year-old grand-child and busy. She's got two children – Becky who's 22 and Connor who's 18 and a step-daughter. Four years ago, she went to her doctor complaining of back ache and was expecting the MRI to confirm psoriatic arthritis, instead it showed that she had metastatic breast cancer. She hasn't had a lumpectomy, or a mastectomy. When she was diagnosed at the age of 45, it had already spread to the bones. There was little point going through breast surgery, as the horse had already bolted, so to speak. Gill was on tamoxifen and zometa and that managed to keep on top of the cancer for three and a half years. More recently a scan showed more spread in the bones and so her treatment was changed to letrozole and dematrasab. Now six months later and there is a suspected lesion on the liver. She's currently waiting for the results of an MRI and is hoping to get on a trial.

Gill says that she has 'taken it all in my stride, tried to remain strong for my kids ... my quality of life is not really any different from before I knew I had it, other than tiredness and aches.'

And here's Rose G.! So here in Rose's words is her cancer story:

I was first diagnosed in 2012. 20 weeks of chemo, bilateral mastectomy. I was working as a consultant at the time and my contract wasn't renewed so I found myself bald, lost all my fingernails and no job. I was out of work for almost a year. It reared its ugly head again exactly 4 years later. I've lost 2 brothers and a sister to cancer. This last year 2 good friends. I refuse to go down without a fight. Fight for fun that is! I've been out of work since September. I tell everyone I'm retired.

I try never to turn down a party invitation. Oh, and my husband and I adopted my granddaughter. She came to live with us the week I started chemo 5 years ago. She's what keeps me going. When I mention #1, #2, #3, #4 on Facebook they are the grandkids. #3 is the one we adopted. Oh, and I love tattoos and wine.

Rose is 56 and about to start on another round of chemo, the fourth since October. She now has mets to the spine, pelvis, ovaries, peritoneal and liver. Oh, and also ascites (which is a build-up of liquid related to liver function.) She told me 'my sister passed from esophageal cancer, my little brother from non-Hodgkin Lymphoma and my other brother from throat cancer.'

And do you know what she's doing? She's planning a 4th of July party. She hasn't done one in six years. In preparation, she's taking the week off wine, until Sunday. Sounds like a great party, her husband's going to grill burgers and hot dogs. She's making salads and kielbasa, a Polish meat dish.

well as you can see, we're all living with cancer
More tales from living it up @ stagehand40.com

(P.S. RIP to the hilarious Rose G. No doubt living it up just around the corner with our very own Bud! They never met in person, but were online sisters and kindred spirits.)

July 4, 2017

MYSTIC ROSE & the Mondayitus

Mystic Rose and her crystal ball will reveal all...
So, can you tell me what I have in store, Mystic Rose? Can you see what kind of day lies ahead on Monday?
'Well, I can see that you have a nasty case of... wait, it's coming to me! Yes of course, plague of almost everyone in the western world, a particularly bad dose of MONDAYITIS!'
Yes, tell me about it and do you know what? It began at about 9pm on Saturday, so this one must be really bad. I know the cause of it, of course, but that doesn't actually make any difference or seem to help in the slightest. Mine has been brought on by the usual stresses of Monday and back to the office – oh scrap that, should read Monday at the hospital. I've been having a few 'Oh shit' thoughts about what may be in store. What can you see ahead?
'I can see a room, you have been there before. It's in a basement, there are machines'.
Oh yes, that's what I'm dreading, a repeat performance of what happened the last time when I foolishly tried to escape the Radiotherapy department. This time I may not even get as far as the lift. On the last occasion, I was immediately prescribed a new dose of 10 sessions

of radiotherapy for my crumbly left hip. My battleship coordinates - L5, T2, C3 - of the spine had successfully

been dealt with and, moving downwards, they had of course correctly identified the need to examine the ball and socket, or is it femur, or is it iliac, pelvis or wherever ....well anyway, my freedom was very short lived.

In contrast to my left hip, my right one is titanium or something and in perfect health, thanks very much. From the age of birth on, it had been the problem child - an undiagnosed congenital hip, leading to traction, plaster, operations, and finally in 2012 a hip replacement. Since then, it's behaved impeccably.

Mystic Rose, can you actually tell me what's going on inside my left hip?

'I can see, it's not clear ....a bit obscured by crumble and fluff and a quantity of atoms, radoms and stuff whirling around ...sorry, it's too misty...'

God, she's useless, this one. I'll tell you. The reason for my sense of foreboding about Monday is based on the fact that my left side now feels worse than when all the zapping began 10 days ago ... oh and also because I want to be able to get on and enjoy the summer, doing exactly what I want, when I want and not when the hospital wants me to. I would much rather be going to the beach tomorrow, than going on a 200km round journey to be zapped and then god knows what.

Rose, do you think I'll make it out of there intact, or will I be recalled? Might I even get as far as an upper floor, like ground and daylight and be able to make a run for it?

'I can see a lift, a hand is reaching towards the magic number 2. There's a man and a woman, they're discussing something. Wait, let me tune in, oh yes, the weekend and the best beach in the area ...'

I bet you do. If and that is a big IF I get as far as the lift, I will be taking it to level 2 and missing out on ground and still not heading out of the front door. I'll pay a visit to my oncologist Deniz and his assistant Ozlem; we'll catch up on stuff, holidays, family and then get down to basics. I think a blood test is due.

'I see a flight of stairs, going down down, past the light and into the basement'.

Yes, well it's more than likely that, on leaving Deniz's office, I'll be heading for level -1 and the orthopedic department. Still missing out on the ground floor! This is like a game of Monopoly, where each turn you do not pass GO and end up going straight to jail. Well, I do have to get to the bottom of what the hell is going on with this cruddy hip. I sit on the loo — it locks. Get into the car — it locks. However, it doesn't lock when I'm swimming, so hoping to get plenty more of that in over the next few months.

'I see doors. There are people inside, but you cannot gain entry. I can hear music and the sound of laughter and can smell beer!'

My my, she really is a wonder this Mystic Rose! Do you think it may mean that my clubbing days are over? Oh well, think I'll survive. I'd be a little put out, if she tried to tell me no more days in the Mediterranean

'I see a couch, a man is touching your leg. It isn't your husband.'

Oh great, that'll be the nice orthopedic guy, seeing if he can figure out what's up. So Mystic Rose does he get anywhere, any ideas from him? Is he wearing glasses by the way and wearing a white coat?

'Oh actually he hasn't got a clue, but I can see a machine. Sorry, not see, but hear. This one is different and very very noisy!'

Oh brill, that'll probably an MRI. Have you ever had one of those? Makes a total racket, but a good substitute for clubbing, as a bit like trans music. The strange thing is that although my hip obviously isn't doing exactly what it's meant to be doing, for the nano-second or so that it is totally frozen it doesn't actually hurt; more like a surprise, which is getting more and more predictable the more often it happens.

'So here you have it! My predictions for Monday.....'

Thanks Mystic Rose for the reading, I'll be letting you know what really happens - she's a total charlatan that one. Wouldn't trust her as far as I could throw her ...

Let me tell you all what really happened on Monday ... well, the best news of the day was that I was indeed let out of jail and was signed out of radiotherapy! Whoo Hoo - as a friend says, 'let's all do a happy dance!' I quite agree. I was escorted off the premises to a fanfare, at least that was what was playing in my mind. The parting word of the Big cheese was to be very careful with my hip! I did ask her just how careful can I be; I do need to do at least basic things like walk and sit on the toilet. At least now, no matter what, for at least the next few days, I won't have to do the 200km journey every day ....only a couple of times a week. Result!

And do you know where I went next, Rose, without more than a couple of minutes wait, I was ushered into the orthopedic surgeon's office, one Mr. Kunt and yes, that does rhyme with runt! After much giggling and sniggering, because I had my mate with me, he did a thorough examination which involved banging, prodding, and manipulating, and came to the conclusion that we haven't got a blimmin' clue what's going on in there and that the best course of action is to have an X-ray and an MRI. I had the X-ray done immediately and the MRI could have been done later in the day; however, I chose to go back and have it done on the Wednesday instead, with results to follow on Friday.

Just as I was leaving his office, he, rather like The Big cheese, warned me to be careful, and said something about break, snap, implode, fracture, pop, splinter ... none of those are good things when applied to your hip. He also doesn't mean break as in riding accident, or on the downhill slopes doing the grand slalom, he means through walking, sitting and doing normal stuff!

I've never felt fragile before; this is a whole new feeling for me to get used to!

And do you know what, Mystic Rose, you were right about nearly all of it! I then went up to level 2 and, without any wait, saw Deniz and Ozlem and caught up with what's been going on, had a debate about the use of cannabis and had a blood test. I didn't bother waiting for the results, as Ozlem always whatsapps them to me. Service, this is 20 carat gold and all as you predicted Rose, you clever girl.

Oh, I forgot to mention that, as I was leaving my orthopedic surgeon's office, he called out to me 'c u next Tuesday!' I corrected him and said 'No, cu on Friday!'

And so it goes ... today, this afternoon, I'll be back in the Med.

My mate Jan had never seen the like of it, no GP referral, no hanging around in endless queues to get bloods or other procedures done, this system flows along seamlessly, with the government insurance fitting most of the bill and a contribution made by the patient. I think the MRI will cost me the equivalent of 10 pounds; what a steal!

Akin and the Bud. One of the superstars at Medstar

July 5, 2017

HAPPY WEDDING ANNIVERSARY, MY BELOVED

    Today is an important day in my life - a day I thought I'd never see! It's my 21st wedding anniversary. (In dog years). Still here and living it up with advanced breast cancer.

The Rose Bud & Her Brilliant Adventures

What really happened on Monday? Well Mystic Rose was right about almost everything!

Today I'll be back swimming in the Med, the hip is buggered and under investigation. I didn't have to wait to see the orthopedic surgeon, a Mr. Kunt, that rhymes with runt by the way and I was finally escorted out of radiotherapy and told not to come back for a month. Whoopee ... There was a big and very loud internal cheer and some virtual and wild dancing took place. All in all, a good result.

But today, there is something much more important that I want to share with you. Today is my third wedding anniversary. In normal years, one is paper, two cotton and three leather; but I think we are working on at least dog years for me, so today is my twenty-first and according to tradition, that is celebrated with a brass gift.

But how can Ali and I measure our years together? We have shared some of our best and worst days. We have had so many extra years, bonus days, celebratory parties and many, many last hurrahs. We've lived a life on borrowed time and still continue to do so. Who would have thought that I could still be here? I certainly didn't ....We've crammed so much into so little.

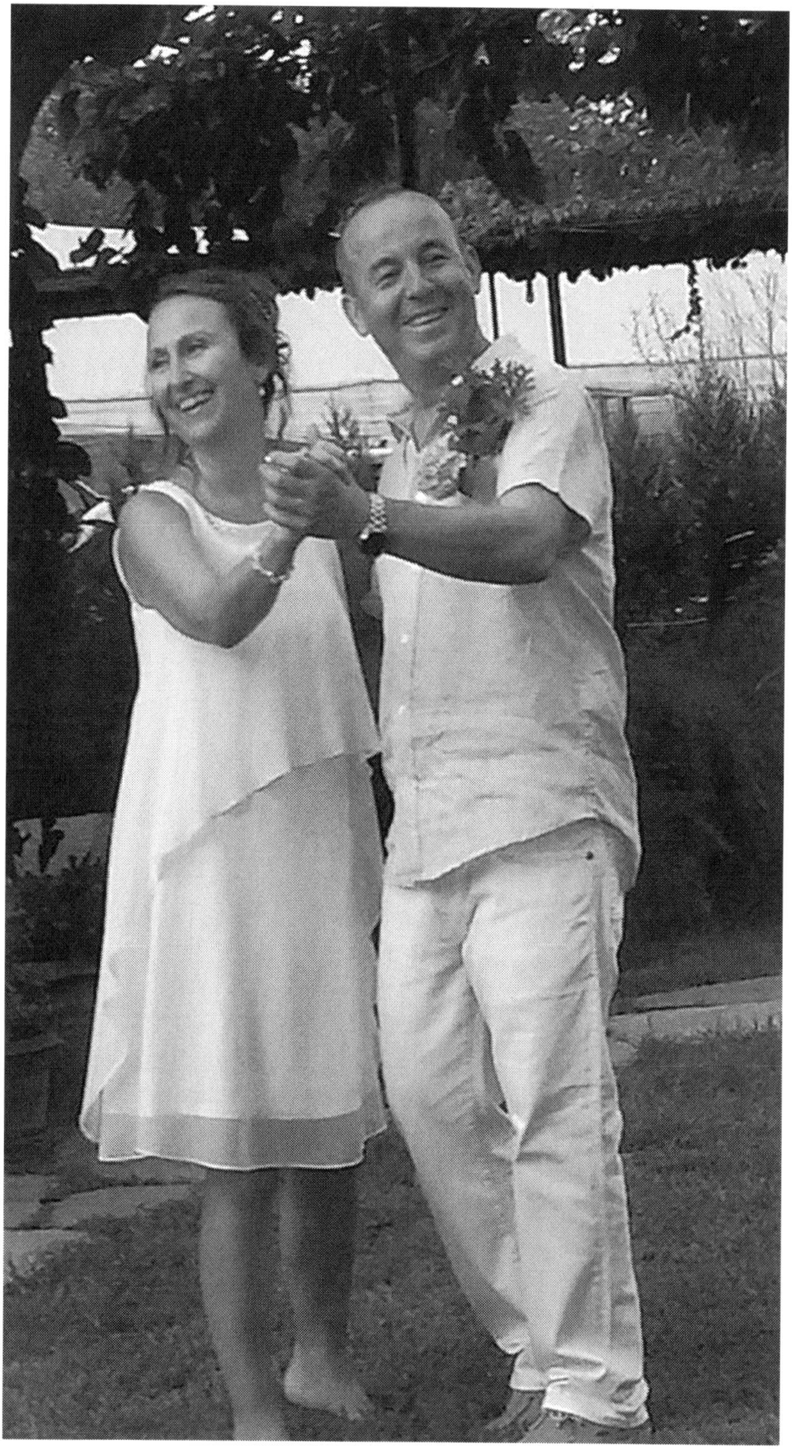

So, I don't want to focus on illness and cancer, but I want to tell you something about my beloved husband Ali. Why do I love him?

He's true, honest, an amazing father, a man of principles, he will never shirk his responsibilities. He's funny, he tells extraordinarily rude jokes in Turkish and in English, he never responds in anger, he has a huge collection of friends. You can be up a mountain and bump into a shepherd who of course Ali knows, he has hundreds of relatives and has stories about each one, he is loved by many many people, he is a self-made man, he loves me, we look after and support each other, and we still continue to enjoy our days together no matter what. Like me, he can sift through the gloom and find the silver lining and still see the light in everyone and everything.

Ali is quite simply the single most amazing thing to have ever happened in my life and all the riches he has brought to that, most importantly Dilgesu, my lovely-lovely stepdaughter. Thank-you my beloved for the years.

Ali & Bud (eyes up!)

July 8, 2017

VIRTUAL FRIENDS

From Sue ... 'My amazing friend Rosie ... love reading her blogs which are a source of inspiration and invaluable information for many ... this one is especially poignant for me as it includes my equally amazing cousin Keri who is also battling this dreadful disease'.

Girls ... you all know who you are; but for all the others not in the know, let me fill you in. I have a gang of entirely virtual friends from all over the globe ...

We are united by one thing, our breast cancer. This is a sympathetic, warm and loving bunch, ready to respond at any time of day or night, as someone is always awake somewhere in the world, ready to listen and share virtual hugs and laughs.

You've already been introduced to some of the stars of this group, Norma and Rose, but there are so many more. I'd like to introduce you to Jill who guides the group and keeps us in check, Ethel who provides the group with wonderful turns of phrase and humour, Keri who always finds just the right response and tone with everyone in all situations and so many more besides.

We are from America, the United Kingdom, New Zealand, Australia, Sweden, Canada, Norway, Turkey and the Middle East. We are an international and pretty classy bunch, sharing our daily trials and tribulations, both good and bad news, rants, tears and sometimes things not even connected with our breast cancer.

The other day, reflecting on my own treatment in my adopted country of Turkey, I counted my blessings once again for the zillionth time - Monday was a case in point. I was signed off from radiotherapy at 9.30 in the morning and, without a single appointment, by lunchtime had seen the orthopedic surgeon, had an X-ray, given blood and got the results and had seen my oncologist. This has always been my experience here since my very first diagnosis and surgery in 2003, that took a record breaking three days!

The average wait seems to be between 2-3 weeks; however, one UK-based member of the group who had a particularly aggressive tumour type reported that, during her three and a half-week wait, her tumours actually grew. How terrifying! Another member from Australia was diagnosed on the Wednesday and they wanted to book her in for surgery on the Monday; however, she postponed it by two weeks as it was the school holiday and she wanted to spend the time with her grandchildren. We are all different and react differently.

However, almost without exception, we are all agreed on one thing:

WAITING is hell! Waiting for a scan, an appointment, a biopsy result, surgery - it's all a nightmare. It is unbelievably stressful, and speed is key for everyone involved. So, I decided to find out what the experience of my band of virtual mates was in terms of how long they had waited between their first diagnosis and either surgery or the beginning of active treatment, and of course what their feelings were at that time.

Here are some of the comments which the women in our group shared about how they dealt with the wait:

The voice of reason in my head kept saying 'Stay calm. We will figure this out. One day at a time. We need more information.' The fear centre of my brain (amygdla) was screaming 'get it out now!'... It felt exhausting with these different parts of the brain battling it out everyday. The anxiety has felt almost overwhelming at many times... And the sadness ... oh crap ... and the anger ... The wait between diagnosis and surgery was a COMPLETE BITCH.' (Ethel)

'It was agony, yes. Diagnosed April 30, 2010. Had to wait until June 6 for surgery. Nearly lost my mind with the wait. Somewhere, there is a drawing I did of what I thought was going on with my body during that time. I drew cancer all over my body. Not knowing for so long really messed me up, gave me sleepless nights, played havoc with my psyche, robbed me of any peace of mind and made me a diabolical mess to be around ... I still haven't quite got my head around that nightmare.' (Big Sister Lucy – USA)

'I cried everyday and would wake up every morning with a knot in my stomach, reminding me I had cancer and was soon going to lose my hair and look ill.' (Emma)

'I cried the whole 5 weeks from diagnosis to operation day. I was a mess and I'm not ashamed to say that I was in the gutter, I'd hit rock bottom. But it took me to hit rock bottom to turn it around. On the operation day, I thought, right, I can just constantly cry or fight this b******d and that's what I did. I'm a really strong person, but this floored me. But I'm better now than before all this ...' (Jan)

'The logical bit of my brain was saying you don't know how long it's been there and its being dealt with in 2 weeks. The non-logical bit had me talking to my right boob and asking what the hell was going on in there!' (Val)

'I found the wait unbearable... I went from Oct 18 to Nov 8 with no surgery date. At my appointment on the 8th, they told me surgery was on Nov 30th. I nearly lost my mind! After all they'd told me it was very aggressive and that it was in my lymph nodes... seriously?! Wait 3 weeks? No way. Luckily, my surgeon is a woman and could see my distress ... got me in on the 10th ...' (Melissa)

'It was summer and at that time I felt it gave me time to try to get my head around the cancer and try to have a normal summer for my kids. I knew they would be back at school when the chemo side effects kicked in. I didn't want them to see my all-day-ever-day struggle'. (Mary)

'Torture'! (Rennie)

'The wait for my amputation was agony ... it was probably 5 months by the time I had my operation'. (Norma)

'I remember being in the doctor's office, getting the news of 'area of suspicion' and crying and thinking 'why me?' and saying 'I don't want to die' ... I just wanted it out as soon as I could'. (Carol)

And here is an extract from Keri's 'CANCERVERSARY'......

'My journey is going to begin quite some time before my official diagnosis, in May/June 2015 when I found a lump in my right breast.

Knowing that these things can occur due to hormone changes, I monitored it for a while to assess if it would change size, shape or texture at different times of my cycle. I was also a bit scared and tried to put it to the back of my mind. After 4 months, I decided that I should get it checked out and went to my GP. I was quickly referred to a breast surgeon and waited for an appointment. When the call came, the appointment was booked for 3-weeks time and the gravity of the possibility I may have cancer started to dawn on me.

Two weeks later when I received a letter postponing my appointment for a further week, it became too much to bear. I was lucky enough to have private healthcare through my employer so I called them up and asked if this would be covered. It was. Various calls between AXA, my GP and the consultant's secretary later and I had an appointment for early the next week. Phew!

....

A week later I went back for my results. By this time, I'd convinced myself it was going to be bad news and had started planning how on earth I could say those words to my loved ones. I was kicking myself for having kept them in the dark, because it would have been easier if they were at least expecting it. I had also started to think about the positives. I had a critical illness policy that would pay out and my childhood home was up for sale for little over what my policy was worth. I daydreamed about buying it and living there once more.

The surgeon told me it was good news. It was a fybroadenoma (fibrous lump) that had formed. It would never turn into anything sinister and was nothing to worry about.

In March/April 2016 I found a lump in my left breast. It felt different to the other lump, but I monitored it for a couple of weeks ...

That room is where I unofficially learnt that I had cancer. I asked the radiologist a question:

Me – Do you grade these?

She – Yes, we do (looking a little shocked that I knew about this process).

Me – Are you allowed to tell me?

She – We usually report back to the surgeon and they will tell you.

Me – Oh (disappointed).

She – I can tell you if you want.

Me – Yes please, I'd like to know.

She – I am concerned about this one

(A couple of weeks later.......)

So, 20th June 2016 comes around and Kim came with me to get the results. We were called into the surgeon's room and there was another lady present who I don't recall seeing before. The surgeon's words were "we've had your results back and it is a little cancer". Right then, in that moment, my whole world changed. I couldn't look at Kim, because I couldn't bear to see the hurt in her eyes or for her to read the fear in mine. I couldn't break down because if I crumbled, I might never be able to pick myself up again. So, I threw myself into the practicalities of it. "What's next?" I asked. The answer was surgery on July 12th, more tests today, radiotherapy and possibly chemotherapy first...

So here I am – 1 year cancer patient. Due to have my follow up mammogram on July 11th. Dreading how painful it'll be, when they have to squash my already sore breast into the machine. Trying not to think about the possibility that I might still have cancer, but also not being able to think positively about being told that I am NED (No Evidence of Disease) because I'm well aware of the fact that just because I may be NED now, it could always come back. My diagnosis was not terminal, but I feel like I have been given one.

Bud, Keri and Sue at Kybele

July 10, 2017

LIFE IS TERMINAL

'Life is terminal and it's sexually transmitted.' (John Cleese)

'Terminal illness is a disease that cannot be cured...'

Another lovely day and another piece about seizing life, no matter what.

TERMINAL - DISTANT - STAGE 4 - ADVANCED - METASTASIS

Call it what you will, but what does all this jargon actually mean for you and me?

According to wikipedia:-

'Terminal illness is a disease that cannot be cured or adequately treated and that is reasonably expected to result in the death of the patient within a short period of time.'

What idiot wrote that? They have obviously never met me or any of the other women like me. If they had, they might be tempted to revise their definition of the word TERMINAL!

This next one is a better description and sticks to facts instead of inaccurate predictions:-

'Stage IV describes invasive breast cancer which has spread beyond the breast and nearby lymph nodes to other organs of the body, such as lungs, distant lymph nodes, skin, bones, liver or brain. You may hear the words 'advanced' and 'metastatic' used to describe stage IV cancer.'

However my favourite definition is this one which seems to sum up where I'm at and have been for years:-

'Depending on their condition and treatment, people may live with a terminal illness for days, weeks, months or even years. They are likely to be receiving treatment to help reduce or manage their symptoms, rather than cure their illness.'

BLA BLA BLA ... does it matter? No matter how much you Google and read up on the having cancer thing, there is no compensation for living it!

3 years ago, I was horrified when I first saw the word palliative on my medical reports! Of course, I thought it meant I was going to 'pop my clogs' - 'kick the bucket' - 'bite the dust' - 'cash in my chips' - any day soon. I had visions of a hospice, surrounded by my nearest and dearests, looking pale but gorgeous, or that scene from Beaches where Bette Midler's more attractive friend is dying, sitting wrapped in a blanket looking stunning in a beautiful beach house! Oh yes, I've played out my dying scene several times.

But today is the first time I've actually bothered reading what 'Palliative' really means:-

'Palliative care is given to improve the quality of life of patients who have serious or life-threatening disease, such as cancer. The goal of palliative care is to prevent or treat, as early as possible, the symptoms and side effects of the disease and its treatment, in addition to the related psychological, social and spiritual problems. The goal is not to cure. Palliative care is also called comfort care, supportive care and symptom management.'

I've been having palliative care for the last 3 years. Almost 3 years ago I was in such excruciating agony that I couldn't imagine life beyond the pain that I was in; however, the diet of radiotherapy and fentanyl patches (a slow-release form of morphine) solved the pain. Since then, I have had classic and pill forms of chemo, several hormone treatments, radiotherapy on various parts of my body and effective pain relief. They have thrown everything in the arsenal at the cancer and do you know what, despite a slow but constant spread of my breast cancer, I feel better today than I did then.

Today I have tumours in my spine, pelvis, iliac, femur and everywhere else in that area, plus a few other spots; however, I'm pain free and still living and loving every day of my life. My life includes swimming, driving, eating and drinking everything I want and, as I write, I'm planning yet another visit to see my dad, sister and friends in England.

So, my message to all you terminals, you stage 4ers, is do not pay any attention to what name is given to our position in the cancer staging system; it's about the quality of life we lead.

Look at me, not in the blue, but in the pink of condition and I've had terminal cancer for 7 years. Can anyone beat that? I'm sure plenty of you can and soon we'll simply refer to it as a chronic condition that you live with, for as long as you can, but until that day, don't be afraid of words:
'Sticks and stones may break my bones, but words will never hurt me!'

Bud and friends in one of her fave places

July 13, 2017

Winston and Lucy –

A match made in Solace and a tale of recovery, love and hope. Today's tale is how a woman recovering from breast cancer saves a horse – a story of love and hope. Today's piece is dedicated to my big sis. Lucy and Winston, her horse. Lucy is a breast cancer survivor, animal welfare activist, Animal Champion and my big sis.

Winston and Lu – 2011

July 15, 2017

CHEMO JUNKIE

Ever wondered what it feels like to be living with stage 4 cancer? Guess what ... I haven't got any hospital appointments for a month, a whole month. I can't remember the last time I had a vacation like that from chemo. Wait ... what am I going to do with myself? It's like I had a full-time job, and I just gave in my notice.

July 17, 2017

YOU LOOK WELL!

Is something you should never ever say to someone with advanced breast cancer ....

July 16, 2017

There's nothing to be afraid of!

As a former English teacher in my local town, I know many people and, if I don't know them, that doesn't much matter, because they know me or more likely my husband Ali, or my now dearly departed father-in-law 'Gök Huseyin.' There's a typical conversation which can be had many, many times in any given day and goes something like this:-

Them: *How are you?*
Me: *I'm fine thanks and you?*
Them: *I'm fine too.*

And everyone goes on their way or there are a few variations on this which may include reference to the weather, price of tomatoes and state of tourism.

However, with me, there are sometimes other interjections based on what people know of my health and these can go something like this:

Them: *How are you? You look really well!*

(YOU LOOK REALLY WELL!)
That is red rag to the bull and my least favourite expression ever!

Me: Oh you know!
(I'm trying to discourage them from continuing with this line of questioning.)
Them: *So, have you finished your treatment?*

And at this point sometimes, instead of giving them the uplifting tale of the battle and then winning against cancer, I give them the truth and I find that I enjoy setting people straight. The minute I begin to give them the real story, which is actually what they thought they wanted to hear, they realize that they don't want to know after all; but it's too late, they can't escape.

Once my alter ego 'Naughty Rose' kicks in, there's sometimes no stopping her. She takes great pleasure and insists on telling them all the details of the treatment, there's no need to exaggerate as it's all true; all chemo options tried, last chance saloon, bones, spine, liver and and nothing left out and you can see that they would like to get away, but they can't. They are regretting asking.

Me: Is it something I said?
And I know that that person will never ever make that mistake with me ever again.

Sometimes I come across another type of woman, the other day I met one of these at the hospital, who themselves have had breast cancer and are now cured. Lucky you! The woman in question was such a pushy know-it-all that I just had to put her straight on a few points,

Her: *Oh, I had breast cancer!*

Me: *I'm sorry to hear that.*

Her: *Once you finish your treatment, you'll get over it. You'll realize there's nothing to be afraid of! You just have to make sure you stay positive!*

So of course it's Naughty Rose's duty to set this stupid woman straight! Who is this woman to tell me what I should do or feel?

Me: Well, my situation is a little different from yours. I've been having constant treatment for the last three years, it's now spread to many places, all over the place actually, organs, bones...... So far there's no sign of it in the brain, I note cheerily!

(She's looking increasingly nervous now....)

She wants me to stop but I don't. I blab on and tell and make her listen and, in the end, I almost feel sorry for her and try to put Rose back in her cage. She is terrified, a rabbit caught in the headlights, my headlights, and finally when Rose stops, the woman is actually speechless. I very politely wish her a good day and walk away. She has been forced to face the reality that this story is never over and, once again, she has to look something in the face which she thought she had packed away years ago!

But that's where NEVER-NEVER LAND is and I don't want to and have never wanted to live in 'The Land of Make Believe.'

I describe myself as a positive realist. This, in itself, is a true blessing and in part I put my longevity down to it. It means that I can honestly contemplate my future, my own demise, without being thrown into a downward spiral. I don't expect, wait or look for miracles, I count living up to now as nothing short of a miracle. I attribute my continued good health (it's a relative term) to my ability to focus on and indeed count the positives of my own situation:

- We make plans for the future, although we may not be able to stick to them and we accept invitations with the proviso that we may have to cancel
- To be amazed and thankful for my good health
- To count the things I can do, rather than those which I can't
- To try to be content with simple things; the most important is a peaceful and loving family
- To have fun
- To swim as often as possible
- To eat and drink whatever I want, when I want

There are many people who may have better health than me, but I never envy them because, when I look at them, I realize that they are not as happy as I am - I know very well what I have in my hand, and I feel lucky every single day.

During my last course of radiotherapy, one of the technicians asked me whether I had sought permission to go swimming. I was absolutely astounded that anyone should think that, at this moment in my life, I should seek permission to do something which I love so much. I've swum in the sea since my first chemo, I've been in the sun during radiotherapy, I've ignored advice about meat, drinking and many other things ...

If I had not done all the things I've been told not to do, then where would the fun in living be and why would I want to continue doing it? While life is this good, I fully intend to continue to disobey all the radio techs and enjoy every minute for a little longer.

July 21, 2017

CINDERELLA IS STILL ON HOLIDAY!

Another day of great Greek food, wandering around Molivos which is a beautiful Ottoman and Greek town. Of course, plenty more swimming, although have to say, this is NOT the Med ... the Aegean is bloody freezing in comparison!

July 22, 2017

CINDERELLA GOES HOME!

Like all good fairy tales, this one must also come to an end. It's time for Cinderella to hang up her ball gown and get back in her kitchen. That's totally figuratively speaking, since Cinders never really got into the kitchen in the first place....

July 24, 2017

I'M A POSITIVE REALIST

Most of the time ... and sometimes a grumpy, difficult and demanding so and so, an irrational, self-centered know-it-all - however, having got my worst attributes out the way, let's look at my best one. I am a positive realist!

So, with the ringing of the bell, maybe a cake, and a final zap and a buzz many women come to the end of their active breast cancer treatment with a last session of radiotherapy. They leave the hospital with a follow up date in the diary or two, a three month appointment and a simple 'BYE.'

And then what?
A big black hole is what.
And what does that feel like? Empty, hollow, you've won the battle, you are victorious but ...
You are adrift is where you are.
During the treatment phase there is surgery, chemo, bloods, scans, enough radiotherapy to keep you going for a lifetime and you are busy. You've also had a lot of support in the form of make-up days, feel good sessions and interest from specialist groups, family and friends, the hospital staff and not to mention all the women you've met there.
In fact, this has become your job; but this job is different because it has enforced bed and rest days built in, like 'unofficial holidays' you can spend the whole day on the sofa in your pyjamas watching daytime TV and eating whatever you feel like ... you are allowed to do this, you can behave like a total slob. Utter luxury ... if only you felt well enough to enjoy it!
A friend explained that 'Everything was planned for me for 10 months,' and she's right, during that period you are not required to think for yourself, if you're lucky you have loved ones and hospital staff running rings around you at your beck and call and now? Well now you probably just feel scared and alone in a vacuum. You are meant to go home quietly, celebrate this close shave with the deadly C and not look back over your shoulder.
But at this moment, although externally there may be a party thrown to mark the end of this journey, internally this is just the beginning of another round of anxiety and waiting until the first three-month check-up which confirms that, yes, you're still clear and then the anxiety begins again until another check-up and once again the 'all clear' and so it goes. However, these check-ups often involve nothing more than the

most perfunctory look, a quick how-are-you-feeling and you are escorted off the premises until the next date. Hmm, that may not be enough to put your mind at rest, but it'll have to do for now.

The end of treatment comes with so many mixed emotions, it's often the point at which we crumble. During the active part, the busy part, the hard part we are rocks, bricks, amazing, warriors, amazons and everyone marvels at us, and they ask themselves 'would I be as strong in the same situation?'

And then you are spat out and back into the real world, but you are reborn as someone else so as well as having to deal with the physical changes you also have to try to work out who this new person is. Everyone around you has moved on and out of sympathy mode and back to normal life, but you are not there yet, and you may never be. You are being pulled out of the cancer cocoon and having to face a new reality as a person you and your loved ones may not recognize.

It's an emotional roller coaster and you may have got off the ride, but you are still suffering from vertigo.

But just STOP for a minute and turn all the awfulness on its head for a moment and think, isn't this the perfect moment to make your dreams come true? You've had a brush with death, is there a better time than this? What are you waiting for?

My sister made her childhood dream of owning a horse come true and I opened a school.

Whether you are a cancer patient or not doesn't matter....

Which of your dreams are you going to realize?

Rosie's school vizion in Kumluca - with her lovely staff

More tales of living it up from the POSITIVE REALIST

July 29, 2017

NOT A BUCKET LIST!

I don't have a bucket list, but when I reflect back on what I have done since 2003 when I was first diagnosed, I realize what I have achieved. Cancer made me focus on undertaking things which were more important than navel gazing ...

July 31, 2017

ANTALYA BREAST CANCER SUPPORT GROUP

After my most recent visit to see my dad, I was angry because, despite the amazing medical care which I have always received as a cancer patient in Turkey, there is no support outside the onc office!

The only difficult thing in life is to decide and get started! This weekend, we had breakfast for our Antalya women with breast cancer group. 2 months ago, we didn't exist and now look!

Rosie at the Pink Lady Breast cancer event

August 3, 2017

ROSIE'S TRAVELS - DAY 1

Another of my last visits? Or one of many more? A special day with my gorgeous girls. London Zoo = what an amazing day, rained the whole time, but that didn't dampen a thing!

August 4, 2017

ROSIE'S TRAVELS - DAY 2

London with dad and our favourite Regent's Park. Just squeezing a little more out of life.

In Regent's Park with Dilgesu, Dad, Rosie and Mary

August 7, 2017

ROSIE'S TRAVELS - DAY 3

Another 'last' trip to a place very special in my heart with some of my favourite people. A wonderful weekend up in stunning Stathern with my sister Mary and my lovely friend Charla, her husband John and Alfie.

August 9, 2017

ROSIE'S TRAVELS

Day 4. Do any of you have one of those mates who 'just gets you'? Well, Nikki is one of those friends. A fellow stage 4'er living life and defying labels. Still squeezing one more drop out of life. My fellow stage 4er, advanced, terminal, life-loving buddy ...

Nikki and Rosie – always laughing also sister Mary and friends Charl and Di.

August 12, 2017

HERE WE ARE AGAIN!

Homeward bound and back to Antalya and treatment. Ended my holidays with a final night with more special friends - Mo and Rich. Brilliant mates!

August 20, 2017

KNOW YOUR LEMONS!

(Firstly, I would like to apologize to anyone who doesn't have a Facebook - currently I think, in the whole wide world that equals my dad .....)

Morning everyone - just checking ... do you know your lemons? If not, take a leaf out of 'Coppafeel' (it's a thing) and get better acquainted with them. No time like the present! Have a great Sunday ...

August 21, 2017

SHOULD I EAT SOYA?

It's a minefield - a diagnosis of breast cancer simply leads to more questions! Someone HELP me - should I or shouldn't I eat soya?

August 25, 2017

WHEN REALITY COLLIDES

At 9.44 on Tuesday, I realized that there are many ways to die – life isn't all about dying from cancer! Living with cancer can be a little like living in a bubble. You are somehow both in and out of a kind of reality.

August 31, 2017

DOMESTIC BLISS?

Well, as I'm still here and haven't yet been wiped out by either the Big C or in an accident, then real life must at times prevail.

September 3, 2017

LIVING WITH CANCER

... I apologize but I've become a lazy blogger. There are a couple of reasons, and both are good, the best being that I've been having a really good summer!

This is what stage-4 cancer looks like on Ibrance

September 4, 2017

LAZY BLOGGER

Have you finished active treatment for breast cancer? Are you struggling to pick up the pieces?

September 8, 2017

A CONVO WITH ROSIE AND NIKKI

Did you know that there's a lot to laugh about with stage 4 cancer? Be a fly on the wall with this little snippet from the other day - Facetime on the beach with Rosie and her cancer bud Nikki.

September 12, 2017

FIRST DAY BACK!

Bud and her oncology team at Medstar

Feels like the first day back at school for me after a long summer holiday. There are a few tests I need to pass ...

September 13, 2017

This is the sequel to Monday's 'Back to School' post. With much giggling and all things scatological ... read on ;)

StageHand40.com

September 13, 2017

STOOLS AND NOT THE KIND YOU SIT ON ...

Diagnosis, living with cancer stools and not the kind you sit on ... and so, to continue with the school vocabulary, it's clear that I currently have wobbly stools ...

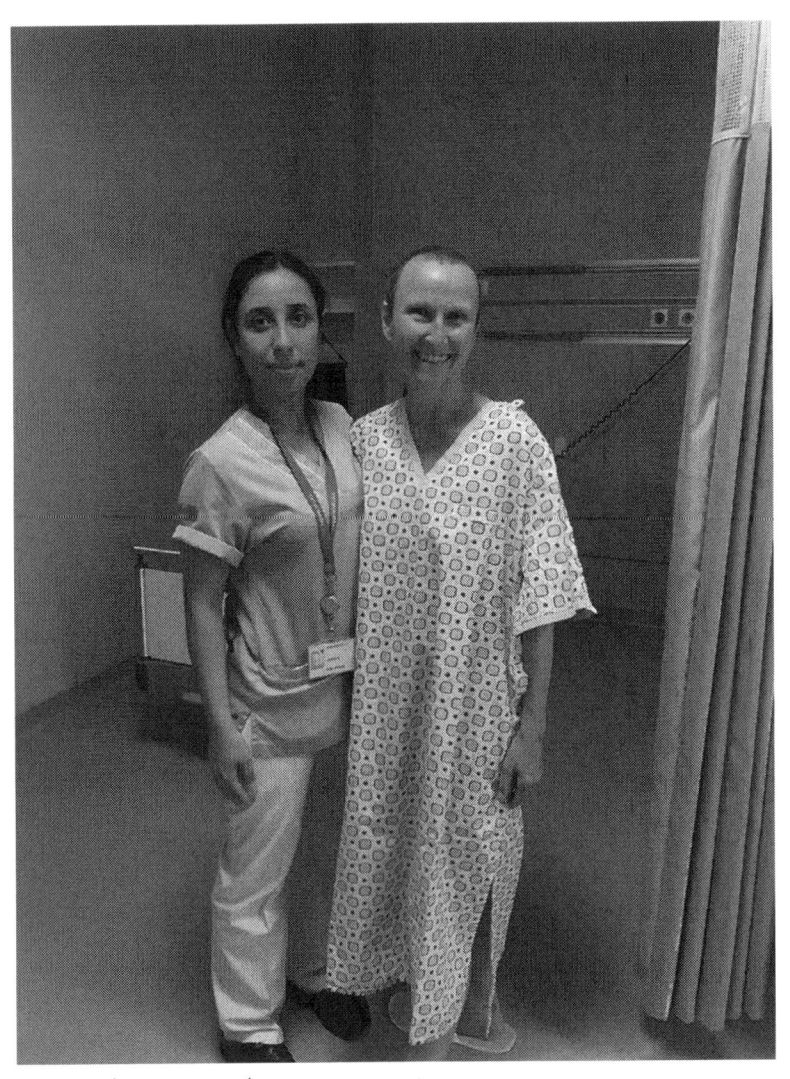

Bud at 'my hospital' Medstar in Antalya

Bud working on her blog in Cirali

And here, ending suitably with one of Chemo Bud's fave topics, the blog came to an end and Rosie stopped blogging and carried on with her lovely life. As she duly noted, the hip was buggered and all kinds of areas inside her were becoming pretty buggered too. She had no more time for writing about her life with cancer; she had to crack on with living it.

(Some of the blogs were discovered in the laptop and will receive better exposure, others were just the Facebook headers I stole from her page that I chose to use anyway.)

In any case, as Rosie would say ... 'you get the gist' .... Lu

SECTION 5

SOMEWHERE TOWARDS THE END

Framing Moments

Published in South County Newspapers, February 2016

"Come and join us in Istanbul!" she said. "It will be too much fun!" The old Lucy would have found a swift excuse to not make that happen. There would be work, home, life, bills – all the regular excuses to not grasp a hold of the day and change its map for a week. That Lucy obviously left home, because this one gets immediately on the computer and seeks the perfect flight. San Francisco to Istanbul is one long 13 hour flight; but a super route they opened up if you have relatives in Turkey. I slept well on the journey and met my name-plaque at arrivals in perfect sequence.

It wasn't until I was in the cab - stop and go in screeching, irritated traffic and pouring rain, that I just realized something rather key. Here I was in the middle of a city I knew not a bit. I didn't speak the language and also didn't have the address of the apartments where we were staying. My life was in the rather emphatic hands of the driver who swerved in and out, as if on a race to somewhere I knew not. I couldn't reach my sister on the phone – the code was wrong or something. I had to briefly giggle to myself at my newly wild and irresponsible status – whizzing through a foreign city with a foreign man, headed to who knows where.

We stopped in a dark alley and I gestured at the doorway. "Here?" I asked a little nervously. "This is where I am supposed to go?" I felt like a school girl dumped in the middle of nowhere. He nodded, dumped my luggage on the pavement and took off. I lumbered myself up the stairs. "Rosie!" I called. "Rose? Bud?" I heard the cackle of London girls, a very sweet sound to the ears after my long journey and out-of-body cab experience. I held my baby tight in my arms and kissed everyone else. I had arrived. I was so proud of myself. The champagne had already been corked, British cheese was being consumed and the folks were prepped and ready for 'Rosie's Peeps Gone Wild in Istanbul.' We had two lovely apartments above one another and a super long weekend ahead in this exotic city.

Soon we were out of the door for dinner close by – a delicious meze, or compilation of dishes to wet the taste buds, along with lots of gossip. We went on to have our desserts in the vibrant downtown district and mixed in with all the Turkish folk enjoying the calm evening airs. Sometimes you can taste happiness and frame the moment – we had lots of those moments that evening. Sister was sparkly with happiness. Here she was with her very best friends, her husband and her big sis – all together for a few wonderful days. I could literally see her cup brimming over with contentment.

Saturday, we explored the old city together and made our way to the Grand Bazaar which was quite the spectacle. Very few Westerners were to be found on the streets, though they bustled with locals. The Bazaar and Spice Markets were super quiet and little business was being done. We did our best to help out the local economy just a bit and then rested up for our big family dinner that evening. Everyone had bought along their glad rags for this special evening and a photographer had also been hired to frame those priceless moments we knew we would witness and save for later……

Dancing with sister-in-law Dilek in the streets of Istanbul

Framing more Moments

Published in South County Newspapers, February 29, 2016

After the delicious family dinner, I left my baby sister to go out dancing with the 'young' ones and limped my jet-laggy-self back to the apartment, bleary with lack of sleep and too much of everything else. Never let it be said that sis doesn't live every moment of every day with abundance. She was absolutely exhausting all of us. The photos I saw of her the following morning made me giggle and wish I could have found the stamina to have witnessed it with my own eyes.

But sister allows little rest for herself or anyone else and it was time for boat-breakfast on the Bosphorus. The morning had threatened us with a few rain clouds, but they soon blew on by and gave way to brilliant sunshine and azure skies, as was on photographic demand. Sister-in-law Dilek had organized an enormous breakfast onboard and the event was a beautiful blending of English-Turkish culture and food, all surrounded with lots of love. Being Valentine's Day didn't hurt it one bit and us girls performed our rather lamely choreographed surprise-song "All you Need Is Love" to the galley of rather stunned males. Then it was time for outdoor photo sessions in true Titanic style and the rather poignant singing of the girls' theme song 'When you need a friend.' The four of them had been friends for decades and here they were celebrating my sister and all of us being together on the boat in Istanbul on that special day. There were many uplifting moments framed that day; making me glad I love to snap a shot, steal a moment and frame it for always in more than just the memory bank.

Off the boat and it was time to find our tour guide who would be taking us out and about. The Blue Mosque was quite something to behold. We had been warned in advance about the Muslim requirement to 'cover up' if you are female and I realized at the threshold to the building how much I really resented doing that. I nearly didn't make it through the door. But then I tied the blue rag around my head in semi-protest and was allowed to enter. Not so long ago, women were not allowed to enter the mosque at all; so this was, in fact, progress. And, inside, it was quite a spectacle to behold. I am always surprised by the depth and passion of people's religious ardors. I could have pulled up a chair and people-watched for the rest of the afternoon; but we were off again, quickly losing our blue rags at the door and allowing our hair to once again flow freely.

Sister let us rest for a little while after our boat cruise and marathon gallop around the city. I have never seen a terminal person with so much energy. If I had not known how ill she was, I would have said she was in training for her next marathon. She continues to defy diagnosis.

Sunday night was our luxy Valentine's banquet. I'm not sure how many courses we enjoyed between the eel, shrimp, mature beef and the chocolate roses, but it was a feast for the eyes, the senses and the taste buds that I shall never forget. More candle-lit moments to frame. Lots of laughter and clinking of glasses. I do remember wishing I could have boxed up the entire evening with all of its colors, aromas and love and taken it home with me to chew on later.

Monday we were leaving this eclectic city for the balmier airs of the south. We were headed to sister's home, where we could rest, re-group and where she could annihilate me – twice – at *Scrabble*.

On my return, people would ask me – "How's your sister doing?" It was hard not to reply that, other than being terminally ill, she is doing incredibly well. She continues to be bursting with energy, enthusiasm and passion. She walks like a speed-racer, eats like a horse and amazes all of us who have the good fortune to be around her. Now that is living. Be sure, when you see it, to frame it.

Dilgesu, Charla, Mo and the Bud

Still talking ... we graduated from email convos and went to texting and then from July 2015 to Rosies's death 3 years later, we chatted on FaceTime and What's App a lot. It was easy and free; and we could either be in group format or just the two of us, also an easy way to send pix.

Summer 2015

Me: Happy Anniversary, you two, from Grandma and Madison Rose!

Her: Ah, cutie! Anniversary is Sunday with a party for at least 50, live music, BBQ ...

Me: Yay, happy days, sis. Don't dance too much ☺.

Her: Twas fab, but totally knackered. Been on sofa watching wimbles.

Me: You look like a rock star, singing your heart out with a bottle of beer. Looks like super, fab time. Relax now, Dancing Queen!

Winter 2015

Me: In the City with Madison's Rob! How are you, sister?

Her: Good - busy, busy with getting ready for Xmas, cut down tree today, will decorate at weekend, cooking and planning and wrapping. Having girls Xmas brunch and they fly on the crack Friday. Have PET scan on Monday and so fingers crossed.

January 2016

Me: Our Mare says she's headed your way end Jan. What's your openings for Feb or March? Might come over via da Bull if you can stand another visitor ...

Her: Feb am meeting Charl and all the usual suspects in Istanbul 12-15. Should be a blast.

Me: Actually, thinking would be fun to see girlies in Bull, n travel back with you, if not too many peeps for you at one time?

Her: Also would work for me too.

Me: Yay!

Her: Cool, I will add you to our nuts what's App group - all plans n stuff discussed there from spice market to oil wrestling and whirling dervishes ...

Me: Crying with laughter this morning with your Xmas group ... omg, we are going to need a videograph for this lot ... X

Her: Yes, this is quite typical chat! You should have been in on the underwear chats. Legendary!

Spring 2016

Her: I am banning crying in my presence as it's all about me. That includes online convos.

Her: Sister - okay want something from you! Actually, am asking everyone - I want you to spend a peaceful 5 minutes every day sending me your good thoughts and energy! We can't be together all the time, but I think it's a way I can ask you and my mates to help ... I will of course be sending my loving thoughts back to you all ... I am a great believer in the power of positive thought and think it will help you as much as me. Could be when you out with the animals, in the bath or even on the throne! And remember, sis, these thoughts not sad and maudlin, but strong and full of your energy. It will be global lurv web - and of course can also chant, dance naked around fire and do as one wants, however I think just a little moment in your ordinary day will do just fine. I'm sure to feel it.

Me: Did you feel it today while I was mucking out? How about when I was filling the water troughs or playing ball with the dogs? What about when I was driving to work – that was a huge lurv fest. Tonight had candles in the bath with Badedas .. that was a strong and long one. Of course, of course. Lots and lots all day every day and at night too. Love you, baby .,.. xx

Her: Thanks sis - I'm feeling it, but remember not to cry at the same time - interferes with sending of vibes ... PP Love you too - already feeling v strong and ready and sun shining on me today, a gorgeous day .. PP

Me: No tears, just energy and light. And sometimes music and bad singing. Strong and ready for good starts to the day.

Her: I love the bad singing .. I like that too. Thinking new anthem track will be a Coldplay track ...

Me: Love Coldplay. Love and light and beautiful, pure thoughts from the Win too – they are on the wind, as we speak, and will be with you shortly.

Her: Hey, sis, morning! Feeling good .. dana dana na na

Me: hey, baby. Good sleepings?

Her: Good, not bad! Just feeling hungry-need hot cross bun.

Her: A gorg morning! Chemo 2 - rather like a yummy cocktail. Chat my night. xx

Me: Your beach looks amazeballs!

Her: Yes, down road from shabby beach shack. Final answer today, but seems happening! And weather really warming up. Sea calling - if I can get bloods up, will be in soon.

Bad ass

Early summer 2016

Her: Just off to court – last hearing in our case ...

Me: You mean there will soon be a verdict?

Her: Fingers crossed for good outcome, just have to listen to Carol's statement then we should have ticked all the boxes.

Me: Hugeeeeee.

Her: But Judge may fudge, as could be scared as quite big case and he is young, but needs to happen. If not, new judge and won't get hearing until September. Bloods are up – nurse Dilgesu just done last jab just now!

Me: Bless that lil punkin. No sleepies last night, gotta go zzz now. Fires n crap.

Mid-summer 2016

Her: I am at hospital waiting to do bloods, then will see if liver behaving or not.

Me: Yesss, liver better be behaving!

Her: Down to 66 from 170 ... yay, chemo here I come!

Me: Bless, yayyyy!

Her: Go back night night!

Me: Amazing Day. Your liver is the Queen of all livers!

Her: Off on turtle watch and swim ...

Me: Love the thought of you turtle-watching. Very universe-aligning. xx

Her: Hi sis, feeling lazy this morning! Not sure if going to go on turtle watch or just swim. Ali and I going on romantic boat trip this evening, fishing, swimming n home late. Do love not having that Sun nite/Monday feeling. It's great to be a retired princess. I'm thinking cuppa tea be nice.

Me: Retired opera-singer/actress/princess ...have your slaves get you one.

Her: Sadly, they all asleep.

Me: Hmm. Real princesses don't tolerate others sleeping.

Her: Actually, I'm sure even Queen makes herself cuppa every now and then.

Me: Ha ha, probs does. Always tastes best if you make yourself.

Her: Last hour on bus - heading straight for the Aegean and Dilek's gorg balcony.

Late summer 2016

Me: You feeling a bit off today, Bud? Maybe too much traveling.

Her: Yes, right after put phone down had terrible runs swiftly followed by more, then felt sick so got kindle and went to bed. Still there now, but feeling better. Have Amazon Prime and got myself all 7 Harry Potters for free, so reading no. 1 again. Love it and so funny. Haven't stepped foot out of door all day! Perfect.

Me: good, might need chillax day. Let them what do do everything ...

Me: Hope feeling better, sis? Just had lovely bubble bath. Reading 'The Rosie Effect' .. a riot and a must-kindle, if you don't already have!

Her: Brill, will load.

Me: Also., 'A spot of bother' by Mark Haddon. A good laugh. Feeling any better?

Her: Much better. Fingers crossed for chemo tomorrow pp

Me: Yay, Bud. Good girl! Frou and I off to the City to see Adele.

Her: yayyyy, pics please, if you gorgeous girls all dolled up xx

Me: We will be. 50 going on 15...

Me: What are the new drugs from the US you haven't tried yet? Going to see onc tomorrow and wanted to ask him about them.

Her: Hey sis, can't remember. Will check, as in fridge at Ali's shop. Ok, so good news on tumor markers, down a bit. We think chemo prob keeping things stable. Onc said I can travel and actually said now better than later, so going to London with Dilgesu August 21-28. Bloody sleep f-ed up here! Ali up half night watching Olympics, then I spend next half night-reading until it's time to get up. Have too much stuff planned for today – breakfast, playing with mates at beach house, then night boat and stay on board, then taking Ali's Mum to see some relatives tomorrow. Think I am going to get off night boat thing as also a bit crowded and bloods will be at lowest point. Gotta stay good as traveling next Sunday!

Me: Yay, sis. That will make dad so happy! Hope you can also get some girlfriend time in. Yes, we are a bit Olymp-obsessed too. How many damn swimming races can you watch? Yes, quite a lot apparently.

Her: Back home and at the beach house. Scan Thurs, but results not until Tues, so def no chemo til next week. Niceeeeee ☺.

I thought first night Rixos, will check in early n then be there to meet you with room picnic, wine, beer, yummies from 7 Mehmet – can think about where you fancy from there and of course there is always the lovely Cirali too ☺.

Autumn 2016

Me: What did scan show, sis?

Her: Need Ipapepilone.

Me: Got it. Infusion done?

Her: Done .. home in front of tennis.

Her: Hey sis. Challenge for you – can you send me pic of mother and a pic of the shepherd's bag? Got talking last night ... amazed that your second name is Penelope.

Her: Hey photos!

Me: Ha ha, hey bossy

Me: All hooked up, Bud?

Her: Good to go! Chemo table – melon, tea, water, biscuits, music.

Mid-autumn 2016

Me: Best hols eva, sis. You have taught me so much about how to live and how to die. I shall forever carry your heart inside my own. Love you bunches, moon and back. xx

Lucy Mason Jensen

Her fave meal in Finike. Breakfast!

Early winter 2016

Her: How are you feeling, has California built a wall yet to keep the rest of America out? Awake early. Will be at hospital at 8.30,

Me: Ha, ha, yup, working on it. How you doing, Bud?

Her: Good, had lovely few days and ready for chill at hospital. Converted Moo to Scrabble, so have enjoyed thrashing her, ha ha. She thinks she may have a chance to win when chemo drugs kick in later, ha ha!

Bud doing her ceramics

Me: Doing okay, sis?

Her: Good sis ... chilling at Incircik and was at ceramics today, so feeling good too. Signal here pants, so catch you later in the week from Antalya when Charl arrives.

Me: Who is coming to see you after Chrimble/New Year? Looking at pressies I have already bought .. might be cheaper just to bring them over myself, plus need to see Baby Bud!

Her: Hey sis .. you serious? Wow. Can you fly direct in and out of Istanbul?

Me: Ya, serious.

Her: Why don't you come a few days after Xmas and avoid silly prices. We will celebrate all in one on NY Eve.

Me: Fabbo, would love it!

Her: Hey, but you won't eat Xmas pud or cake! Will just have to make sherry trifle!

Me: Hate Xmas cake n pud. Sherry trifle yummers!

Her: I make v nice meringues too. Oh n spiced red cabbage, bread sauce ...

Me: Can't wait already!

Her: Brill, excited too!

Me: Yeeee. Had like an epiphany .. looking at Suzy Q's big ol Bearpaws .. like whoa, that is going to cost a plane ticket to mail and ..... I'm coming, sis. I'm coming! All done, all in. Window seats all legs of way .... ZZZZZZZ.

Her: Haven't slept. Been reading all night. Had bit of dry toast n tea a few hours ago. White food rocks!

PS Have our turkeys for New Year. Feeding them up!

The Rose Bud & Her Brilliant Adventures

Pre-Christmas 2016

Her: How do you feel about opera, sis? Just a thought?

Me: Love opera!

Her: Brill ... okay, thinking let's do opera on Tues and spend Tues and Wed in Antalya. And ... radical ... maybe stay in different hotel! Actually, the white one rather amazing ... and white! But has fab sushi bar.

Me: No chemo that week?

Her: Will have chemo on day you go. Spoke to one, he say ok ... could really do with week off now, but onwards and upwards.

Me: Aww, honey. How's Daisy?

Her: Nuts! She needs a mate. She especially likes burying things in the garden.

Me: Yeah, she needs a buddy for sure. Burying symbols equals loneliness. Then she can dig things up and visit with them again.

Her: No voice!

Me: No voice means worn out, no can do ... must rest voice for much laughing when sister arrives ☺.

Her: You go night, night. Am poised for ever-elusive bowel movement ..

Me: Oh crap. Literally ...

Right before Christmas 2016

Her: Hey sis, I'm just having a bit of warm milk, n honey with crumbled up bread. My version of instant rice pudding, but less yummy. Good for icky stuff.

Me: A bit less icky today, sis?

Her: Bit better, voice still grainy, but better and less coughing. Finally hope to make mince pies n do a few bits of Xmas prep!

Her: We all booked n sorted for Antalya ... 2 nights Su Hotel .. literally 2 mins from 7 Mehmet and on first night opera ... my Xmas pressie to you!

Me: And indoor pool?

Her: yep

Her: Slug! Surely time to be getting up? It's nearly Christmas.

Christmas Eve 2016

Me: You manage to get some cough relief, honey?

Her: Yes, they have given me nice cough medicine and throat spray. Didn't do X-ray as seems clear, problem is throat, so all good. Quiet evening. Ali home and snoozing, they had lovely time trekking in snow today. Hey, could you pack a couple of odd gifts for next Saturday... we will play a game and nice to have maybe a bar of Hersheys or something v American?

Me: Of course, will throw in some random things.

Christmas Day 2016

Her: Happy Xmas, sis. Where you peeps now? We had lovely lunch at Katie's - turkey, pressies, now home on the sofa. Perfect! How's your Chrimble, love? Passed out on the sofa, too much food?

Her: Hey sis - might be slight change in plan .. Dilgesu coming tomorrow, she's got proper flu. May be one of Ali's boys who picks you up so look for sign SIS LUCY and any chance you could bottle whisky from Duty Free? Turn your phone on in Bull ...

Me: Oh no, poor Suzy Q. She is really worn out, poor thing. Have to keep her away from you. Oh dear me, Auntie will be her beck and call girl. Will buy whisky, ya ya.

Her: Any news, you up and away?

After New Year 2017

Me: Having flat white n free internet in Starbucks. Looks like on time. Bloods good? Miss you already.

Her: Hooked up ☺.

Me: You nice and snuggly at home, Bud? Miss you.

Her: V nice and snuggly and managed not to feel icky this time!

Me: Yay to no icks.

Her: We won our case! Crazy day - anyway now, instead of settling for 250 lira we will be looking for a lot more. If not, I have the right to sell all of the assets and take my money back. Super good day, but also knackered!

Me: Oh my, fab news Bud. Wish I was there to drink champers with you and squeal with delight!

Her: Just back from Antalya ... Ali's surgery on Wednesday. Looks like also in lymph! Oh well, still easy op and recovery.

Me: What, cancer?

Her: Yes, thyroid cancer, the best one to get!

Me: How's he doing in the brain?

Her: Fine, I think. Hard to tell. He says fine.

The Bud's 47th birthday, January 16, 2017

Me: Happy Birthday, Bud! Did you have a lovely day?

7 Mehmet Restaurant in Antalya, her fave!

Her: Yes, in a way, but actually flew back to Antalya, spent afternoon at hospital having Ali's pre-op tests n then drove home in pouring rain. Totally caked out and have a feeling there may be more at ceramics tomorrow....

Me: How is the patient doing?

Her: Patient very good. Daisy loves Aslan!

Me: Yay Daisy n Aslan. Love love. Need pic!

Her: He's huge and has properly put her in her place. He's a sweetie too, just when they play together, they are a bit boisterous!

Her: Had PET ... get results Thursday.

Me: Patient Ali doing better?

Her: Good, good. Was at work today!

Me: Oh perfect. Love a man that goes quickly back to work.

Late January 2017

Her: Haven't passed my exams ☹

Starting new chemo now. Just to try to keep on top of it a bit, but this chemo much better life quality. 2 weeks on, week off and v. light, only 2 hours. No ickiness, fab. But think this will be last chemo as have run out of ones haven't tried and, in the end, liver won't cope. Looking forward to having nicer quality of life for a while.

Spring 2017

Me: All good with the bloods, Bud?

Her: Yes!

Me: What did the onc say?

Her: Good .. lots of stuff to get sorted when get back to Turkey! New biopsy most important and then beg/borrow/steal the new super expensive drugs. Fink have to buy private! Was enrolled for about an hour on drug trial, but they rejected me because I have had more than 3 rounds of chemo ☹

Her: Palbociclib or Ibrance, if you can't say fancy name ... can get in UK - very cheap at 4,425 per month POUNDS! Have PET today and should get results latest tomorrow and then possible biopsy Friday. Need to be sure that my cancer still hormone positive. Buggers can change!

Her: On da road again – back to Antalya and today's excitement is biopsy and special radiotherapy right into liver tumors. No new tumors, but growth so going to try to zap right into them – also one of the treatments recommended by Dr. J. We all over these little buggers ☺.χχ

Me: Wow, impressive. Kinda like the laser knife, Bud? No pain meds necessary? Yeah, get the buggers. xx

Her: Certain needles will be involved, so sure all sorts of meds. And may be in for the whole day – don't know, just going with it. Love swift and decisive action, certainly is that!

Me: How it go, baby Bud?

Her: Yay, had lovely drugs, biopsy, angiogram ... went in ambulance to other hospital. Before they can give radio into liver, they have to check it doesn't go anywhere else, that's why angiogram. Have to stay here with sand-bag on leg for a few hours and just allowed to eat something!

Me: Oh, good girl. White night, was worried. xx

Her: Oh poo, sorry!

Her: Just having lovely tea and bics. Lovely drugs, no pain.

Me: I love drugs.

Her: My Scrabble app gone nuts and has accessed your FB address book and thinks I am you! I have actually begun a game against myself. Somewhere you are I. My system and I can't delete you ... if you have Scrabble app, can you delete?

Me: Will do. I am you and you are me.

Her: Look at who is playing! I can't make a move though because who am I? Do I exist in the Scrabble astral plane? So, is someone else me?

Me: I deleted the app, so I don't exist either ☺.)

Me: onc says to call Pfizer-UK direct. They have discretionary drugs they can allocate in emergency situations.

Her: OK your FB has now taken over my Messenger, WTF? I'm bloody you again. I just want to be me ☺.

Me: Doc J wants your most recent pathology reports and onc report. Can you get?

Her: Will get. Looks as if cancer may have mutated and become HER2 positive and that probs treatment that I need may also be different now (maybe Herceptin). They are getting 2nd pathology report from another lab done to confirm findings. Plus having RFA (one lobe of liver irradiated...) It's all go, sis ....

Late spring, 2017

Her: Weird achy thigh muscle but gone today— no other radioactive side effects at all! Hoping liver will be all good to go for some nice drinkies in London ☺.

Her: Gotta get that designer drug — no other treatment options available to me. Sob sob. Gonna have to raid the bank of dad ...

Me: Oh well! He's always ready for that!

Early summer 2017
Me: See the Pfizer article in the Times? They are giving it away free to NHS patients, while awaiting NHS approvals. You are kinda NHS?

Her: Doc J putting me through! Doc J said to apply to start at 100 because of tendency to drop white blood cells. Also having MRI n bloods to see how liver doing after SIRT treatment. It's happening!

Her: Got bloody osteopenia in the hip, dang it. Oh well.

Her: Hey sis - v exciting - we getting breast cancer support group set up, have site and place for first meeting. 1st ever in Antalya!

Me: Fabbo. Check out Relay for Life over here. Our big walk is coming up – I'm walking 10 miles for my Baby Bud.

Me: Maybe you should do a cancer support blog too? People would love it, because you are so entertaining ☺.

Her: Thanks, sis. I know I find me funny too ☺.))

Me: Glad you are blogging. Be big help and support for lots of peeps.

Her: Yes, have to get it to the peeps n I may not be v good writer, but pleased with most of the first post!

ME: You are a good writer. My friend Rika was just diagnosed. People like her will benefit hugely from a forum where she feels less alone ...

Her: Bald shots pre digital, do you have any? Or particularly fab or funny shots. Need some before pics for blog.

Lucy Mason Jensen

Bald Bud in the Wendy House

Me: You mean both of us bald?

Her: Yes and no. Just some shots of us n def one of you bald or with eccentric head gear.

Her: Wowzer, nearly 300 people have looked at my blog today, just in the last 5 hours!

Early summer 2017

Her: Sis, can I post your column in the blog? 'Tis so lovely...

Me: Course you can!

Her: Will have time later today to write new blog, going to look at your stuff. Let's chat about a new piece and maybe a joint writing thing?

Her: Spoke to Doc J today. She v. positive about Ibrance. My cancer mate Nikki went to see her today too and thought she was v fab.

Her: Next entry will be hair – do you have pic of me with pudding bowl? Moo as Bo Derek?

Summer 2017

Me: Wow, sis. Totally great discussions today on the BC site. Well initiated! Love-love Mystic Rose. What onc n dox say about bad hip?

Her: Yeah yeah, usual mixture of good and bad. Hip not bad, other bits of bone more crumbly.... Doc J still prescribing magic drug for me tho, so fab!

Me: Husband was talking to his mother about you this morning and he said 'Yeah, Rosie is like stage 8 or something ... she's defied all the other stages' lol

Her: I love that ... stage 8 hehe. Off on hols tomorrow – Greece and Retsina here we come!

Late summer 2017

Her: Sister, bring me Reese's pieces please ... a few ... 🍬

Early autumn 2017

Her: Bloods low, but had treatment. Go low with the Ibrance. Diff one here panicked, what with poop issue too. Have short course antibiotics and back tomorrow ... slight firming of the stools!

Me: How's poop today?

Her: Pooperdooper as us plopsters say ☺.

Her: Hey, sis. Can you send me your gene testing results and reports? It's v v eppensive to get done, but if I have mutations, they may be able to treat me according to that, but really need to see how likely that is and whether you have any?

Her: Ali has the man flu. Freaking terminal, I'd say.

Me: Yeah, def worse than cancer, cos your wife will kill you way before cancer does ... ☺.)

Late autumn 2017
Me: Our mate Rose Genereux died this morning (from the BC group site)
Her: Went out like the fireball she was ... on her own terms.

The heart project

Published in South County Newspapers

    We didn't expect great news – she had warned us that the cancer markers were up, so we weren't imagining an all-clear diagnosis by any means. But I hadn't anticipated something so earth-sliding that I would be left numb for the ensuing days and entirely sleepless in Soledad. Not only were the markers up, but tumors had increased in the spine and, additionally, spread to the lungs and liver. It was so crushing to me that, with this type of almost hopeless news, I finally hit the brick wall I'd been imagining in our family's pathway for the last several years of her disease. Life without baby sis was inconceivable; but, increasingly, poking its ugly head through the clouds of our family's reality.

    At times like this, you lean heavily on friends and family. You find comfort in the shared grieving process that some find themselves at the beginning or middle of during such times. It's a journey for sure. Your whole body aches with doom; even the bright Cali sun and azure skies can't bring a sparkle to the dour truth present in every waking moment. She lives in Turkey with her family, and I live here. It's not practical to run to her side every couple of weeks. She has her own life over there; I have my life and family here. You feel so completely helpless and hopeless when the diagnosis comes in and it is not a good one. I warned everyone in my professional life that I wasn't on my game. My work was likely to be below par. I would conceivably miss deadlines, forget paperwork and be less than on most fronts. Nothing got accomplished. The taxes remained on the dining table where I had started working on them before the call. My front room still had remnants of Christmas lingering and boxes waiting to be packed up and stacked in the garage. My life was a nasty, moldy mess, sinking quickly by the minute.

    "I need your help," a message came from sis in the early hours from her home in Turkey. "I need as many people as possible to send positive messages, a love fest if you like. I need to try and buy some time. I need hearts across the world." Rosie never asked for anything before, so this was a serious request. And so, Team Rosie was born, and hearts were being constructed the world over from flowers, rocks and simple objects. Folks made a heart sign and sent the photo across the ether. Little Rosie shrines were built in bedrooms all over the planet and shared with the other members of 'Team Rosie'. My own has a rose rock, a unicorn, toys and photos from our youth and a candle. "Feeling the love!" she jokes, "Totally feeling the lurv fest!" And with all this positive enthusiasm and photos of beautiful things moving back and forth across the internet, a little hope crawled out of the dark and gave us—her friends and family—some belief in the power of hope, the tenacity of love and a collective effusiveness in the strength of a shared effort.

    I do believe she will buy some time. She managed her first chemo this time around just fine, and there is another scheduled for the coming week; so we will all be throwing hearts around the universe in the next few days in our collective effort to make sure her bloods come in right where they need to be. Any hearts you'd like to throw at the project would be more than appreciated. I find myself looking for them wherever I go.

    Rosie Emma Alexandra Mason Arican is my baby sister.

From Kate:

To: Lucy

Re: Special days with sister

    Ahh Bella, you will have to be super strong and allow Rose to express whatever she needs to, however hard that is for both of you. There is such a strength and courage in that honesty and speaks volumes of how close you two are that she can offload anything at this time. Parting is difficult at the best of times, let alone in these extreme circumstances. Go on autopilot if you need to. The fridge here is practically falling over waiting for your arrival, loaded with bottles of vino that will need to be drunk! Thank god, we live in an age of FaceTime and you have had these precious days with her. Safe journey, darling ...

K

XX

From Carey

To: Lucy

Re: Special days with sister

    What guarantees are there in life honey. None whatsoever is what. Step off a kerb looking the wrong way, change the CD in the car and lose attention, walk along a pavement below a piece of loose signage. So many ways that life can coil, twist and burst — just like that. And then imagine if we all lived our lives as if each moment were our last; that's no way to live. We don't know, we have no control, and all that we unknowing, uncontrolling individuals can do is live in the moment, love in the moment, and make sure that those we love know they are loved so that if the kerb, the CD, the signage — the cancer — claims us we will — up to that time — have lived a life and brought the very best we can to it. Rosie is doing it. We should all do it. She is beautiful, vibrant, resilient, and strong. And you will always see her.

C

xx

Lucy.....

Be hard to say goodbye tomorrow. She seems to act as if we won't see each in person again.

L

(As David Kessler notes in his excellent study of grief, "Finding Meaning: the sixth stage of grief" ....'People who have been in the deepest depths of despair have the broadest bandwidth when it comes to enjoying life: when you've travelled through the deepest valleys, you surely appreciate the highest hills...')

Bud and Me

Happy Dust – The Last Goodbyes

Published in South County Newspapers, 2017

    People still ask me about my sister. Though she has been ill for an awfully long time now and it is always my 'last trip' overseas and the next 'last adventure', when I go to see her in Turkey, I really appreciate, often complete strangers, asking about her. It all helps. It's like the whole world has threads of hope slung over in her direction that might lift her up for another day, might inspire her to get out of bed one more time, or more accurately, now summer is approaching, coax her to get into that glorious Mediterranean Sea for one final season. It is always one last time with Rosie and that makes it all the sweeter each time we get to taste it. Last year was the 'last' New Year we would likely spend together, and then there was this year – a sweet gift we hadn't anticipated and that didn't disappoint. I never talk about it being the last time anymore, because sister defies all the odds. Despite the fact she only ever plans a month or so ahead in her life, she keeps on keeping on. She has been dealing with cancer for going on 2 decades now and I don't feel that she's about to quit just yet.

    Baby sister was determined to go over to England and visit our father for Easter. "Easy-peasy, sis" she breezes, as she tells me all about jumping on a plane for the 4-hour plane ride right after chemotherapy. We all held our breath a little bit there; but off she went. "Your sister is going to do what your sister wants," my husband reminds me, as we ponder all the nasty super bugs out there and how compromised her immune system must be. And, after all this time of her telling us, we know better than to tell her. So off she went and enjoyed a blissful Easter with her friends. Father was ill at home and a visit was not possible. Then she felt feverish herself and her friend took her off to the emergency room, where she was treated with some heavy-duty antibiotics and told to get back home to Turkey as soon as possible. Poor sis. She tries to live her life like a normal, healthy person; but sometimes her disease reminds her that she is pushing her boundaries. This was one of those times.

She arrives home and has issues, feeling dizzy and nauseous. Thoughts spring into our minds of the brain tumor she already whooped a while ago and what could possibly be going on now. Could it, perhaps, just be the combination cocktail of chemo drugs and the hefty antibiotics having a bit of an adverse reaction with each other. As ever with Rosie's situation, we think on the happy side, we go for the best-case scenario, we sprinkle the happy dust from the combustion of a 25lb champagne bottle. And then we wait.

One of my oldest friends is up a mountain, skiing in France. Grateful for modern technology, that keeps all of us close and in constant communication, I am able to tell her and my other dear old friend about my Rosie fears. They are real friends, never seeming to tire of handing out their love and support towards a subject that will likely never go away, even when Rosie herself has. "I'm so worried about Rosie," I tell them, relaying the latest drama. "Dearest. I am sending every pure particle of mountain air and every ounce of noble fir tree spirit to wend their way to Turkey to find Rosie and sustain her. The good elements are all on her side in her beautiful homeland to enrich her, as is the incredible love and strength of her family and friends. Look ahead to the sunshine, always!" My friend sends her effusive flurry from all the way over there to here and over there. My other friend tells me she is sending out huge amounts of happy dust from the fields of her home. At once, I feel the effects. Of course, the happy dust will find its way to Rosie and help her through this additional challenge. Sure enough, I check in with her the next day and she is making a cake, reading a book, getting ready for an English lesson ... she is back on the Rosie plan and we love that plan. That is not the one with the tired wan face and the wry smile. That is the one that shouts, loud and clear, that she will be swimming in the Mediterranean this year and don't try to get in her way!

I have learned so much from Rosie and her illness over the past several years. I have learned how the power of the mind is an extraordinary thing. If you want to keep living, it seems that your mind may be positioned to help you do just that. If life gets you down, don't complain about it, do something. If your body doesn't feel like doing anything, then lie in front of a fire, listen to music, read or watch something, talk to someone fabulous, eat something divine. Wait just a little until your body is bored of all that and in search of something new. Attitude is all – I have learned that too from Rosie. If you have a complaint, complaining about it is not fun for you or anyone else. The worst people in the world are the ones with the complaints that feel the need to share with anyone who will listen. They will empty a room as quickly as a plague of ants. Not my sister. I notice that people flock to be around her because she is so fun, so funny, so full of life that none of us can imagine anything otherwise being around her. We forget, much of the time, that she does have stage 4 cancer and it is likely to get her one day, maybe one day soon-ish. Except that summer is just around the corner and she loves summer, so that's worth sticking around for. She will find herself in the sea with a snorkel because she can't hardly swim anymore, or lounging on a floatie, because it's hard for her that day to manage the snorkel, but she won't complain about it. No, she will get up and do it, or she will make you feel as if she doesn't want to at that particular time. You just go ahead without her.

 It has been a few years since my own diagnosis and, thanks to Rosie, I was able to look at her and our family's lot at the time and go as radical as possible in my treatment. Maybe that is why I am still here, and I haven't had a recurrence. Regardless, if it comes back to visit, as sometimes it can, I will need to infuse some of the Rosie happy dust and go with the flow. We cannot change what happens to us; we can only change our response. If I get another visit, I want to be as effusive and fun a sick person as Rosie is and make myself a pleasure to be around; so much so that people will forget I'm sick. Just the way I do with Rosie. And if you are thinking that Rosie must be some kind of Saint, trust me she is not. She is an opinionated brat. She is bossy and outspoken, sometimes even narcissistic. Often, these days she is still bossy, but supremely thoughtful and loving. She spares us as much as she can by way of suffering and then she will just purse her thin lips and say, "Just can't take it on, sis. Just can't. If it's upsetting for all of you, then oh well." And that is my Rosie, my Baby Bud, my happy dust, my crazy diamond, my baby sister.

It does not define her

She is up early and to bed late. She sleeps little, if at all. ("Sleeping is boring.") She drives like a race driver and walks really fast wherever she goes. ("No use in hanging about!") She makes lots of plans and executes all of them with forever an eye on the morrow, in anticipation of having fun with people she adores. ("How did I ever find time to work?") Her future planning is limited to a scope of only 3 months, ("Let's just see how things go,") but she makes those 3 months count. In short, my baby sister Rosie lives life with a – hate this classification – "terminal" disease more than most do without.

We recently returned from a precious week spent with her and her family in Turkey. Now, back home, I am feasting on the memories. She lives life with a selfless grace such as I have never seen. Nothing was too much trouble for her during our stay. We stayed in a luxury hotel and were chauffeured by her to a whole plethora of beautiful places. We had boat trips on the Mediterranean, languid swims in azure waters, tours of ancient cities, amazing meals and so much love and laughter – not to mention aggressive Scrabble games—that I came away with my cup flowing over with joy, heartened by her seemingly-amazingly good health and our happy days together. If you didn't already know, you would never guess that she takes lots of pills everyday including the chemo pill, she is on all kinds of medications to try and stop the osteoporosis, that is pervading her bones, she has permanent nerve damage in her feet that means a lot of things, but mostly that she suffers with numbness and sciatica most times of every day and night. She does not let any of those things – let alone the C word – define who she is and how she lives the rest of her life.

"You need to rest, Rosie!" my husband ventured, and I thought she was going to eat his head. "I can sleep when I am dead," she retorted, reminding us that she will always live her life on her own terms, without a modicum of self-pity or fear. She loves enormously and dances through her days, worrying only for the loved ones she will, one day, leave behind; though no one should count her out of the game just yet. For her husband and her stepdaughter, she worries a great deal. They already dealt with the loss of a daughter and sister to cancer just a few short years ago. She plans ahead that they will be taken care of, that they will be able to live in a home that she has never resided in, so will be able to build fresh memories without her. She ensures that they will always be a part of our family, no matter what. She attends counseling sessions with her daughter. She is preparing for her own exit in a fashion that defies convention, while still leading the most amazing vibrant dance on earth. And that is her; always has been. She is my brightest light, my rock star and I am so proud to be able to call her my sister.

The end of Ramadan

Published Summer 2017
South County Newspapers

    It was the end of Ramadan in Turkey; the culmination of a month of fasting for the Muslims. We were invited to Mama's house in the evening at dusk to celebrate the end of the fast. We had previously witnessed a restaurant full of people awaiting the dusk, the break of their fast—salads, water and bread in front of them — and literally counting down the moments until they could finally eat and drink. It was quite something to behold. Especially when the temps were so high and the need for water intense! I could not imagine the pressure of thirst like that.

    Sister and I had spent a quiet day at her home in the mountains, eating a lot of home-made lemon curd and tahini ice cream – no fasting there – and enjoying the cool flagstones and the luxury of a cold shower whenever we willed. I was a little concerned about what they might be serving at the feast that night and broached the subject. "Of course, they won't give you goat, sis," she chirped. "They know you have goats for pets." At ease once more, I prepared to meet the family for dinner, learning how to appropriately greet Mama as my elder, (kiss her hand, she kisses your head, you kiss the hand again ...) to the great entertainment of the gathered family. My dinner was a fabulous BBQ chicken, never mind what everyone else was eating. Soup, salad, yoghurt, rice. The Turks really do know how to eat good, fresh food.

    The next day we were going on the boat from Adrasan to spend the day cruising around the Bay and swimming off the boat, one of my sister's favorite things to do. We were celebrating a friend's 70th birthday and there were lots of familiar faces on board. Sister got in her party mode and flitted around from one friend to the other, catching up and spreading the cheer. In those social situations, she reminds me of our mother greeting everyone in the room as it were, making all feel welcome and included. At times like those, you could also forget how ill she was. And there she was up and down the steps from the boat into the azure waters of the Mediterranean – at least 4 times that I counted – without a care in the world. No matter she has tumors all over, including the recently annoying boogers in the hip and pelvis area; she was going to enjoy her day out on the water. We ate fresh fish, sang happy birthdays, swam and swam some more. I fell asleep on the deck to the sound of sister chatting with her friends. It's a memory I shall always hold dear. Then she was exhausted and needed several games of Scrabble to come down off her cloud, (she still mostly beats me).

We returned to her favorite place in Cirali to rest up some more and hang out with her husband, daughter and friends. It was extremely hot by then and we spent much of the time playing Scrabble in the shade, or she worked hard on her blog, cheering up the members of our online Breast Cancer Support group that we both enjoy. We would swim in the sparkling silver millpond of the Med first thing in the morning and then again once the sun started to dip down at the end of the day. It was too brutal and white-heatish in the hours between and I was so grateful for my small, air-conditioned cabin at Cirali and the lovely cold shower that gave me respite. High summer can be quite taxing in that part of the world.

As I was leaving for Antalya, early in the morning, the sun was rising. A huge, brilliant orange ball soon blazed in the skies. I remembered that it had been a while since I had witnessed my last sunrise and I needed to amend that. Special days need to be marked by special things. I am grateful for every extra sunrise I get to spend with my sister these days, never knowing if we will get to do any of those things again. In the meantime, she is still floating off the boat with her friends, cooking nice food and making every day count. This week she has a party for the official closing of her school and 'only one doctor's appointment', she noted with glee. For now, her days of daily radiation are over, and she is happy to be able to take back her days and fill however much longer she has with lovely and meaningful hours.

The Last Gifts

Everyone is getting a gift. She is getting ready.

Today she gives me my present – it is Granny Evelyn's cameo earrings. They must be super old – and came to me, encased in a tiny, very old wooden box I gave to her for Christmas when I was at boarding school. I remember buying it in a dusty old antique shop for 50 pence circa 1974. The box itself has to be extremely old. I strangely remembered it. Bud always liked boxes. 'For secretive people' she said. I do remember our Granny Evelyn wearing those cameo earrings.

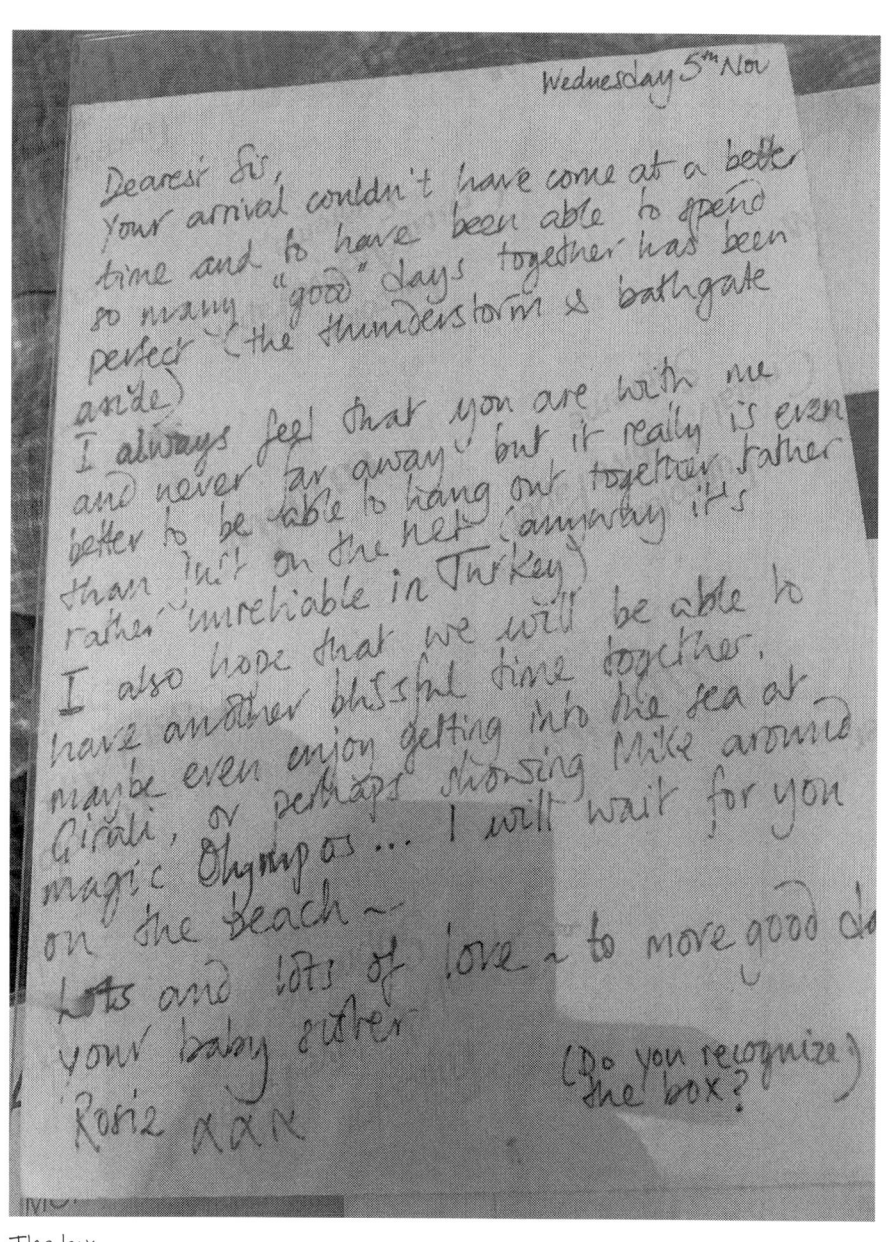

> Wednesday 5th Nov
>
> Dearest Sir,
> Your arrival couldn't have come at a better time and to have been able to spend so many "good" days together has been perfect (the thunderstorm & bathgate aside)
> I always feel that you are with me and never far away, but it really is even better to be able to hang out together rather than just on the net (anyway it's rather "unreliable in Turkey)
> I also hope that we will be able to have another blissful time together, maybe even enjoy getting into the sea at Çirali, or perhaps showing Mike around magic Olympos... I will wait for you on the beach ~
> Lots and lots of love ~ to more good da
> your baby sister
> 'Rosie' xxx
>
> (Do you recognize the box?)

The box

Later she started slipping into her tunnel. God, how I remember that too.

"I have many heroes in my life," she tells me. "These are people who continue to keep me alive. There's Mustafa Ozdogan, my oncologist, without him I would have been dead many years ago. But there are many more besides. I would like to tell you about Akin, he is one of my secret heroes working behind the scenes. He is head of nuclear medicine at Medstar and is responsible for interpreting my PET SCANS and measuring increase and decrease in tumors and cancer activity ... it's his detailed diagnosis which enables the Medstar team to offer me the best treatment and to keep me going.

Thank you to all my heroes ... it's all about teamwork and I'm very lucky in that TEAM ROSIE is second to none. And thanks to all my other team in California - another rocking crowd!

Who would have thought that chemotherapy could be so much fun! A lovely day of art and chemo and the results are not too bad! Thanks to all the Medstar team and especially to Aysun Gurol Erdogan - you rock!

Lucy in her Team Rosie hat, proudly worn until it fell apart.

Lucy Mason Jensen

Art during chemo at Medstar in Antalya ...

November 2017

Her: Need to give the Ibrance back to Doc J. Back to treatment ...

Me: How are you today, sis?

Her: Ick. Trying porridge.

Me: Better today, Bud?

Her: Better ... had spinach and yoghurt for dinner, may have mashed banana on toast later. Tomorrow should be proper turning the corner.

Me: Onc asked if you can get eribulin over there?

Her: Thanks, sis, already had that one. Freakin Queen of chemo has had 'em all.

January 2018

Me: Thanks, sis, for another lovely New Year in your beautiful home with your beautiful peeps. Just had my simit and coffee. Love you bunches xx

Her: Sis, was about to check on you! 'Twas lovely - time goes sooooo quickly, but better too little than too much!

Me: Ha ha, better too little than too much ...trueeee xx

Me: Just white food?

Her: White food, chicken and rice, but feeling fine.

Me: Great! Chemo recipe please, sis?

Her: It's called Ac chemo on Macmillan site - cyclophosphamide & Adriamycin.

Early Spring 2018

Her: Hi sis! Another amazing meal at Nicole's. Gorgeous time. Breakfast with Dilek, Levent, Zeynep and co. Meze and raki in a Meyhane restaurant (although think may be resting liver tonight, bloods tomorrow!)

Her: Just had one more of those night chemos. Results good! Seeing head onc in 2 weeks and then he'll have another think ...

Me: All-night chemos? Kinda like an all-night party, but lying down?

Her: Hehe, kinda. Well, results show bones same and just growth in one liver tumor, but also, I didn't realize we can nuke liver with this cyber knife thing - but not while having chemo. Think may squeeze one more chemo in and then we'll probably play some star-wars and zap any new growth ...

Her: Sister, just booked to go to UK after next chemo. V exciting and get Easter and chocolate and eggs too!

Me: Yay, the Bud!!

Her: Going to celebrate now with slab of homemade cake, cream and raspberries ☺.

Her: Hoping to bring your dragon flies to UK with me.

Late March 2018

Her: Chemo done and dusted.

Her: Hey, sis. Well, hols not going quite according to plan. Between father and I, we can't get our act together. I've had an off-on low level temp for days, so went to brill Grantham A & E yesterday - no infection but began antibiotics and really couldn't face trip to London where dad still hacking. So, flying back from Nottingham tomorrow. Was a gamble to come so close to chemo and didn't quite pay off. But been very relaxing up here and of course still managed to have fab time ...

Easter 2018

Her: Results all good - a little more here and a little less there. All as expected. So, continuing with our new plan, will begin tomorrow - daily pill, no radio necessary, so fab. Yoga and swims tomorrow.

Me: Well done, Bud! I see a swimming summer ahead. xx

Late April 2018

Her: Sister, I'm making flying visit to UK, arrive 4th leave 7th. Will I see you?

BTW, dragonflies flying in ... can bring too. 61 bucks.

Me: You will! I'll be at dad's on Sunday the 6th, yay!

Her: Sadly, Moo doesn't arrive til 7th, but prob just as well, as it all get rather exciting for Dad and he may have to miss his party again ☺.)

Me: Oh, I know ... we will have to slow our roll .)

Late May 2018

Her: Checking out the brow later today for our micro-blading. Also need little botox update too. I'm such a princess, so high maintenance!
Me: You are ☺.

Early June 2018

Me: Bud, what drug are you on currently and what are they proposing next? One is curious.

Her: About to start using Pemetrexed (Alimta) from UK. I am the 1st person in Turkey to use it for metastatic breast cancer and have received full funding for it!

I've had 2 rounds of Temozolomide (Temodal) - it's used for treatment of brain tumors (which I don't have). Hope it may have had some systemic benefit.

Me: Whoa, look at you. Info at your fingertips!

Her: Eyebrows are on - gonna have to drag you outta bed tho! 600tl. Bring dollars, TL is crap.

ME: Yay, Bud! How fun! Have dollars, will travel!

Her: One last small request - Reece's pieces - just making last of mine into ice cream ☺.

June 9, 2018

Me: TK 80 arrives in Ist at 17.15, then change and flight to Ant arrives at 20.45. Let me know if you want me to get a cab and, if so, where are we staying?

Her: Cab to Alp Pasa hotel in Kale ici - that means old city, but it's poss that someone may be there to get you. Don't be alarmed in taxi when you start to drive down wiggly road - it's the only way in!

Can you bring some small dollar bills? A few ones and fives ... trad to give to kids as presents on the family dinner night. Oh, and mozzie stuff ... pp

While I was there, our last days together ...
Grains of time

    I'd watch her sleeping on her back. Peaceful, still, like a shroud. She is still breathing though, lightly. I study her chest moving up and down – tiny, smooth breaths. I quietly move across the room to the bathroom, trying not to wake her. But just like forever, my movement would provoke one eye to open and a smile to spread across her tiny, pale face. Stairs are now a problem, a little breathlessness. Swelling from the steroids, swollen stomach, gas, irritation. Difficulties with the bowels, as ever. She stays away from salt and sugar to help her systems, but I see her body struggling now as never before. We are staying in a cramped bed and breakfast in the old part of Antalya. Its classic old town beauty belies its trickiness and functionality, when the body isn't working right anymore. The stairs are an issue, she feels crowded in the room; it's humid outside. She wants to go home and, as her driver, I need to make that happen. We go to the hospital, and she has the brain tumor zapped, though, ironically, the tumor is the least of her current issues. We talk to her chief oncologist, and they are putting their heads together, wondering what next they can do for her, while there is a little time left. Is there any time left? Her liver levels are up. They will not give her chemo under those conditions. Without chemo, yes, she knows, her time will run out. I take her home and, immediately, she feels better. She is calm and accepting again of whatever comes her way.

    She wants to go to the sea and walk down the beach. She can no longer swim, but she can float with her noodle, and she is happy with that. It's enough to be in the clear blue warm waters of her home. She is calm, accepting. We spend hours in the warm azures of the Mediterranean, and we are so happy in those moments, watching the silver twinkles on the water, looking at the changing moods of the sky. We are in one of her very happiest of places – a small tropical seaside place called Cirale right on top of the historical Olympos. We stay at Tunay's pension – good friends of the family – he and his wife Dulgur run a special place with delicious food, comfortable cabins and lovely gardens. She and Ali were married there in the gardens almost 4 years ago to the day. We sit in a café nearby and play Scrabble, hide a little from the strong rays of the June sun. She can sleep on the beach there, as much as she sleeps anywhere. I watch her from the sea, lying on the sun lounger, and I wonder if she is still breathing. I wonder that a lot these days. If she would stop breathing there in the sun lounger on the beach near the water that she loves, then she would die happy. It is there that we find ourselves these days. This is a magical spot and always will be. I tell her I want to bring my granddaughter here one day. She smiles.

Her other happy place – and perhaps the crown in her kingdom is their home in the mountains, overlooking the bay and the agricultural area of Kumluca, not dissimilar to our Salinas Valley. Her husband custom-built the home near his village a few years back, when he was losing his daughter Didem to leukemia. He had hoped the mountain airs and organic produce would help her recover, but she died, just a young teenager. Her death nearly broke him. But the mountain home is a happy place now. My sister adores their house. The wide-open social kitchen, the huge flagstone floors and high wooden ceilings, fireplaces and wood stoves, views galore and cozy reading and snoozing spots. She loves to cook there, to pick the fruits and vegetables from their large garden, breathe in the mountain airs. Breakfast is enjoyed on the verandah or terrace outside, overlooking the bay below. It's a very important meal in Turkey – eggs, cheeses, tomatoes, olives, breads, yoghurts, fruits and, of course, multiple glasses of chai tea. The family always eats together – it's a lovely custom. It's the peaceful time, before everyone starts rushing around to wherever they have to go. My sister's family rushes more than most. What are they rushing for; why do they not savor the moments? Is time so short?

It's the season of Biram, a time of festivities. We are headed to Mama's house for the special dinner to be held at dusk on the last day of fasting. The smell of roasting goat makes me want to run outside, but it is their custom and I behave. I tell myself that I do not have to eat it; they have kindly made me an alternative, as they did last year. The children play, people laugh. Everything seems like a normal family celebration, but then we are rushing again. We must up and out early, we must visit relatives. Why must we, we did that last night at the goat feast. Isn't our time together so short? I give my sister a look, she catches my vibe and she changes the plan. We will be sitting on the terrace, enjoying a leisurely breakfast together, savoring the views and the food and the peace. We will not be rushing up and out. And so, it was a much better day after that. She showed me where Ali's daughter and father are buried and where she will be too, before sundown on the day she passes. "You won't make it, sis", she tells me, reading my mind. A surreal conversation that you should always have, like it or not, when time is so short. And her time here is now limited, we know that. How limited though?

I am leaving her again. It's 3.30am when my cab arrives to take me and, this time, she gets two hugs. As usual, she has made me my cup of coffee, as she always does when I am staying. Her tiny frame is so fragile I hold her gently, as if she might break. I do feel as if this will be the last time I hug her in person. "I don't want people rushing to my sick bed," she tells me. "Just sitting there watching me sleep ... ugh!" The sand is running out on the timer; there are only grains left. Don't waste it, don't waste it. There's not much left.

I'm home and she is back in the hospital. Things seem to be failing, body parts are worn. The liver isn't working properly, the bowels either. And let's not even get started on the brain tumor. The issues seem to be growing and multiplying, compounding problems cascading swiftly on the downhill slope. They put her on a drip – a deep cleanse of the liver. No food or drink for a few days. She is woozy, dry-mouthed, tired. I wonder, if I were in her hospital room now, would I see her short breaths ease and stop? Why do I keep wondering that? Something in the human condition is preparing me for that, I'm sure of it. They give her 1.5-2 months to live. What do they know? Do they know something I don't? My mother lived 3 weeks of a 6-18 month diagnosis. I don't believe in that stuff and, if sister knows it, she's not dwelling on it. She has consistently defied all expectations, these past 16 years of fighting her cancer battle and smiling along the way.

She arrives home after her marathon drip week in hospital. She is craving watermelon. They have the best melons there. In the sunset light of her terrace, her skin is no longer grey, but bronze once more. She has a little more energy and brightness. She is home. A few more grains are added back into the timer. Time. But how much more time?

Lucy
Turkey, Summer 2018

June 12, 2018

Me: Miss you already, sis. Have some lovely days with Ali and Suzi Q. Insist upon it!

Her: Sister! You settled in, checked in, having coffee? Beautiful morning here - not a cloud, but think I will stay in bed and finish my book. Been snoozing. I will insist on special days. Plenty may re life stories to be shared from your end and mine - excited to hear of all of yours as it unfolds and would like to catch up with Mikey and Frouie one day when we have a decent connect! Happy homecoming, sister! Thanks for always being there for me, sis.

Me: Ha ha, having an Efes! Always always always be there for my baby sis. I'm just a short plane ride away. Like anytime. All totals relative. I'm a good driver ☺.

I love you soooo much.

Big sis

xx

June 19, 2018

Her: Rigged up on a serum and being treated for chronic wind and build-up stuff in bowels ... zero in mouth for a couple of days and exercise and it should also bring the liver down. Well happy with that. Have luxury hospital room, footie, all mod cons ... I'm fine!

Me: So, liver doing its job, just needs a little help?

Her: This should bring liver enzymes down - it all needs a bit of a clear out. Feel less swollen already - just waiting for ward to wake up as think then I can crack on with my exercise ... walking and farting ... xx

June 20, 2018

Me: How are you, Bud? Outta hospital?

Her: Still in. Just had foot rub from Ella. Improved results already! Menu still liquids at mo - have done a little poo, but still a bit swollen. Got zapped and had session with Almila. All good. Liver still coming down in the right direction!

Me: Well done, Team Bud!

June 21, 2018

Her: Team Bud here made decision that need to drain off some of this liquid swilling around, so will have radiotherapy and then in the pm a stent will be fitted, and it will drain off ... should help and then hope also to be allowed proper food and liver will continue to come down. It will be temporary, but the drain will stay in place for a while. Got everything crossed that will be home Saturday - now have nurse Ali installed and nept football match!

Me: How are you doing, Bud?

Her: All god here. I mean gooooood.

Me: Yeah, don't go all god on me.

Her: Gawd, noooooooo!

June 22, 2018

Me: Well done, baby. Now go poo and you can return home to your peace of earth ... and watermelon!

Her: Done the poo, but think they're planning to keep me in until tomorrow. Will have to be patient a little longer. I'm about to have hospital breakfast, def no watermelon until I get home. Done another poo! Hope you've had a good day. Luv ya sis - crack on ... xx

June 26, 2018

Me: What head onc say, Bud?

Her: V pleased - think could even have chemo next week. Drains good!

July 2, 2018

Her: Morning and night, big sis! We off for final zap! After serious session yesterday, now rocking new improved footballer style - the half monk ☺.)

Me: Final zap is the best zap. Go, sister!

July 6, 2018

Me: So lovely to see you at peace on your gorg terrace. Totally hear you, sis. You are going to make your days about you and your Ali, as it should be. You have shared so many joyous days with so many of us over the bonus years we have been gifted. The memory bank is full to the brim. You and I have had so many wonderful times, I shall always carry your heart inside my own, you will always be my naughty little sister. I shall hear your voice and laughter everywhere, just as I do now.

July 7, 2018

Her: Good day- sorted out bag of rubbish and now also have v fab disabled access bathroom downstairs ... plus of course England won at the footie!

July 14, 2018

Her: Hey, big sis. When we chatting? Dilgesu home. Very happy people.

July 17, 2018

Me: Baby sis. I will see you everywhere, for always. You will be with me everywhere and for always. I will carry your heart inside my own and we will always be together. Always. Of that, I am sure. Happy trails, my love. Come swim with me sometime, if you're not too busy out there on the ether. I'll see you out there regardless ... my hummingbird, my dragon fly, my baby sis. Love you forever,

Big Sis XXX

July 19, 2018

Her: Buzz me when you free?

And with that she started to shut down all her open windows to the world. Fortunately, sister Mary was there for a few days, so I could check in with her and Bud's great friend Katie also; but Bud herself began checking out the week before she passed. In fact, photos from that time made it seem as if our Rosie - our

A convo with Katie

Bud - had already left Rosie's body. There was a vacant quality to her look, as if her spirit had already fled its decrepit shell and she was already out there, free from her body, and getting ready for the next adventure.

And then, thank god for Rosie's friend Katie, who was the communication bridge to my Bud after sister left. She made me feel as if I was there, even though that was not possible. Katie saw her every day and helped me watch her go. Bud wanted it to just be her and Ali and Dilgesu at the end and I honored her wishes, though it was so very difficult.

Katie: I spoke with Rosie about my feelings towards her today and she shared hers about me, we cuddled, I cried. I invited Dilgesu and we cried, we spoke of the family life Rosie found with Dilgesu and Ali and they taught her how to love. We spoke about Rosie and where she was going. She's going to nature, she said, flying freely over the Himalayas and swimming in all the oceans, in the air, all around. She's got plans already. She and Dilgesu told each other how much they love one another. And then she told me she wet the bed last night.....

July 18, 2018

Me: How was she today?

Katie: Hey, very weak today. Slept most of the day. Completely different to yesterday, but again peaceful and smiley. A doc came up and examined her. She's not in any pain. They took blood to see if she needs to be put on any serum.

Me: Is she properly conscious? I noticed she no longer checks messages.

Katie: She knows what is going on, but drifts in and out. She definitely didn't have the energy to really chat on phone either.

Me: No, I guess we won't speak again until her spirit leaves her body. Now Dilgesu is home, she is at peace and will likely leave us soon. Her body is failing.

Katie: It is. But one thing I did notice, as she drifts in and out of snooze, you can see she is laughing to herself at something and smiling.

Me: That's lovely.

July 19, 2018

Katie: Rosie was so much better today than yesterday and when we spoke about the piece you sent over, she knew it.

Me: Aww, she FaceTimed me late last night, couldn't believe it. Brief but beautiful. She thanked me for the message, told me she loved me, blew a kiss and was gone.

Me: You are such a good friend to her.

Katie: Rosie is such a special friend to me. More than a friend. I'm so thankful to Adrasan.

Me: You two are sisters and now you will be our sister too.

Katie: She's so comfortable with the people who are here to take care of her. She likes them all and they are looking after her so well.

Me: Aww, bless. The best exit for the Beach Princess.

July 20, 2018

Katie: She's very weak. She said to me she just feels so tired. As the days go by, more and more.

Me: Awww, my baby. Do you feel that she's close to passing?

Katie: I really don't know. We have some nice chats, but they don't last long. She gets confused, but can then understand that and have a giggle at herself.

Me: Her body is done. I'm feeling like I should be with her.

Katie: It must be so difficult.

Me: It so is.

July 21, 2018

Me: How was she today?

Katie: Not great today, I'm afraid.

Me: Mary said she was talking a lot of gibberish, but still sometimes funny.

Katie: Yes, she was. Not sure how long we have left, but I will say again that she is in no pain. That's so important. Lots of love to you.

Me: That is everything, thank you honey.

July 22, 2018

Katie: We had a message from Ali this morning saying that Rosie is a lot better today than she was yesterday.

Me: The Rosie Rollercoaster Ride — she'd love that. I think she's just prepping us all for losing her.

Katie: We were going to pop up in the afternoon, but Ali said she was sleeping like a baby, no pain.

Me: Aww, my baby. It is so weird knowing that she is still on the planet earth, but out of touch, out of reach. A sub reality. I feel I should be with her.

July 23, 2018

Me: Obeying her last wishes is super hard.

Katie: I went today, but I only got a lovely smile. Late morning, they washed her body and hair. She had some lunch and then went to sleep. I was there from 2-6 and she was soundo.

Me: Aww, poor baby. Her body is worn out. Glad you got the smile though.

Katie: You're right, her body is tired.

July 24, 2018

Me: Did you see her today? God, I miss her already.

Katie: Just got back, love. She's sleeping, she's been in a deep sleep since yesterday evening. Don't think we have long XXX

Me: Haven't slept thinking about her. She likely won't wake up again, will she.

Katie: Omer, the nurse, said he doesn't think she will.

Me: Such a strange mixed feeling of relief that she's on her adventure already and sadness that we couldn't keep her around any longer ...

Katie: Feel the same, so mixed. Want her to be at peace, but don't want her to go.

The atmosphere at the house is so peaceful.

Me: Yesterday I went to the ocean and wished her spirit out of her worn-out body,

Me: Can you tell me what the funeral procedure is in Turkey? I know nothing except that they are buried before sundown the day they pass.

Katie: Yes, of course ... so they will first wash Rosie's body and she will be taken to the mosque next to the graveyard in Incircik. There will be a prayer said there and then she will be taken to the graveyard to be buried. Generally, only men go to the prayer and graveyard, but we will go too. Some women do and will go. After that it's a tradition here that you 'open' your house for guests to come and give their condolences. We will open the Kumluca flat for about 3 days.

Me: Oh wow. Lots of chai to be made!

Katie: I think it's a tradition that you put a headstone a year later, but I will check. Will ask Ali about Incircik.

Me: Ok, good to know. Practical things to stop you losing your mind.

July 24, 2018

Me: Ali just sent me a message that she was restless, so they were giving her morphine.

Katie: Oh really.

Me: Yes, no open eyes, just restless.

Katie: Day 3 of not opening her eyes. He also said her arms are really cold.

Me: Mary told me she researched the final stages and cold limbs are part of it.

Katie: Yes, I did too. Don't know what else to say.

Me: It's strange, as it has been. She's on her new adventure already, just waiting to be shot of the useless container that is her body. We have been already mourning her for days. We know it's time.

Katie: It is time.

Me: It is. I can almost hear the wailing from the village.

My Dragon Fly

"Baby sis, I will see you everywhere and for always. You will be with me everywhere, for always. I will carry your heart inside of my own and we will always be together. Always. Of that, I am sure. Happy trails, my love. Come swim with me sometime, or all the times.

My hummingbird, my dragon fly, my butterfly, my baby sis.

I shall love you forever. Big Sis XX"

(This was read to her for me before she passed.)

    Strange things happened the week my sister fell into a deep sleep. "She won't wake again," the nurse said. "What do you mean, she won't wake again? She's just sleeping, isn't she?" Of course, you awake from sleep. Except that sometimes you don't.
    The week we spent together in the middle of June reached new heights of sisterhood. She could no longer drive per the

doctors' orders - her brain tumor had just been diagnosed — but, apart from that, she did not seem to have slowed at all. She was still rushing around cooking and chatting and firing on all cylinders. We still raced from here to there to see Mama, celebrate Biram, visit so and so. She was such a busy little bee, as she was her entire life. The last two days of my stay, we stayed at her very favorite beach place on the planet and there she slowed a little, let herself snooze in the sun and play 'Scrabble' with me in our favorite cafe. Our last swim together was in the Mediterranean of course and she floated around quite happily. I watched her a lot that week, knowing, for sure-for sure, that these would be our last few days together in the flesh. My favorite photo of the two of us was taken unknowingly by a friend, who was walking behind us, as we returned from our last swim in the sea. Also, I believe, her last swim on the planet. There we were like twins, side by side wearing the same hats, completely in step with one another. It was a precious moment captured forever.

  After I left, the doctors said there was nothing more they could do for her. Never mind the brain tumor and other tumors throughout her body, her liver was shot and there was no coming back from that. They did a procedure to ease her discomfort and sent her home. "Good news and bad news, sis" she Face Times me, as she would every day. I was almost used to those good news/bad news calls after all these years. "Good news is I don't have to go to Antalya and have treatment anymore. Bad news is that there's nothing more they can do for me ... but" she went on," I CAN eat and drink anything I want now, No more damn steroids!" Oh, that girl - always seeing the bright side of life. I scrunched up my mouth. "Now, sis. We knew this day had to come sooner rather than later," she cheered on. "It's all good! It was always about the quality of life, not the quantity." I stayed calm and cheery through the call, then, when she hung up, I sat down in the manure of my stable near my horse's legs and yelled at the universe. "48? Really, that's all she gets? She loves life! How dare you take her away!" I was furious for several moments sitting in the horse manure, and then I cried hot, salty tears that my willing dogs licked away.

    The 24-hour nursing staff arrived at her home and took care of her round the clock. Our middle sister was there. Baby sis started to sleep a lot and began shutting down the world outside. She signed off from group discussions, had farewell tea parties and said her staggered goodbyes to friends and family. She was closing the doors and windows to her world. After our middle sister Mary left her home in Turkey, she slept even longer. We joked that she needed so little sleep during her life, that her body was grabbing it when it could. She would then only FaceTime for a few seconds and sometimes it didn't really seem like her anymore – the words were not that clear and the sparkle had already left the building; the shell was in auto-operational mode. She would sometimes chatter on almost deliriously. She told people she was flying above the Himalayas, she was swimming in all the oceans. We knew she was already on her journey away from us, but we were still in a holding pattern in the waiting room of her life. This was a most distressing time.

    Then she stopped waking up and chatting and taking nourishment. It was day 2 of the deepest sleep ever and I was in agony. I couldn't sleep, work, function. Flowing tears and numbness set in. My husband told me to cancel everything – we were going to the beach where we had sprinkled my Mum's ashes nearly 18 years ago – Mum's beach – and we were going to have a little chat with the universe. It was the strangest of most strange and magical days. I ran along the beach to our Memorial spot, looking for dialogue. The skies changed from blue and sunny to thick swirly fog. Cormorants, pelicans, gulls swooped overhead, sandpipers scattered at the water's edge. I found a piece of old driftwood boat and decided this would be Rosie's boat - my own personal monument to my mermaid who loved the sea and boat trips on turquoise waters so very much. I lay on my back in the sand and talked to my Mum, watching the sun be consumed by the fog and the gulls crossing over my head. A group of horse riders strolled quietly and calmly past me. I watched them move slowly into the fog. There was one rider moving slightly to the right of the pack.

The slow march reminded me of the Grim Reaper escorting home its dead in a slow-motion majestic way. "It's okay, sis. You can go," I said to the rider on the right, as she slipped away into the distance and out of sight.

About 11pm at night our time – 9am in the morning the next day Turkish time, our middle sister called me to say that Rosie had finally gone to sleep-sleep. According to Turkish custom she would be buried before sundown. I felt oddly calm and peaceful myself that day. The colors of the sky and the flowers all around were sharply enhanced, the birds' song extra sweet and the cuddles of my animals more comforting than ever.

Her new adventure had just begun. We will see each other again.

(July 25, 2018 at around 9am Turkish time, my baby sis passes away)

July 25, 2018

Me: Was it a lovely ceremony? I feel strangely calm and peaceful.

Katie: It was. She's in a stunning place, you will absolutely love it.

Me: Did you see her before she was buried?

Katie: No, I didn't. I didn't need to. I'm glad you are feeling calm and peaceful, because Rosie is too and that's just how she would want you to feel.

July 27, 2018

Me: Today I am hollow and sad and ripped off. Tears trickling down my cheeks. I guess this will be how it goes for a while, until I am all cried out.

Katie: To cry and grieve is a good thing.

Me: Yes. Last two days I was numb and peaceful, today I can't stop crying. I'm also furious at the world that took her from us.

July 28, 2018

Katie: How are you today?

Me: Better today, calmer. How are you?

Katie: I'm good actually. Is it okay to feel good? That's odd too, isn't it. We were with Ali and Dilgesu today.

Me: It's good to feel good. Waves on a beach, sister. She wouldn't want us all weepy and sad .. (can't you hear her now ...'oh for fuck's sake ..')

Katie: Ali said to me he realizes that Rosie was the center of their family – Rosie, him and Dilgesu – so they need to adjust. We plan to go to Incircik one day in the week for a sort out – that's going to be really difficult, but also lovely.

Me: Make sure you keep some nice things for yourself. Do you have a dragonfly?

Katie: I do and Rosie's first present to Ece Mira was a dragon fly sensory toy. Didn't click until the other day.

Me: Dragonflies are very magic. I had a huge one over my pond yesterday. 'Hi sis,' I said to her, like a nutter ☺.)

Katie: I keep reading all the beautiful things people have written on Rosie's Facebook, so so so lovely.

July 18, 2019

Katie: ALI JUST TOLD ME THEY FOUND THE LAPTOPPPPP! YOU CAN ACCESS HER BLOG, WAHOOO, BRILL NEWS!

Me: OMG, I cried. I feel sick with excitement. I'd given up on being able to access it. I've already started my 'Rosie Book' (not its actual title) but this is what I really wanted. 1 year away from her passing? No coincidence I'd say. (Bud be like 'wtf, found underneath all that mountaineering shit ...')

September 23, 2019

Me: Saw an enormous electric blue dragonfly this morning. She's so happy I'm headed over there to see all her peeps.

Katie: She will love the fact you're coming – it was very important to her.

Me: I know. It's important to me too. I'll always come.

Lucy Mason Jensen

SECTION 6
AFTER THE END

The Grief Study

Published by Lucy after July 25, 2018
A textbook for grief

    I remember my daughter telling me that there are many things they don't teach you in school. She was referring to balancing a checkbook at the time and making a budget for life. True, they don't teach you that. They also don't give you a textbook on how to handle a part of the human condition we all experience; and that is grief. This is not my first Rodeo. I am middle-aged plus; I have lost plenty of people in my life. I should be pretty good at it by now; but nobody taught me the class, nobody had me write a dissertation on the subject. In short, I did not graduate from this topic in any shape or form. And every time I go through it, it's a little bit different; but no less agonizing.

    "Well, she had been ill for a very long time," said someone. "Probably a bit of a relief that she's no longer suffering." I nearly choked. "She's in a better place," another helpful soul ventured. (How do they know?) Some people say nothing — they don't know what to say. And we all feel so inadequate at times like this; when we should be adept at finding the right words, consoling the person, providing the necessary comfort.

    I find myself doing strange things like cleaning. I'm always looking for something — that one special photo of her I can't find, the bracelet she gave me, the story I wrote about her. I don't sleep much and my brain zips around on special alert in an obsessive way through my white nights. I can't stop thinking about her. I wade through multitudes of photos trying to prepare for her Memorial, as if she'd care if it was totally perfect or not; but I want it to be. I'm constantly losing things. So far, I have lost my driving license, my ear plugs and headphones — among other things. Also, my mind. Some I find again; some I locate in the most random of places, as if I sleepwalk at night and move all my possessions around just to drive myself mad. I am possessive about her memory in a quite bizarre way. I suffer leg cramps and survivor's guilt. I wake up crying. I drive and cry. I am an angry mess.

So, while I am traveling through this strange, lonely journey located somewhere between dementia and hyperactivity, hoping that one day I will find my driving license and be able to calm down and sleep a little better like a normal human being; I thought it might be useful to contemplate the compilation of a textbook for grief. It should be a living document since life and death are subject to change and we must keep our tools sharpened for the next loss, which, let's face it, is always just around the corner.

Please do ask the person how they are doing, whether via text, phone or email. But just do it. After all the hoorah has died down, the flowers have wilted, the messages of sympathy stop and everyone moves on with their lives, that person is still back there in their own private pool of agony. Grief is a lonely place; don't forget that. They need you after the party is over, as it were.

1. Please do send them your memories of that person. Dig up the old photos and quirky times. Share the treasure with that person. They are so precious, when no more memories are going to be made. I remember, after my Mum died, a friend of mine wrote to me and told me that my Mum taught her how to swim. I had not known that; the information was precious.

2. Be kind to them. If you know them through friendship, family or business, know that the heart is tender thing and loss can take a while to process and grief to heal. They may not be on top of their game, they may be fractious, forgetful or downright inefficient. Watch them and help them to get back to where they were before, if possible. At least guide them towards a place where they can function better in the world that never stops, even though they may have checked out.

3. Invite them to do something fun – something that will stop them dwelling on their loss and how on earth they are going to carry on without that person for just a little while. Maybe take them out to lunch, to the beach, to a

movie. Something that will allow them to put their sadness aside for a short time and do something 'normal'. One of my friends took me out to lunch when my sister passed and then we went and bought some memorial items – a beautiful, fitting, wine glass, artwork, earrings ... it was a fun and thoughtful idea I shall pass along. Flowers die, my memorial beauties will not.

4. Help them to see down the road and plan nice things. In the midst of planning my sister's memorial service in England, my friends are planning other fun things to do together as well. We will be seeing old friends, going paddle boarding, singing songs and playing the piano, drinking and eating yummy things – in short, celebrating life in the way we know how; because this is all we have. Our loved ones would not want us to waste any time getting on with our lives and being as happy as possible. That much I know to be true.

5. Now is not the time to share how your grief was for you; you will have your time down the road. This is their time. Let them be as self-indulgent about it as possible. It's all part of going through the torture chamber in order to come out the other side and be able to continue life without that person in it.

6. So, the textbook for grief has begun. Feel free to add to it and pass it along, because, as I said, it is a living document. It seems to me, we all need a bit of a reference guide to this universal subject. We are not good at it at all. The more we come together in 'Project Grief', the better.

Do not stand at my grave and weep; I am not there. I do not sleep. I am a thousand winds that blow. I am the diamond glints on snow. I am the sunlight on ripened grain. I am the gentle autumn rain. When you awaken in the morning's hush, I am the swift uplifting rush of quiet birds in circled flight. I am the soft stars that shine at night. Do not stand at my grave and cry; I am not there. I did not die.

Author Unknown.

Messenger from another realm
Written and published by Lucy after Rosie died

'The Dragon Fly Is the messenger of wisdom and enlightenment from other realms.'

We all wonder what's next, don't we! We struggle with this being it once our mortal bodies are done and tired. The thought of just going to dust and being nothing and nowhere doesn't sit well with most. The Faithful have strong beliefs about where they are going – right or wrong, who knows until they get there – but at least they have a theory. Until I found magic, I didn't have much of a theory. After my mother's death, her spirit visited me a lot in random shapes and forms. Often with a whoosh through my body or an uncanny coincidence. Once the magic gates are open, they are always open. Now I reside in the Magic Kingdom, I feel sparks and pings from loved ones in the most unusual of places and ways. We can't see them in the same format, when they are on the other side; they are certainly not existing in a human form that we can understand. The new entity is behind a screen, around the corner, in the tree, located just a short distance away – but you can feel them when they pass by, or call in to visit and it is the most wonderful unearthly experience.

I looked for my sister after she died, remembering some of her last words that she would be flying over the Himalayas among other places. And why not? Her traveling was a bit curbed towards the end there; and I know she wasn't able to visit Japan – a place she had always wanted to go. I think she would go there first. She always loved Japanese food and culture. Even as a young 'un' I remember her sporting her bright red quilted Japanese jacket. After she took her last breath, she was quiet for the first couple of days, as we adjusted to the thought of her body already being buried in the ground and her spirit free. "Where are you, sister? "I asked her, walking the dogs over the land. "Oh, there you are!" And there she was in the shape of the most ethereal, exotic cloud mass that drew out a large 'R' for Rosie in almost angel style and sported colors of turquoise and gold in its midst. I laughed to myself, 'Typical, drama Queen!'

    I spoke to her friend in Turkey who had the unenviable task of cleaning out her closets. It was the first time that any of them had been back to their home since she passed. "Was she there, Katie?" I asked her. She said she wasn't, and I found that strange, since she loved her home so much. I step outside to the secret garden to visit with my turtles and there in the most resplendent orange-red color was a large dragon fly. I gasped. We have a thing about dragon flies, as I have likely mentioned before. Sister gave hand-crafted silver dragonflies to many of her good friends and me to many of mine. They are an out-of-worldly creature and here, I had a red one fluttering over my pond. In a flash she was gone. "I saw an orange-red dragonfly," I told anyone who'd listen. They knew I hadn't been sleeping well and figured I was likely hallucinating. When my sister and Ali had their engagement party, she wore the most stunning red-orange gossamer veil. It came to me in a flash – this was the same color. I had to find that photo. I went a little manic in my search. Fortunately, Father is organized and laid his lands on it swiftly. Yes, there was my dragonfly – that was exactly her. The next day I returned to the pond, and she was there again. This time, she rested calmly on the green bush, eyeing me, not flapping or moving at all. We were so close – an arm-length only – I could see her eyes. She watched me and let me photo and video her. "Well, hello, sister! It's about time," I told her! "Where you been, Japan?" We visited for a while. I showed anyone who would look the photo of the red-orange engagement veil and the red-orange dragon fly and people had to admit it was a most inexplicable and magic gift I received in my secret garden that morning. The next morning her children were there – one red and one light blue. The magic continues to flow.

    "I know where Rosie was when you went to the house," I told her friend Katie. "She was in my secret garden, and we had quite the chat. I'm sure she's on her way home now and you'll catch her in the morning." Katie laughed and agreed there was something just a bit special about my little story, illustrated with photos of the orange-red dragonfly and Rosie in her engagement veil.

And so there you have it. Look for magic out there in the universe with your mind wide open. Receive the gifts when you can and embrace the universe for comforting spirits and bizarre coincidences.

Ali and Rosie – their engagement party

Our magic dragonfly in the secret garden the day she was passing.

Bud's self portrait of her engagement

Letter through the ether

Friday, September 14, 2018

Dearest Baby Bud,

I haven't written you a letter in such a long time. Normally we would send a quick What's App, pictures, or texts... Face Time being our most very fave. We were always seeking out the perfect spot for reception between the US of A and good ol' Turkey. I can't FaceTime you anymore, unless I want a one-sided convo – lol–so I have resorted to the old-fashioned word – pen to paper, as it were, if my hands weren't so crap. The old scribe is sadly long gone in the modern-day vernacular, but this old broad is going to dig up some dinosaurs to break through the plaster and talk to you the way we always do. Carey recommended I do this as a way to reach you and fill the void a bit, ease the ache, curb the grief. (To which I hear you say, 'Oh for fuck's sakes ... you knew I was going. Had to go, love, it was time. Past time in fact .. ha ha!") I love hearing your voice inside my head – it makes me smile. A lot.

 Looking back in my phone, you last sent me a message on Thursday, July 19 ... "Buzz me when you free?" It was 9.38pm – we always love to chat at my night, your morning. You are always such an early bird. "Morning, sistaaaa!" you'd quip, like a little chirpy bird, normally clasping your beloved chai by your fingertips. I might be holding a glass of red at that time, or boiling water for tea and thinking about a bath. We always have so much to say to each other, even though it had been only a few hours since our last chat. 'Talk to me as you always did. There is no difference. I am just around the corner, the other side of the wall. I can hear you still.' I am reminded of a variation of this when I listen for you, as I have been for about 6 long weeks now.

 This morning you were two pale lemon butterflies flibbery-jittering around the Secret Garden. Who knew they lived such short lives? Some large hummers cruised through our zone as well, though no dragonflies, those magic creatures were off someplace else. Dad even said he saw one in Regent's Park. Everyone, the world over, is looking for you in the form of a Dragon Fly. I know you like that! Before you gave me my special silver filigree, I knew nothing of them; now I see them as messengers from another realm, special-magic creatures sent to show the living that you are not gone; you are just free of your mortal body. You are still here–your spirit, your essence–and you want us to know that. The orange-red You that came to me as you were passing over – gosh that was a special look, honey. Totally matched that yummy orangey-red engagement veil and dress you wore, next to Ali's greens at your very special party. That was the happiest I ever saw you pretty much, and there you came to me in that special dress-up, when I so badly needed to chat. The canvas replicas of those two pictures sit side-by-side at home and I shall never forget the magic and hope they inspired that dark and agonizing day and still do.

And now onto the tattoo. "You f-ing nutter," I hear you say. Ha, ha. It has created quite the ruckus honey, or did, before I threatened the husband to shut it, or I would divorce him. I wanted you by my side and close to my heart forever and always, which of course you are and will be, but I have now immortalized it in permanent ink of the most glorious magic red-orange-green dragon fly with an essence of woman about her, you, that woman, that marvelous unique creature you are. As did your beloved Frowie. Blame her, she was the one that sowed the seed of the idea and then we did it. We just freaking did it, without telling anyone. She did tell me I was 'bad ass,' which I took as a real compliment for a near 55-year old chick. And then the old man accused me of being 'gangster' and 'flying my freak' ... well, I ate his head, as you do, and put him back in his corner where he belonged. I think I surprised him with my 'bad assness' – not bad for 20 plus years of marriage. He has since cooled his jets and made me lots of nice meals, been very quiet and accommodating, ha! Men don't have the emotional capacity that we do – I knew that, but I have really been reminded of that since you took off for the Himalayas and all the oceans of the world. He doesn't really know how to manage me, my grief and my emotions. Like at all. He got told. Carey reminded me that we need different people in our lives for different things – he failed the supportive grieving spouse class, sadly.

    I think my tattoo is a beautiful work of art and I shall always cherish it and the glorious, magic memories it inspires. Friends of mine agree. Oh god they have been so lovely and supportive since you took off. Not that I would expect any less, because, like you, I have the best friends. But what would I do without them? There's that awful time when the flowers have wilted, the messages and cards stop and you are still left back there in your pool of grief, missing your loved one, while the world moves on without you. We all go through it, and we basically suck at it. Without my friends, I would be even more of a mess. Oh, I know ... I hear your voice again ...'Can't take it on, sis. Just can't take it on.' And nor should you, baby Bud, but I would always tell you anyway, cos that is just who we are and always will be. Our dialogue flows like a swift moving river in perfect tune with each other and our feelings....laughing at our inside jokes, quipping about all kinds of crazy stuff. The best sisters, a special sisterhood, not broken by anything, least of all death.

    Oh my god you would have laughed today. Your buddy, crazy Keri and I were messaging back and forth, (thanks for hooking us up on the boat that day ... you were just determined to connect us, though I was reluctant to let you go to hospital by yourself, while I went off gallivanting on the boat. You just knew we were going to be friends!) A kind friend of hers painted a picture of you for me. It's one of my fave photos of you – a typical Bud pose on the boat. Yet the nose is way off and the mouth is more like mine, so none of it works except for – we both agreed – the really fab hat and sunglasses! She messaged me in a right conundrum about what to do. I howled laughing, as I knew you would too, and thanked her for the kind and thoughtful gesture. I shall hang my 'off Rosie' pic on the wall proudly when I receive it and it will always give me a giggle. (Thank god for giggles. Where would we be without them?) Let's face it – people are really hard to paint! You would be the first to say that, you talented creature.

    And so now we've had a nice chat and I have heard your voice for a while again and your amazing laugh that simply makes me laugh in response; I really must do some work. That stuff has to happen once in a while, lol ..'Yeah, Lu go on then. Get moving lass ..' There you are again, making me smile.

    I'll sign off now and likely see you tomorrow in the Secret Garden. Thanks for making the time to meet me there, our special spot. Soon your Memorial Platform will be in place ('A bloomin Memorial whaaat?' I hear you say.) Yes, it will add to the magic evolution of our Secret Garden. It will be a work in progress. Will be looking for magic in Alde to bring back and add to make mo' magic ..

    Love you always, my baby Bud ...

Big sis
X

    I carry your heart with me. I am never without it ... here is the deepest secret nobody knows, (here is the root of the root and the bud of the bud and the sky of the sky of a tree called life, which grows higher than soul can hope or mind can hide) and this is the wonder that's keeping the stars apart ..

    I carry your heart inside my heart ...

e e cummings

The Dragonfly in the Secret Garden.

Day 55

September 18, 2018

Dearest Bud,

It's been 55 days since you started flying over the Himalayas and swimming in all the oceans. I think you have been quite busy with all that fun stuff, because I haven't seen much of you these long 55 days and counting. I hoped, by now, you would have come to me in my dreams and told me all about it, but I see only stars when I look up at night and often a dog's wet nose. I see you as dittery white butterflies and my very gorgeous dragon flies, but I want more. We all want more. I shall try and wait patiently.

    God, I'm strange without you to bounce off of. In the evening, about the time we should be FaceTiming, I go very quiet and very sad. Thoughts get darker and darker. If I sit too long waiting for the call, I will cry, so I make tea and rush off for a bath, where things are warm and comforting. Anger drives me to eat and drink more than I should, to try and feel better. I understand the call of the addict. You are looking for anything to make you feel better, but it never does. You are quickly back there in your black spot.

    I just went off driving today for the hell of it. Didn't really have anywhere to go, but didn't want to sit in my office and gaze out at the mountains. Still losing things. Can't listen to my music — each song seems more annoying than the one before. Everything is sharper and darker.

    "Oh for fuck's sake!" I hear you say in your wry way, smiling widely. "Lu, get over it! It's done and over with. I live here now. I'm not gonna be able to FaceTime you from where I'm at, I don't even have an Iphone anymore". "Yeah, I know. It's hardly a surprise that everything feels a bit pointless these days. I'm a hair away from near madness and yet the world is carrying on as if nothing has changed. EVERYTHING HAS CHANGED, PEOPLE! MY SISTER HAS DIED. She was in my life for 48 years and a bit and now she lives somewhere else, where I can't get a hold of her when I want to. I don't even know where she is. "She's in a better place?" Oh, don't give me that fudge.

I ask my other sister how she's doing. "Well, busy. Doing my course.' No, not that. Everyone handles loss differently and I feel so alone with mine. The counselor tells me that is a 'normal' feeling'. What's normal? I feel like I'm drowning. Grief isn't making me any nicer, is it, lol. I know. Can do better, will do better. Maybe not today though.

Love ....

The Rosie Day

Published October 2018 in South County Newspapers

It was a baptism of sorts the day I crashed my neoprened body into the North Sea in front of most of my family and oldest friends. I needed the adrenalin splash of the cold water, the pressure of the waves around me. I needed to submerge myself in a familiar place where I always think I'll see her again. I feel close to her in the water, a passion we both shared. We were both swimming fish from a young age. Beclad entirely in flattering black rubber, my friend and I took the paddleboards out on the sea, looking back at the shore at the long shadows of various groups of familiar people, who were standing on the beach, holding champagne glasses. It was a view I will never forget. Blue skies, rolling clouds, long late summer shadows and everyone who had showed up for her in my most favorite place – some of us from across the world.

It was the day of the Celebration of Life for my baby sister Rosie Emma Alexandra Mason Arican. My friends and I had already been in the seaside town of our childhood for several days, preparing for the 'Rosie Day'. Fortunately, a smarter one than I had suggested having the event catered; thank goodness for that wise old owl, Charlene-Darlene. That, in addition to decorating and prepping, would have likely taken me over the edge.

The rental house where we were staying looked stunning. My Baby Bud smiled down at us from every inch of wall space. My friend Kate had made sure we had bunting for the amazing array of photographs from Rosie's 48 years of life and she alone constructed two enormous photo collages and large photo books for the masses to enjoy in the Rosie Palace, as it became known. We had prosecco and even glasses for it. The catering crew were busy setting up a fabulous high tea with a spread that impressed even the most hardcore British tea critics. It was a memorial fit for a princess. (I smiled at that. Early days in Turkey she used to call herself 'The Beach Princess'.)

I was so excited at the prospect of seeing all those people who loved Rosie as much as I did, I had forgotten that this was our version of her funeral; that Rosie wasn't actually going to be there. All of a sudden – about an hour before the folks were due to show up – I stopped and gazed up at the sky. My eyes filled with tears. How could I have forgotten she wouldn't be showing up to her own party? A party wasn't something she would miss for the world. I sat outside in the little back courtyard of the house and gazed up at the sky. Sure enough, there were swooping angels, butterflies and dragonflies all around if only you opened your eyes to see. I felt her tell me that, of course, she was going to be there. She wouldn't miss it for the world.

"What's going on, Bella?" My friends appear with a glass of bubbles to calm my nerves. They always know when to show up at my parade. I was panicking just a little. I couldn't remember a word of what I had thought I might say, and I certainly didn't want to cry, as the introduction to the Celebration of her life – because that would make others cry and that wouldn't do at all. I hadn't prepared anything to wear – I had bought along a few Turkish outfits that we had purchased together, but I felt ill-prepared and out of my league. Who hosts their own sister's funeral? But that was what we were doing, and we better do it right. There would be no second chance to do a better job.

And what a lovely gathering it was in the end. Her husband was there, as were her oldest and my oldest friends. Our oldest family friends were there too, our father, aunt, and cousin. My daughter was there. It was perfect. I had no cause for concern in the end. I didn't say everything I wanted to – do we ever. We laughed, we ate, we drank and told funny stories. The Rosie Day ended with Father talking about her down in the courtyard with everyone gathered around. I'm so glad my friend videotaped it. The afternoon was truly a sunshiny memorial to a fabulous life well lived and everyone said they wouldn't have missed it for the world. Rosie loved every second of it. She also enjoyed the random polar dip at the end of her amazing day and had such a good laugh at me in the neoprene wet suit, looking completely like a beached whale.

3 months on – a letter through the ether

October 25, 2018

Dearest Baby Bud,

How the hell is it 3 months since your spirit left your old body? And where have you been anyway? I look for you in my dreams, in my garden, in my bushes and in the moon at night. You haven't even visited me in my restless nights and told me you are okay, you are busy, you can't talk right now; but you are still around, and you will be back. Even the dragon flies have been noticeable mostly by their absence. I feel abandoned, absent. You, of all people, should be able to break through the curtain and visit. If you are flying over the oceans and across the seas, get back over here where I can talk to you again. It's so quiet without you. The numbness and painful aches are back. Life is impossible.

    After your Celebration of life, I thought I would be able to stay busy and stay up, but I am now feeling the way I was before. Thoughts of leaving, selling, going ... not constructive thoughts, come and go. I miss our nightly chats over FaceTime – your morning, my evening. You were always so perky and optimistic, no matter what. I don't feel optimistic at the moment. I just feel sad. Sad and angry and ripped off. Everyone else moves on – things will get better, they say. They don't see the gaping hole inside me, the fractured heart. You were stolen from us; when you had so much more life inside you.

    Thank you for the dragon fly today though—gosh, it was nearly the size of a dinner plate, swooping down the road. The butterflies were delightful too – flibber-gittering around. Was that you? Wish we could chat again like we used to. Yeah, I know it had to happen at some stage, sister, but I hate it, I hate life without you. I miss your voice – there is a cavern where your presence used to be. I look for signs you are still there, out there somewhere, finding your way back to me from your new planet, but the small signs have not been enough.

Grief is such a lonely place, and everyone navigates it so differently. I am lonely in mine. I hear your voice – 'Can't take it on, sis. Can't take it on...' You knew we would find it hard without you; you were a very bright light. My husband is checked out and hopeless. He doesn't know what to do with me, so he does nothing but stays away. My friends are doing their best to prop me up from afar. Heck. Gonna have to do something radical to dig myself out of this hole. Without my animals, I would completely lose my mind.

Love and miss you too much,

Big Sis
xx

Carpe the diem

Now I'm older, I talk a lot about seizing the day. Buy the shoes, make the trip, eat the cheesecake. Life is so brief, and we don't all get the same time allotment. That's a for sure. My father is cruising in his 90's. My baby sister was under 50 when she died. Sis always talked about the quality, not the quantity, because she knew that her life was going to be a short one in length and a tall one in depth. That's the cancer gift for you. My mother died at 67, still wearing her blue jeans and sneakers and catching all the new movies when they came out. To make it count, you have to live each day as if it were your last. Rosie taught me that. And I certainly try to live in that vein, weaving in the necessary paid work focus and piles of laundry and domestic tedium into my daily life; but not letting stress compound or issues weigh me down that I can do nothing about. It's a much freer way to live that breeds an indescribable feeling of peace and happiness. You are not just crawling through one day and onto the other; you are living your best life.

One of my besties flies in from London. I pick her up from the airport and we go to stay in our favorite hotel in our favorite city on the bay, as we do every year. We adore the tranquility of the lobby, the same friendly staff, the cookies and apples, the milk for our tea, the ting-ting of the cable car outside our window, the funny sights we witness of humanity doing their thing. We also love the shopping and the food and the buzz of the city, but it's really the small things we crave so intensely when we are not there. Normally after our January visit, we are immediately booking and planning for the next trip, putting dates in the diary a year ahead of time. That helps with the winter blues and the optimism, perhaps, that we will both get another year out of this crazy little thing called life. Armed with a laptop, a phone and some internet and the world is my oyster.

Our other old bestie friend invites us to her daughter's wedding at a classic beach hotel where her parents married 60 years ago. This is in a place called Hyde and I'm not sure exactly where that is, but I'm going. I'm no longer going to miss the weddings and the special days; I'm going to be present, just a plane ride away and a new pretty dress to boot. I've already missed too much – my friends' weddings, my baby sister's wedding – shame on me – funerals and more. I'm going to do my best, for the rest of my life, not to miss the important days, where possible. Though we all live all over the world, the world is so much smaller these days, the travel easier, the communications better. The way I see it, there is no longer any excuse.

My cousin Cornelia died young. She was my age; early onset dementia, wrapped around some cancer at the end. That hit hard. My age. At my age, we are just babies; we have so much more to do on this planet, places to go, people to see. Watching the phenomenal film 'Bohemian Rhapsody' with my friend a few days ago took me back in a time capsule to the 80's, dawnings of so many things in the world and our own personal era, as it were, when things were simpler in a way and more complex in others. Freddie Mercury died aged 45 – a pioneer of his time. The music and the band live on.

'Girls Gone Wild' are discussing plans for a Fall tour of Turkey with me at the wheel. As we speak, crash helmets and racing suits are now being ordered.

Carpe the diem, seize the day. My life has taught me that the hard way. Thank you, Rosie, for continuing to show me the way to live. You already showed me how to die.

Cleaning is good for grief

Published in South County Newspapers

"Cleanliness is next to godliness," I think I heard my Granny say that more than once and, growing up, I never understood what it meant. It could have even been the other way around. She was full of irritating little phrases ... "A change is as good as a rest!" That was another one. "Waste not, want not." I could go on and on. The more annoying they were, the more I seem to retain them into my middle age. Thank you, Granny, for the lasting legacy! She never said anything about cleaning being good for grief though; that I had to write for myself.

Who knew? As I found myself neck-deep in mouse turds in my garage, hauling out paint cans and old mouse-chewn shoes that hadn't seen the light of day since we moved in years ago, the story I'd read came back to me, discussing the lack of control you have when you are grieving and that is why you, instinctively, turn to things you can control – like cleaning. My mother would have a really good laugh at that one, since cleaning has never been super high on my priority list, unless it's a stable; but I'm finding it unusually true at this juncture in my life.

Case in point—the other day, I have 20 minutes before I need to leave the house. "Oh, I'll clean out a cupboard!" The thought danced through my mind. Who thinks that way? But sure enough, I cleared the cupboard space of all the china and crystal we never use and bang, all done in 20 minutes. Some of the crystal had been left over from our wedding decades ago and never been touched, so it was past time that it find another home. I already find myself thinking about the next cupboard to clean; this is not me.

The garage was a lofty project for a Sunday afternoon when I could have been relaxing with a remote control and some good football to divert me; but no, I'm sweating buckets, hauling out decades of useless abandoned stuff and filling up garbage bags like there's no tomorrow. If my body had not drawn the line and started complaining loudly, I would still be out there into the wee hours, because the job is never-ending.

"Oh, find something more fun to do, for heavens sakes!" I hear my sister barking at me from Saint Elsewhere, wherever she is these days. "You don't have the kind of free time to spend it cleaning. Who does that? Nuts ..." Her voice fades away and I hear myself telling her, "But you didn't lose you, did you?" I've been doing all kinds of weird things and thinking all kinds of strange oddities recently, that cleaning has to come in as doing something fairly normal, no?

"Do fun things," the grief columnist continues. "Make time for you, take time out of your day-to-day to have some good old-fashioned entertainment. Laugh! It's good for you!" I realized I hadn't done much of that recently. Truthfully, I laugh so little these days that my laughter lines have started turning the other way. So, I did just that – I booked something fun. "Beauty and the Beast"–the Stagehands production down in King City. I wasn't expecting much, except to see my neighbor and other familiar faces perform in that nice, cozy theater, a play I have never seen that I knew would impress my granddaughter. My husband just raised his eyebrows when I told him where we were going – a facial expression that said, "She has really, truly, lost it now!" But how pleasantly surprised were we! Not only were the music, set and characters impeccably staged, but the play was fun and funny! It was so delicious we didn't want it to end, and I immediately urged others to make the time to go and see it. It is so nice to be pleasantly surprised, that I smiled all the way home, as the tune 'Be My Guest' buzzed through my head. I could easily have gone back and seen it again the next day. And the day after.

Grief is a process. We all know that. It's not easy and it's not quick. But, if you are in the same place as me and life without your sister is pretty sucky, I'd say, curb the cleaning just a little and make more time for the fun. It doesn't change anything, but you'll be glad you did. I know I was. This week I will try and find the fun again.

2018
Get the tattoo

"So, Mum. You ever thought of getting a tattoo?"

"No."

"How about a dragonfly tattoo?"

"Oh."

And so, the idea sprung, just like that. In all my many years on the planet I had never, ever, ever contemplated getting my skin inked, burned, colored – or whatever it is they do to your skin to ensure that that part of your body never looks the same again.

I remember, clearly, barking at my daughter the multiple times she inked her body, under-age and without my permission, on various parts of her anatomy. Later, I had even attended tattoo removal sessions with her, where I witnessed her go ashen grey and clammy sicky white with the agony of it all; let alone the expense. My friend took me along for her first tattoo – a dove on the shoulder. She dug her nails into my skin, as the scratcher worked on her, and frothed, nearly, with the pain of it, going a sickly grey color as well, with me wondering what on earth I would do with her when she keeled over on the ground in front of me, vomiting on my shoes. She didn't even care much for the tattoo later on, calling it a 'fat pigeon' and wishing she could undo it.

But it felt as if I would and could do this. I wanted to do this. Since my sister's passing, the dragonfly has been an important symbol of her existence in the afterlife in some shape or form. Often, she is flying through our secret garden – perhaps as an electric blue Mama, or baby, or, on occasion, as the very strong red-orange character creature reflected in her engagement veil, the special visitor from another realm I saw the day before she passed; the one that calmed me and told me it was going to be okay, her spirit was going to be okay, we were going to be okay in the end. Friends, the world over, seek out the dragon fly as well. "She was at breakfast with us today," her old friends in Turkey tell me. "What color?" I ask. "Orange." (No wonder she wasn't in my garden this morning!) "She was there today," another tells me from the north of England. "What color?" I enquire. "Green." Aha. She's making the circuit, checking in on everyone, making sure we are not losing our minds, or falling apart as we promised her we wouldn't. She's showing us, from the other side of the curtain, down the road, around the corner, floating just above the earth's surface, that she is still present in our worlds. She is still with us and coaching us through the early months of life without her earthly body among us.

My daughter would send me various images of dragon flies. No, the wings are too low, it looks too evil, the body is too short ... and then she came across the perfect mixture of person and dragonfly, the merge-purge of sister-auntie and dragonfly we felt to be our reality. "Yes!" I exclaim, "Yes, that's it!" And here the idea grew further and developed a tail and a name. It would be 'Bud' for me, since that's what I called Baby sis, and 'Rowie' for my daughter since that was forever her name for her auntie. Our distinguishing marks would now be matching tattoos. But it was still a dream. Were we really going to do this? Like anything a little tricky, we didn't tell anyone of our well-designed plan. She found the tattoo parlor and artist – a well-established professional establishment in downtown San Luis. I found the days to come down and visit. "It's just for a consultation, Mum', she tells me, to which I thought to myself ... not if I have anything to do with it. If I step inside one of those parlors, it is because we are doing this thing. I didn't dare tell anyone, lest they try and talk me out of it, or I lose my nerve. This was a fine line we were treading.

We step inside for our consultation. The artist was kind and helpful, interesting. Like your own physician or psychiatrist, we felt comfortable with him. "Come back later today," he tells us. "Today, like really today, no more sleeps? That today?" "Yes, today." We were going to do this thing today. Except we were not, as it turns out. A customer went a little long, his colleague didn't really get where we were coming from and, a bit deflated, we rescheduled for early the next morning. Not today, as it turned out. But we played tennis and braved ourselves for an early morning the following day.

Up with the birds and the lure of the ocean, we arrived early and got in line at the local coffee shop, where it was publicly announced that everything would be a 25-minute wait. We grabbed the quickest cup of coffee we could and received a text that our artist was going to be 25 minutes late. We giggled nervously and waited some more.

As he proceeded to etch out the approved design and coloring, I felt a bit euphoric. Here I was, well over middle-aged and getting my first tattoo of my dragonfly, my baby girl, my Bud. And that, somehow, helped with the discomfort. The pain of the needles was lessened by the pain in my heart and, actually, in a strange way, it felt good to experience physical pain of some sort at this time. Nuts, I know. Like a burn or scratch or irritation, it wasn't exactly pleasant, but I thought of sis and how she would react and how this was the best tribute to her and the love I feel for her. (Grief is just love with nowhere to go, my counselor told me.) It's also a gorgeous piece of artwork, representing a magic creature, magic colors, and just sheer magic during a period of painful loss. We thanked Brian for his talent, artistry, and thoughtfulness with us. He told us he was honored to be a part of honoring Rosie and it became a special day.

Make everything count! That's what we would say, after our adventures of the last few days. Life is short: take the vacation, make the move. Get the tattoo.

A letter through the ether

November 7, 2018

Dearest Baby Bud,

Gosh, how the scabs of healing get ripped off quickly where you are concerned. I can be doing alright with my day and then, I come across a photo, a memory, a place where we went – and I am off the cliff again.

    This morning, I friended Melissa and I remember you talking about her so fondly. We are chatting away, and I send her the wonderful vid of us karaoking at Street Café. Next, she exclaims, 'how can you not be alive when you are so alive and right there on her screen?' I had to watch the video again and I crashed. So appallingly raw. Where are you, anyway? Flying over the Himalayas and swimming in all the oceans? Wish you'd fly over my place again and make me into a believer; wish you'd come and talk to me in my dreams. It would really help if you did.

    I started thinking about when I come over next month and how strange it will be to be in Turkey, your home, but without you. I needed to book a room for the night in Antalya when I arrive and found I couldn't possibly stay at the Rixos, or anywhere we had stayed together. I felt up a river without a paddle. You always took care of that stuff and made sure I had all my coffee stuff and personal what-not when I got there. I had to plan this alone. A lump filled my throat, and it wasn't good.

    Now to get really busy again and stop thinking about you or how angry I am that you are not in my sphere to bounce ideas around with or share the good and the bad. Ugh. One of those days, Bud.

    Back to work and back to busy I must.

    Love you, Bud.

Big sis
xx

A New Year
2018–2019

"I laid her way down in there, wrapped in muslin cloth, swaddled like a baby. Her open face was tilted towards the sun, just as she would want." It was New Year's Eve in Turkey and my brother-in-law took me to my sister's grave for the first time. Nothing can really prepare you for seeing your sister's name on a grave marker, but I sat down on the warm rocks by her grave and put my hand where I thought her little head would be. I turned my eyes to the sun also and told her how much I loved and missed her. Just when I thought I was all cried out, a few hot tears rolled down my cheeks. Her grave was located next to her husband's father and daughter, situated in the small village graveyard near their home in the mountains. The last time I had seen sister in June, she breezily waved in the direction of the graveyard as we drove past, gesticulating at where she would be buried down the road. ("Don't even think about trying to make the service, sis. It will be before sundown on the same day!") But I was ill-prepared all the same. That conversation took place only a month before she was laid, stone cold, in the ground.

We drove to visit his mother in the town of Kumluca. She doesn't speak a word of English, but love is the same in all languages. As soon as she saw me, the tears streamed down her cheeks and she flapped her worry beads around. "She can't even talk about Rosie," Ali said. "She took it really hard." Mama was soon smiling again though, as we drank Turkish coffee together. She continued to smile and point at the painting Rosie had done of her a few years ago – the love and the humor so entrenched in the art.

Mama, Bud and Suzy

The two of us drove quietly back to the house together and arrived to a kitchen full of people cooking, drinking and chatting. The turkeys were being boiled, the pilaf and salads prepared. A huge log fire was blazing in the wood stove and lights twinkled on the Christmas tree. The only thing missing was Rosie. But we did our very best without her; we really did. 'We done her proud,' as the English might say.

Rosie loved Christmas and New Year.

Friends of hers had come over especially to spend New Year with us, her step daughter Dilgesu had her friends over, the neighbor brought their young baby to see us and another her toddler. We played bingo for random prizes, we sang karaoke. We even sang the old English New Year song 'Auld Lang Syne' and I was reminded that there is never going to be room for all on the planet – as the babies are born, others die – and that is the essence of the human life cycle as we know it. Rosie would be the first to say that, though her life wasn't that long in the general scheme of things, she had enjoyed an amazingly rich life, and an especially happy one, the last 10 plus years she spent with Ali and Dilgesu and all the adventures they had enjoyed.

We settled into the scene of festivity at their home in the mountains, just a short trip from the graveyard, but all of a piece in some ways. Though sister wasn't there in physical body, her spirit was all around, both in her house and out. It was in the paw shake of her dog, the screech of her cheese-loving cat Elvis. It could be found around the baubles of the Christmas tree she loved and up in her favorite picture window overlooking the valley and the bay. It could also be found in the smiles and hugs of her friends so happy to see me, yet teary all the same. So many people loved her and that is no exaggeration. You read obituaries and hear how, through death, people reach the stature of near Sainthood. Sister was no saint, but she was an amazing person, especially in her later years as she refused to allow her illness to define her, and she navigated what remained of her life with an amazing grace and acceptance. During the customary 3-day period of mourning, when the family gathers at the house in Turkey to receive the mourners, over 1000 people came by to give condolences to her husband and his family. That's a pretty good turnout for a foreigner living in their community. In time, we hope to put a nice bench and tree in her honor in a local park in the town where she founded her English school. She'd like that. I can see her students sitting on her bench and talking about how much she taught them – and not just about school subjects either.

New Year's Day, I went back to her grave with two of her best friends. We stood at her gravesite and laughed and joked. We told funny stories about Rosie, and we know she loved it. If we had brought along chairs, we could have stayed there even longer and toasted her beautiful life, well-lived, with one of her favorite fizzy beverages.

    The night before I left her chosen home, I sat on the balcony of my hotel overlooking the Mediterranean. It was stormy and black waves were crashing to shore. I felt strangely calm and fulfilled. I had managed to visit her family and home without having another meltdown, I had spent wonderful days with her people and celebrated the beginning of a new year in the way you should. I had solidified ties with her Turkish family and did my part to close out her estate, as is required in Turkey. I came back to my home feeling as if I could move on a little now; my heart still a bit fractured and spirit a tad whipped; but with the knowledge that I did my best, as her big sister, and I have no regrets.

Magic

Very soon after Winston Churchill Sebastian Mason Jensen – aka Sir Winston White Horse – went to sleep on April 2, some funny things started to happen on our ranch. Previously, the llamas and goat were his hang-out buddies on the land below. They would move around together, as grazing animals are wont to do, presenting quite the most eccentric combination of hooves and coats. Neighbors passing by our 7-acre parcel would remark on my motley crew and ask how I ever managed to put that gang together. Occasionally the 3 llama boys would come up to see what Win was chewing on at the house, since he loved to graze on the lawn and hang out with us and the dogs where possible; but generally-speaking, the boys were grazing well away from the house in their own rambling world, especially when the land was teeming with yummy things for them to gnaw on, as it was after last winter's rains.

    As soon as Winston died, the llamas were not only up by the house, Harold Malcolm Democracy–chief llama–was positioned on the deck right next to the house. This had never happened before. The first several days after Win passed, Harold had the most eerie hum going, almost all the time – interrupted only by the distraction of his favorite grains – and then the humming would start again. I'd witnessed the hum before, when their brother Rev was passing. I put my arm around his neck and asked him if he missed Win as much as I did. I swear his eyes began to mist over. We showed him a large canvas of Winston and his cycle handlebar ears curved over, as he focused on the photo. I knew he recognized him.

    Nowadays, his 400lb self can be mostly seen on the deck, sometimes blocking the entire entrance way, so the dogs have to alert me to move him if they need to pass by. It is quite the strangest thing. My husband never constructed the deck for a llama creature's weight, so some reinforcements will be necessary in the coming months. When we open the sliding door to the house, Harold will peek in and stand stock still with fascination. I'm sure, one day, he will be in the family room, stretched out on the cool wooden floor with the pups. I know my llama shearer would tell me this is not 'normal' llama behavior and that he has become 'maladjusted', (her favorite word for tame llamas); but I couldn't care less how maladjusted he is in the llama world. I love it and I'm certain it helps me deal with loss. I can groom Harold now, as well as his brother Max, who used to be such a scaredy-cat. They seem to quite like it. Brother Sam will also feed out of the hand now. Things at Solace have changed for sure.

    My sister Rosie used to tell me how much she loved butterflies. "Yeah, but they live for such a short time!" I said to her once. "Yes, sister, that's the whole point. They are really beautiful AND they live short lives. Enjoy them while they are here! All about the quality, not the quantity!" And, of course, at the time – duh – I knew she was talking about more than just butterflies. She was quite the butterfly herself throughout her pretty short life. My Secret Garden has become a plethora of magic since Rosie passed. I built the Rosie boat in her memory – she loved boats, she loved water; I needed a memorial site for her close to me and so the boat was built. I found the abandoned wreck on my Mum's beach in Moss Landing, where we had scattered her ashes. I found the memorial on the day that Rosie was transitioning, so it was all perfect. I lay beautiful things in front of the old piece of boat, including sea glass and stones from beaches I loved, dragon fly images, a Sir Win White Horseshoe, a mermaid and much more. When I talk to my turtles and feed them in the mornings, I am often reminded of what a special place my Secret Garden is, as the butterflies flitter by, the humming birds dive and stun with their glorious array of colors and the dragonflies whoosh through, sometimes with their babies in tow. Ever seen a baby dragonfly? It is the most astounding tiny slip of metallic color you have ever seen. The mama is a green and blue beauty – she likes to come and swim with me, as my sister would – her babies stay in the sanctuary of the Secret Garden and the stalks of the long grasses. I can't wait to watch them grow up. They say that the dragonfly is a messenger from another realm, and I certainly believe that to be true. Dragonflies were special to my sister and me. She knew they'd be even more precious to me when she passed.

When I was in England, my friend and I went night swimming in our clothes in the sea – long story. The Mama Cormorant – my mother's spirit creature – was nesting above us in the basket of a metal groin, as we swam beneath her. I told my friend my mother would never let us swim without her watching us; no matter that we were good swimmers. Sometimes this meant hours of her time, perched on the beach just watching. I felt the same thing about the cormorant. She would have been watching especially cautiously at night. I felt her presence. I called out her name.

When Winston passed, I saw his spirit animal evolve as the elegant white doves that frequent our place – they eat and drink and nest and live peacefully in our trees, lots of them. This gift means that I see him all the time – exactly as I need to. If there are two doves together, then he is with his beloved Abbey Rhode- our gentle brown mare–who passed a few years ago and whose passing made me a believer in the fact that animals do grieve and, boy, did he, for 2 plus weeks.

"Good morning, Sir Winston White Bird!" I chirp, as I go out of a morning. "Morning Bud!" I say as the dragonfly greets me at the gates to my secret garden. "Mum!" I see the cormorant swooping over the Pacific on her way to grab breakfast. And who will tell me I am wrong, or at least insane. My perception of the world and my loss is eased by seeing my beloveds in the bodies of other creatures, since I can't see them in person. They live at my home we call Solace, and they all provide me with immense comfort.

The spirits of Rosie and Winston

Published in South County Newspapers, April 2019

A lot of strange things happened the day the body of Sir Winston White Horse was laid to rest and his huge spirit freed. His flesh was not even cold when we were called to rescue his name-sake Winston, Jr. from Metz Road. The poor pup had been sitting there on the side of the road with a broken leg for who knows how long, watching cars drive by and leaving him behind in the dust. We picked him up — he was so sweet and grateful, despite his pain, and, as protocol requires, after a trip to the vet, he was transferred to the shelter to serve the stray hold, after which he was slated for euthanasia because his leg was so badly broken and infected. We put a stop to that and immediately pulled him from the shelter as a non-profit rescue may. After about 3 months, he is now running fairly competently on all 4 legs, if a little bit inelegantly, after being used to 3 for some time. The infection has gone, and the leg was eventually saved after a scary period, when it could have gone either way. Ultimately, wonderful vet care and love saved him.

After several potential adoptive parties reviewed his medical records and decided that his challenges were likely too much for them to handle, I had to reconcile myself to the fact that, all along, he was just waiting for me. This week, after adoption hopeful number 2 in 3 months turned him down, I decided I could not put him through any more emotional or physical stress. He would be staying forever with us at Solace, where I knew he would be safe and adored, as he should be. I knew that, if he left us, I would always worry about him and his anxiety and how he was managing elsewhere. So, the day Winston Sr. left, Winston Jr. arrived. A canine, not an equine, but a wonderful creature in his own right.

Since Winston Sr. departed this world as we know it; amazing things have happened in his place. Our three llamas — Max, Sam and Harold Malcolm Democracy — used to be quite aloof, as llamas apparently should be. Our llama shearer told us that if they became too friendly they would be considered 'mal-adjusted'. I never quite understood that, since they never seemed to get in my physical space or threaten their humans in any way. But since Winston left, they have been roaming much less on the pasture and hanging out much more near the house with the dogs and ourselves. The peering in became a daily thing for Harold, sometimes more often. He was still looking for Winston. "I think Win may have told him we would need a little more taking care of when he left," husband noted. The huge gap he would literally leave behind would need to be filled in a little. And they have done that, my 3 llamas and my naughty goat; not to mention my Winston, Jr. who has kept me pretty busy with his puppy antics and his big loving self. Though the large royal white spirit of Senior for sure still roams around Solace and I have even felt him on the breeze of a night, the llamas have helped us with our grieving and, I believe, we have helped them with theirs.

It's nearly a year since my sister passed away. Friends in Turkey have told me how many times they have seen the famous red dragonfly that has become a worldwide symbol of my baby sister Rosie. One sent me photos of the dragonfly resting on her toe by the pool. Others told me they were going to start charging pool admission, since the Rosie dragonfly had been frequenting theirs so regularly. There was never any doubt that her spirit would be mostly in Turkey, her chosen home. So far this year, I had only seen a silver blue dragonfly at home; no Rosie red ones, since the day she was transitioning from our planet to another 12 short months ago.

"You have to feel her energy, it's everywhere!" Her friend tells me. "I do," I respond. "But I want to see her dragonflies," I said, and, within minutes, there she was, flying in front of me across my secret garden. "There you are!" I exclaimed. She whooshed in and out of the pond area; then came back and rested close by. She was so close I could see her tiny eyes, mouth, nose and ears. She let me photo and video her. She tolerated my chat and my proximity for a good long while. Then she brought her flashy red boyfriend into the garden and there they played together for a while. I told everyone who would listen. I shared the photos and the video. "She came! She came after all!"

The magic made me so happy. If you are not already a believer, what I experienced might make you into one. It has been a long and difficult year without my beautiful baby sis and my beloved Sir Winston White Horse, not to mention two of my golden oldie pups. Loss of that magnitude can take you to your knees in the worst way. But once you stand again, you might be amazed by the extent of the magic that can be found all around you. The essence of Rosie and Winston and all my beloveds are still all-around me — outside and in. Time and absence of physical presence has no bearing on love. And thank goodness for that.

Well, hello, precious!

SECTION 7
WELL AFTER THE END

Celebrating The Bud's birthday

It was going to be her 50th birthday very soon; we had plans to celebrate. My friend was over from England and we had special festivities on our radar, such as peanut butter birthday cheesecake on the top of the Macy's in Union Square. I knew I wouldn't find the day easy without her. I could imagine what a hoo-ra of celebrations she would have enjoyed with all her bestie friends, were she still with us. Perhaps she and her husband would be heading off to Venice or Palma for 5-star Michelin dinners. But no. None of that would be happening. She died when she was 48.

I also knew my anger would rise; my grief would rear its ugly head again when it was time to celebrate her 50th birthday without her. Grief is like that. Waves on a beach, as they say. Just when you think time is being a little kinder to you, the memories becoming sweeter rather than pained and you are finding yourself able to find more joy in each passing day; then along comes a milestone birthday and the wave slaps you down all over again. I remember when she was born. I was still alive when she died. I feel raw and bitter again. All wrong; just wrong.

The day of my sister's 50th birthday, my friend got the flu and went to bed. The weather was cold and stormy with wet roads and grim skies in place of champagne and festivities. There was to be no celebrating that day. I did not even go and clean up her Rosie boat memorial in my Secret Garden that I had planned on doing. The boat, with its chipped paint and fading colors, is so representative of how long she has been gone, that, some days, I can barely look at it. I felt so depressed and desolate all over again. I wished I could hear her chirpy little voice and see her naughty little face again on FaceTime. I felt robbed; a familiar sentiment these past 18 months. I had a hot bath and an early night. I wanted her birthday to be over. Sleep refused to find me; I was so tormented on the night my sister should have turned 50.

But the dawning of a fresh day came along, and my friend was feeling better. The weather was much improved. We were going to head up to the City after all for a belated birthday celebration. That evening, we ate sushi in her honor. She loved sushi. And then we went shopping. "This is for Rosie's birthday," I said, purchasing myself a nice green parka I had been coveting. "Rosie would love these shirts," I told my friend. "Another part of her birthday treasure trove." I had so much fun shopping for Rosie's birthday — i.e. for me — that my sadness faded into the ether. I had such a giggle buying myself gifts for my dead sister's birthday, I just knew somewhere, perhaps only inside my heart or around the corner, or inches above from where I was currently standing, she was giggling too.

Milestones and memories can be super difficult mountains to climb, when it is only a short 18 months since your sister died and you can quickly feel raw all over again. You catch your breath at an old photo of her laughing, a voice clip, the date of her 50th birthday that she is not on our planet to celebrate with us. We have been denied her presence on a day that should be all about her; her vibrant spirit so markedly absent.

But that's life, is it not. We don't all get the same allocation. Baby sis would be the first to say that her life was all about the quality, not the quantity and she was fine with her allocation. For the rest of us, mere mortals, left still grieving in her wake, time can sometimes be a healer or, at other times, a reminder of painful loss. My father celebrated her birthday by sending us an old photo of us 3 girls together, no words, just a picture that spoke mounds. Fortunately for me, the celebration of my husband's 60th birthday was right around the corner from my sister's 50th and the whole family and dearest friends would be getting together — more reasons to celebrate, but in a different way. Having successfully shopped for myself on my sister's birthday, I would need to stay in shopping mode through the next celebration and out the other side. We can only hope, in the meantime, I don't lose my gusto for the living and their well-earned celebrations, whilst still giving a nod to a life well-lived and one that I shall always miss.

Lu

Enjoy the Journey

There's a plaque leaning up against a tree in my front garden. It's old and weathered; but the message remains solid. *'Enjoy the Journey'*. It will always live with me. It reminds me of my sister Rosie and her successful efforts to enjoy every day, no matter what. It prompts me to be grateful for my lot and to see the bright side of every possible thing. Some days that is not so easy; but it's a task I remind myself of daily, when I feed the birds and water the trees.

The summer of Ibrance is what we called it, when she was able to enjoy the benefits of the most recent wonder drug for stage 4 patients and boy, did she enjoy it! Bud no longer had to go into Antalya, (2 hours plus each way,) for treatments, chemo, radiation. Nope, she just popped an Ibrance and went along her way, planning lunches, teas, swims and boat trips. She dyed her hair blonde, gained some weight and had everyone whispering that she had kicked cancer. 'Oh, don't be silly!' she'd giggle. 'You can't kick stage 4 cancer — you will always have it until you pop your clogs' — a typical Rosie expression. And she was right, of course; but that didn't stop her enjoying every second of her last full summer. She was always the first to comment that this was her last visit, her last birthday, her last summer. She was prepping us for her being correct about that in the coming months. She walked so quickly that summer; rushing from one sensation to the next, as if she were running out of time; which, of course, she was. She drove quickly, rushing from the baker to the store, to the house, to another house. She was absolutely exhausting.

I remember, lying on the beach next to her in her favorite place, Cirali. Finally, she went to sleep, and I watched her, wondering if she was going to peacefully go off to St Elsewhere at this very time. She was seldom that still. I got up quietly to go into the sea and an eye opened. There she was. She wasn't still for very long. 'Want a game of Scrabble, sis?' she asked, and we were off again.

She and her friend Almila from 'My Hospital,' as she called it (MedStar — a whole load of stars could be found in that building) founded a breast cancer support group – the first ever in Antalya. She discovered that there were a lot of women suffering the treatments and near stigma of cancer in silence. Quite different to her and her situation, these ladies were pretty much alone with their disease and their thoughts. Well, Rosie wasn't having that; so, they put together a support group; as you do. They had events, a rally with lots of pink ribbons, flowers, balloons, open air car parades – a show of unity and force in the cancer world. Even the oncology department at the hospital attended. It was a pretty stunning thing to witness, and the event still goes on today.

I met several of her cancer sister friends in Turkey after she passed on and she was so beloved to them. Though we mostly didn't have a shared language; the language of loss and sadness is as one. We embraced as long-lost sisters in our grief.

Sadly, the Bud blog was lost to the graveyard of unpaid blog domains, but I have managed to capture some of the entries and, I like to think, they bear repeating.

MAY 17, 2017

SPEECHLESS!

Just a small word of thanks to everyone who has read, shared and taken the time to respond to my first blog entry. The word is SPEECHLESS! (Not something usually associated with me!)

MAY 20, 2017

ALL ABOUT MEEEEEE! (One of her favorite sayings)

A few milestones to be noted ... move to Turkey, breast cancer at 33, stage 4 at 40, but still here at 47!

May 25, 2017
MASKS, STRAPS AND A WET JELLYFISH
I wanted to share with you the steamier side of my hospital visits ...

(She's talking about being strapped down for radiation. I was reminded again that, God, she was funny!)

And she had a blog-filled summer, boy did she. She had quite the global audience and a faithful following. Until ...

September 13, 2017 (her last blog entry)
STOOLS AND NOT THE KIND YOU SIT ON ...

Diagnosis, living with cancer stools and not the kind you sit on ... and so, to continue with the school vocabulary, it's clear that I currently have wobbly stools.

    She was back to treatment. The summer of Ibrance was over; the super wonder-drug was no longer working for her. With the return to treatments, the blog stopped, but the sense of humor continued to flourish and entertain. I recall being on a boat trip on the Mediterranean with her and her friends. She was surrounded by a huge group of them—laughing and joking—and you would never be able to spot the one most likely to die first. They enjoyed a tea party on the high seas, fundraisers for the local animal rescue, lunches, dinners and – her favorite – breakfasts, as if, this time, the time really was running out.
    I spent the New Year of her last year with her and her family in their mountain home. It was a special time. Not quite as rambunctious as the previous year, truly more poignant; as if we knew, she knew, that the cancer was taking over and likely to soon win the race. Or, at least, before the next New Year. She had more achy bits, though she never complained. She was a bit more tired, a little less energetic; but if you didn't know her well you wouldn't know that. I enjoyed the slower pace with her. It was so relaxing

to sit by the fire, her hearth beautifully decorated and her tree sparkly with white lights. We'd drink some nice wine and watch a film or a football match. She was content. 'Oh, sis it's all about the quality,' she'd say, when talking about her life. 'Cos we know I ain't gonna get the quantity!' And she'd laugh, as she always did, and made it easier on everyone around her.

Working on some of her story – and our story – has been very therapeutic for me. It is delightful to dig back into the blog, some of her writings, letters, photos. I am pulling out the memories from the coffers and feasting on them. I'm hearing her voice that I miss so much, all over again.

Enjoy the journey, just as Rosie did, until she closed her eyes for the last time, (even though she shared big plans for her after life before she left!) Make the best of your lot with whatever hand you have been dealt.

Instead of saying, 'why me', it's as Bud used to say – 'Why not me?'

Everybody Grieves

When I entered the doors of the group grief counseling session, I could not believe what a popular place it was on a chilly, dark Thursday evening. The room was full-to-capacity. Gosh, look at all those people feeling the way I am! That was one of my first thoughts. Then my mouth went dry, and I was not sure that I would be able to talk to complete strangers about how I was feeling. What would they care about my sister, how much I miss her and how the world is way too quiet without her? How am I feeling anyway? I'm not bawling all the time; or failing to function. I'm going to work again, sleeping better, sometimes. I can even raise a smile. I'm a phony. I don't need counseling. All these thoughts cascaded through my mind, as I sat with the group of fellow-grievers and waited for the mediator. I thought I should maybe just get up and leave, but I didn't allow myself to do that. I had made the drive and exercised the courage to walk through the door into the unknown – I would give it a go.

As the mediator went around the room and asked the folks why they were here, or what was going on in their lives, I realized that, for some, this was a life club. They had been coming for years and would likely keep coming for several more. What they had gained from their grief club helped them to the extent it had become a regular event on their calendar. They came to see friends; a safe place to be among birds of the same feather. I came to understand just how many types of grief there are and how normal I was to suffer the loss of my sister so badly I felt I needed a little help.

Joe next to me had lost his wife in March. He felt as if the joy had been sucked out of every day of his life. He cried through much of his testimony. Some days the only reason he would get up would be for his two dogs. "Yes, exactly!" said the mediator. "Your dogs need you to get up for them and so you will. This is progress, this is a path to healing." Maria had lost her baby at 4 months. She got pregnant again very quickly after the loss and her in-laws, and her husband to a certain extent, felt that the new baby should be fair compensation for the one that died. She was still reeling from the loss and attending grief counseling by herself, estranged from her in-laws and struggling to communicate with her husband. Our mediator gave her permission to grieve as much as she wanted for the lost life, her hopes for the little girl, her sense of hopelessness and isolation. Joanna was the caregiver for her father who suffered with dementia. She was grieving the loss of the man she knew and loved, while he was still technically alive – a different type of grief, but equally numbing.

I am familiar with the lonely aspect of grief. Though loved ones try; they really can't help you much, except to be there when you want them and talk to you when you are able. They have their own grief to juggle, their own sense of loss and isolation and helplessness. I certainly know that is the case with my husband. He fails to understand my anger at the world, my feeling of failure that I couldn't save her; that love alone couldn't save her. He struggles with my lack of joy; when I have much to be joyous over.

"It's a slow process," the mediator said. "You must be patient and kind with yourselves. You will never get over your loss; because that is not what happens. But, in time, you will learn to live with the loss and live the best life you can. Because you loved deeply, your loss is great–no way around it–but you can help yourself navigate through the waters of grief, by sharing with others who are dealing with heart ache themselves. The act of sharing is cathartic in itself."

I came out of the lit room into the dark parking lot and felt my progress go backwards a little. Dark streets, dark thoughts, dark places. But I perked up when I got home, and my husband agreed to come with me the next time. It would, perhaps, be interesting for him too and maybe he would learn how to better handle me on my journey.

We are not much good at this grieving thing, I've noticed. After the closing ceremonies of our loved one's life, we expect ourselves to get back on the horse and ride off into the sunset, get on with our lives, function properly. My expectations of myself have lessened royally since I crashed into a crumpled mess after Rosie's Celebration of Life and suffered days when I couldn't stop crying, days when I felt so horribly saddened, I couldn't stand to have my eyes open; nights when I was sleepless and furious, raging at the universe. I am out of my burrow now, cautiously, like a nervous rabbit — still fragile and numb and fractured — but not crying all the time or hating the world. At least, not all the time.

For any of you like me out there, I do recommend the counseling gig — whether individual or in a group setting, or both. Writing things down is also helpful. I shall, likely, be going to counseling for a while and writing things down a lot.

I shall not pass this way again

I shall not pass this way again. I expect to pass through this world but once; any good thing therefore that I can do, or any kindness that I can show to any fellow-creature, let me do it now; let me not defer or neglect it, for I shall not pass this way again.
Stephen Grellet (1773-1855)

None of us know what happens when we pass on to another place or planet. That is one of the largest mysteries of this universe. I always thought that my baby sister of all people would have the ability to come back and tell me what happens when your earthly eyes close for the last time and your heart stops beating; but since I see her these days in other entities like dragon flies and butterflies, and catch a whiff of her essence on the air and as a shadowy reflection in the water; I'm sure her current state of 'being' is not able to communicate with me in that way. She can definitely 'reach' me, but not in the same way. She is often just around the corner from where I am; but I have come to accept that she is no longer of this world. For whatever it's worth to the world at large, that is what I have surmised thus far. I am still working on my acceptance of the fact.

There's something about a nasty illness that gives you a sense of haste and purpose portrayed in the above quote; even more so if your disease is terminal. Rosie rushed her way through the last years of her life with absolute purpose. She would try new things – pottery, screen printing, you name it—to keep her creative juices going. But once it started to be less than an obsession for her, it was instantly dropped. She had no time to waste in this world. But, come to think of it, she was like that her whole life. It was as if, when she was born, she had a second sense that her time on earth would be limited; so, she had better get going and make the best of it. 'Better crack on," she would fondly say with a sparkle in the eye.

But isn't that a good way to live? Live as if you are dying, soon, which of course we all are. We'll never have enough time.

Don't waste the precious time you do have, bemoaning your lot with your eyes turned inward. Strive to be happy every day and make others equally so; whether man or beast. This time of year, especially, there is a lot of lip service paid to doing good for others and then there are the people that actually do the good for others, (and they mostly do it quietly). Look around you! Little free-food pantries are nicely stocked in town for those that need it. Even book and toy stations are set up. Churches establish food drives. No one judges – take what you need, be happy it is there, pay it forward when you can. Help your neighbor! Do they have small children to feed and a reduced means to do so? Could you make them a pot of posole or bake a chicken? That might be an enormous thing to a family in need. Please be kind to your planet. Recycle where you can, water the plants and the trees, feed the birds, save the bees. Rescue the animals! There is so much to do if you turn your outlook in the correct direction. You are passing through only the one time. Make it count.

 If I was a religious gal, I would hope that, once I close my eyes for the last time, every single one of my beloved pets would be able to greet me at the pearly gates–or, in my case, more likely, the rusty old iron ranch gate–with lots of barks, meows, neighs and more at our reconciliation party and they would be as happy to see me again as I would them. My life's work has been dedicated to them; they inspire me every day to try and be more how they see me.

 I still rescue other lives where I can. I will trap, alter and release. I'll always pick up a stray dog in the street, or help fund a surgery, or do what I can to make a small difference in the larger scheme of things. I'm not tooting my own horn; I'm just sharing what I do to make my journey through more significant. If we all do small things with big hearts, what a wonderful place this would be!

 The years 2021-2021 have been so taxing for so many people on multiple levels. Thousands in the world have passed from a horrid disease, families have been torn apart, there are missing place settings at tables across the planet. Others have been unable to work, or their work has gone away. They are afraid they might lose their home, be forced to move their family. They fear that their children will be hungry, that they will fail in their schooling. So much uncertainty, too much anxiety and a lack of clarity and direction pervades. These are unprecedented times. We must bond together as human beings and look out for one another, ease each other's journeys, be kinder than necessary. If we cannot do that, then what really are we good for?

A dear friend of mine is suffering a wretched disease, when she should be enjoying her friends and family during her well-earned retirement. She is not one of the complainers of the world. 'I will give life my all until my last breath,' she tells me. 'Lots to do.' And she's right. There is lots to do, while we are still here. Thank you, Ellen, for reminding me of that simple fact. Let's give our lives our all, while we can. Our passage is never guaranteed to be a long one; the pathway seldom a smooth ride.

Ellen, my brave friend Ellen, this story is dedicated to you.

Sisters

Bud, Lucy, Mary in Aldeburgh

We were always the slices of bread, separated by her jam filling. She was the youngest, the naughtiest, the most demanding of the family's attention. There wasn't much more than a year between the youngest and the middle, so it always felt as if there were the 3 of us, with the youngest being the most high-maintenance child. That was the dynamic we grew up with and became accustomed to.

The baby sister's various surgeries to fix her congenital hip as a youngster was just the prelude to all that would come in adulthood. From age 32 on, until her death at 48, the Bud would be the first to say it was always all about Rosie. She would laugh about it; but we all knew it was true. We would travel from wherever the rest of us lived on the planet to where Rosie's home was in Turkey; as you do when a family member has a nasty disease from which she will likely die in the reasonably near future.

Dad's birthday would be celebrated with all of us together in Turkey. It was always the last summer, the last birthday, as the middle sister noted a little wryly while baby sister was alive, 'The Longest Goodbye,' as it can be when you are continuing to live with Stage 4 cancer and enjoying the benefits of life extensions through developments in medical research. As the youngest proudly observed, on more than one occasion, 'I am a miracle of science!'

And then there was nothing more they could do for her; her liver was shot, and the miracle of science began to fade. I could feel that the family dynamic was about to dramatically alter. I warned our dad that our family unit was about to become fractured; that we had lived 48 years with that demanding, sparky little spitfire and how were we going to manage without her now.

A few days after she died, I wrote to my middle sister, that, from now on, I would try and be a better sister. For so long it had always been about the youngest, and she and I lived in the wake of that larger-than-large personality and all her issues. I wondered what we would find to talk about, whether the years of not paying much attention to each other would have permanently damaged our sisterhood. We had not visited each other's homes in years, we knew not much about the other's lives. Without anything conscious, we had somehow managed to bypass one another, because of our commitment to our ill sister. She was the filling to our bread. And then our plates shifted.

They say that about a terrible illness in the family; that it can absorb the other family members, so they become almost unimportant in the larger scheme of things. In their efforts to save and support the life of the one sibling in need, they are near invisible. And it's true; it happens by default. And then the high maintenance child is gone and the other two start emerging cautiously from the shadows. Grief can be the great separator; I've found in the past. But this time it was different. I admitted to middle sister that I had crashed badly after baby sister's death - truthfully, suffered something of a breakdown - and this was the beginning of us finding our way back to each other. Though our reactions were different, our feelings of loss were similar. We had to learn to move on with our lives, always remembering that sparky little naughty pistol, but still living and carrying on and doing our best to be happy.

And then Middle Sister decided to come and stay for a week at my house – she hadn't visited in several years. We had such a lovely time together, discounting the clumsy falls each one of us had - me in Monterey and her in the vineyard! We stayed in nice hotels, ate delicious food, swam, played with puppies. It was a super special time, and we didn't want it to end. Next, I shall take father over to her home for Christmas. I haven't been there since her wedding several years ago; I haven't been in England over the holiday season for ions either. So, lots of positive things have come out of our youngest sister's death, as she would certainly have hoped and anticipated. This week we celebrate our birthdays – exactly 5 years apart – and I'm so glad that we have been able to reconnect without the jam in the middle.

Families are certainly a work in progress, as are most relationships; but I have a feeling that ours is going to be fine. Though we will always miss our naughty little sister and things in our world are certainly quieter without her, it is good to share the memories and the photos and keep her alive in that way.

The Fabrics of Memory

It was the 1960's in England. The country was still recovering after the war and things were used and re-used; almost until they turned to dust. Looking back, it was a time of great thriftiness and creativity. Hand-me down clothing was standard in every household, as was a sewing machine and knitting needles. The wool shop on the high street was a popular place to stop and chat. Though it was tiny, it was ceiling to floor with perfectly wound bundles of yarn and different kinds of needles. My grandma was a compulsive knitter, as was my Mum. Our early dolls were handmade, as were our hats, gloves, scarves, sweaters and even the odd knitted dress. Many of my early dresses were your classic hand-sewn 60's cotton shift style with bold stripes or floral prints that were then passed down to my younger sisters when I bulged out of them or started to show my undies. Nowadays, a person is considered an artisan craftsman if they make their own clothing. Back then, it was normal life. The past is another world – they do things differently there.

Early in the 70's, my mother discovered the delights of patchworking. Ever thrifty, she had multitudes of pieces of material left over from all her dressmaking endeavors and never could bear to throw anything away. She had hexagon paper templates that she would use to craft the patches, so that they were more-or-less uniform, and then sew them together. Television was quite the novelty at the time, and I remember her half-watching something and sewing at the same time of an evening. She made herself a multi-colored patchwork skirt, an enormous quilt for her bed and patchwork pillowcases for everyone. My sisters and I had our names embroidered on them. I have 3 that have traveled the world with me and survived the passages of time and ravages of change; now a bit ragged and holy, but still mostly intact. I couldn't think how to preserve them. Some would be of the mindset that old and broken things should be part of a household sweep when they have outrun their use. I am more of a historic preservation type gal. These scraps of fabric were part of the precious memories of my youth, and I could not part with them.

Talking to my cousin Caroline – herself a great craftsperson throughout her life – we talked about the fabrics of memory and how they could be just as powerful as photos or music. I told her of my dilemma with the patchwork cushion covers and she offered to put them on the pile of her many creative projects that she would work on over time. That made me feel so much better. I dug out the incredible silk peacock dress that she had custom-made for my mother likely 50 years ago and sent it back to her. As the creator of that work of art, she should have the pleasure of deciding how to best enjoy it. I had schlepped it around the world for at least two decades now, without a clue how to showcase it as it deserved. It gave me so much satisfaction to package up the peacock and the old patchwork covers and return the peacock to the original creator and the covers to a place where they could be restored or reinvented in some way. I knew she'd do them proud, when she was able. Her son was recently married. She worked long and hard on a memory quilt for him and his bride; a work of art steeped in love and family history.

And that is why I have such a hard time throwing away old treasures. My old green candlesticks belonged to my grandmother. To another's eyes, they might be considered ugly. Certainly, they are worth nothing; but she was something. I have old shirts that belonged to mother and scarves that were my sister's. Memory fabrics of any kind are hard to part with, but especially when they were crafted with so much love. That was the dress I wore in 1974 at our school dance, that was the one she made for Mary and, at the time, I wanted in my size. It had cheerful bunnies on it. That one adorned the back of our younger sister and I think the fabric may have come from France. I also remember the dress Rosie was wearing when we got the news that our grandpa had been killed in a car crash. I was 9. How on earth would the memory be able to dig so deeply and recall and immortalize such moments in time?

I imagine, when I am gone, my kids will look at all these antiquated bits of blanket and fabric and pour them all into a dumpster along with most of my other crud. Maybe they will keep the odd story I wrote or a nice photograph I captured; but memory fabric? That will likely disappear, as memories do fade and dissolve from one generation to the next. Ashes to ashes, dust to dust. I shall do my best to share the story of the ugly green candlesticks, or the patchwork pillow cases with whoever will listen; but I hold out little hope for their longevity.

    I wonder what my creative cousin Caroline will do with my scraps of memory fabric. Maybe she will inspire me to do something fabulous with the other nostalgic pieces in my collection. Years ago, my youngest sister made me a sheer silk dress in her screen-printing class. I knew at the time that I could never wear the dress. Now it is a lit wall-hanging that I like very much. The dress was repurposed to art.

    If, like me, you are a sentimental creature and struggle with discarding any slices of memorabilia, be it old t-shirts, green candlesticks or memory fabric, try to keep only what you love-love and repurpose what you can't discard at the present time. Then know that the next generation will likely dumpster much of what you leave behind for them and you must be okay with that.

The past is a foreign country; they do things differently there.
L.P. Hartley

My Water Song

Lucy Mason Jensen

I see her
In the water.
The water's where I see.
The mermaids and the memories...
The water's where I see.

I see the sparkle on the water,
The glitter on the sea.
I hear the laughter,
Taste the salt,
Long for more time in the sea.

I see sunshine on the sea,
A brown-grey slap of waves upon the stones.
I've wished for more time in that sea
with her
And her before.

I see them in my water
While in my water muse.
If spirits are there for the seeing,
The water's where I see.

Lu

After the end —

WORDS OF SADNESS, MEMORY, GRIEF, LOVE AND SOLACE...

(And no matter what she said,
it was not always about Rosie!)

I created this place, at the end of my book, as a forum for grief and love — because the two cannot be separated; a place where we could gather from all over the planet and share our feelings about our own losses, our empty spaces at the table, our shared angers, our lovely memories, our loves and more.

Thank you, all, for showing up to the buffet.

Lu

Rosie always loved butterflies ... "Yeah, but they live for such a short time!" I told her. "They do," she replied. "That's why the quality is always much more important than the quantity." She used that line a lot during her short 48 years on this planet. As I was surrounded this morning by white butterflies everywhere I went, all flibber-gittering around, dizzy with the quality of perhaps what was going to be their last day on the planet, I was reminded of our butterfly discussion and how much we used to laugh together, sometimes until we were dizzy, just like butterflies.

Lu and Bud

"I guess once the tears come for a loved one, they become like a geyser collecting all the mourning inside."

Jeanne

"You added a different color to our life. We love you so much. It's good that you were with us. You were our butterfly."

Dilgesu

Zehnep, Dilgesu, Bud and Ali in Instanbul

"I understand John. We are in the same situation. I lost my daughter first and then my wife. You lost your wife and then your daughter. We are the same."

Ali

From: 'My mate Jan'
    I first met Rosie when I attended a talk at the Kybele Hotel in Adrasan, Turkey on the forthcoming solar eclipse. This was in 2006. Lovely lady, I thought, but we had very little in common. For one thing, I was almost 20 years older, and our lives had taken very different paths. It did not enter my head that we would become as close as we did.
    It was almost a year later when, after a party, a friend of ours had an accident. The police called Rosie, as her Turkish was excellent, and Rosie called me as I was very close to this friend. We spent the next few days in emergency departments, ambulances and hospitals. Over this time, I realized we did have a lot in

common and I warmed to the caring person she was. She also had a wicked sense of humour and we seemed to bounce off each other.

For a very intelligent person, she could be quite dippy; like the time we were driving to Kumluca (to watch the mud wrestling) and smoke started to pour out from the engine. 'Have you put any water in lately?' I asked. The blank look she gave me told me she had not. Our shopping trips were always eventful, going into town to purchase sunbeds for the hotel and coming back with a gorgeous beagle called Bella is just one that springs to mind! Then, there was the time she won the local ladies swimming contest and was awarded various random items, most of which we lost on the bar crawl we did around the bay.

Rosie was nearly always the first to call me when I arrived back in Adrasan and, in her normal infectious and enthusiastic way, it would be 'when are we meeting up? When are we going for breakfast? (her favourite meal of the day) When are we doing a boat trip..... all delivered at 100 miles per hour.

Rosie loved new ventures promoting, in my opinion, the awful fruit/veg Pepinos with Grass Ali. Then, there was the time she was selling above ground swimming pools with German Ali .....not particularly successful, if I remember correctly! I don't think she would have for one minute described herself as the perfect hotel landlady, but, my goodness, what fun we had at the Kybele!

Rosie's real forte was in teaching, which she excelled at, and once she opened the school in Kumluca, she really came into her own! In fact, as she was fond of saying, she had 'got her shit together'.

To sum up this lengthy rambling, to say I truly loved Rosie is no exaggeration. I know people say it all the time now, but I really did. She was not just a friend she was a phenomenon, an inspiration and one of the bravest people I have ever been fortunate to know.

I often referred to her as my friend 'Sick Note' and I am proud to say that to her I was 'my mate Jan'.

From Katie

We must have met in the summer of 2007 when I moved to Turkey for the summer. It wasn't my life plan to stay here, I was 19 and wanting a summer of fun....that was 14 years ago and I'm still here! Rosie sure made it a whole lot easier to stay.

Too many stories, so many laughs and memories I will treasure forever. I gained a sister when I met Rosie. She took me under her wing. I moved into Kybele with her. I was the bar girl ... not that we really needed one as it was self-service, help yourself really lol. Rosie was generally laying around the pool on a bean bag. Kybele was our home. It's a very special place. We had so much fun, drinking and dancing til the morning, laughing until our bellies hurt.

Rosie then started to become a bit more serious .. she fell in love with Ali and life was changing. It was time for us both outgrow Adrasan and move on. That's when Vizyon was born – Rosie's baby, our language school. Just as everything was going amazing .. the f in cancer came back. But obviously that didn't stop Rosie. It never would.

I can't tell you my favorite memory with Rosie, we really had too many. Rosie helped me through some of my worst days, she was by my side through my best days. We were always there for each other. Always will be. We laughed (a lot), cried and grew together. I'm so pleased that Rosie met my first born Ece Mira. I felt that Rosie felt she could leave now she knew I had my baby girl in my life and I'm sure she's looking over us and also loves Tedi Can too. Just like we all do her.

Rosie taught me to do more than enjoy life, live it to the fullest. You really only get one chance, so no matter how long you have, live life how you want. You only get one. She and I spoke of the family life she found with Dilgesu and Ali and how they taught her how to love.

Katie

The Rose Bud & Her Brilliant Adventures

Katie and Rosie

From Gill—Rosie was the sister Katie never had. She made Katie the person she is today. Rosie will always reflect through her eyes.

From Captain Hasan — Rosie was one of the nicest people I ever met — my friend of over 20 years.

From Sue — I'm so happy that Rosie met Ali. I remember the first time she taught him as a student — she came home with that 'look' on her face ... and, from that moment, he probably didn't realize it, but his future was written ...

From Jaynne:-

There are certain beings whom one meets in life where it is instantly palpable that they are Angels on this earth. The warmth that washes over you from their smile and laugh, the light shining from their eyes, the instant feeling of relaxation and comfort one feels when in their presence. Rosie was one such Angel. I will always remember the first time I met her, she was sitting on the bottom of the stairs at number 22, a house I will always have the fondest memories of, and she greeted me as if she'd known me all my life. Like she was happy to see me again, even though we'd only just met. As someone who struggles with shyness and feelings of being an outsider, I was so grateful for her, making me feel at ease and welcome. It was quite something and as I say has been imprinted in my memory because of it!

The warmth and relaxation she brought out in others was astonishing too. I loved seeing John so happy and enamoured, and Rosie's unending, beautiful love for her father. Seeing Lucy's soul just beam with pride and joy, sitting next to her Rosebud on the sofa. Experiencing Mary's light-hearted side as she swapped secret jokes and giggles with her little sister. The whole house's atmosphere changed when Rosie came to visit, every room she was in seemed to bubble with life and laughter, enticing me in whenever I was to walk past. She loved my dogs, and oh my, did they love her. Suki, my little girl, took pride of place on Rosie's knee and no amount of coaxing was going to get her to leave it! They were a force, the two of them together. Suki knew she was in the presence of another special being, one sent to earth to change so many lives.

They say the brightest flames burn out the fastest. With Rosie and Suki perhaps this was true. Those of us who are still on this earth missing them know just how lucky we were to have shared in their time here. How lucky we were to have known such love and experienced and learnt from their inspirational qualities. We carry them in our hearts always, sometimes in our grief at their passing, but mostly while feeling so lucky and blessed that we were able to call them our friends.

Keep sparkling up there in the sunlight, dear Rosie and Suki! We love you!

Rosie and Suki at number 22.

Rosie

One day in the grocery shop I met an older man who owned the big peach-coloured house opposite me. In front of his house was his most beautiful garden filled with many flowers including a multitude of red and pink roses. He had a green thumb for tending this garden with much devotion, coupled with admiration for the beauty each of the flowering plants.

Over the course of time in getting to know him I heard about his daughter in Turkey where I was working several times a year. Perhaps because of having Turkey in common with his daughter, I was introduced to her on one of her regular visits to London.

This was Rosie.

Her father John loved her dearly as he loved his other two daughters.

There was a problem though—

Rosie was having chemotherapy for her cancer.

I visited Rosie and John over the course of Rosie's chemotherapy. During this time, she fought to decorate pottery while sometimes being forced to take a brief nap on the couch. Each time we met Rosie engaged in lively conversations about her friends, food, her language school, her interest in art and our common interest in children.

When Rosie left London, having completed her cancer treatment, I repeatedly said to her father, John, that she was an inspiration to anyone who might get ill. She kept very connected with her friends in the UK. She also persisted with her artistic interests. The chemo effects were always subordinated to her excitement in being with her father and friends. I somehow felt more energised and appreciative of life, after returning home from my visits with her.

Some years later I too had cancer. I continually repeated to her father that Rosie was my model for surviving the unpleasant experience of having drugs, chemo, hair and weight loss. I tried to emulate her by appreciating each moment with my sisters and friends who visited with me.

I resisted any interest in having more than a few minutes of discussion regarding the pain and agony of having a life-threatening illness.

When I look at this flower from Rosie's father's garden I always think how his love for Rosie gave her inspiration to live every second of her life with joy and vigour, while down-playing the pain she experienced (even on her wedding day) and the nearness of her death.

I believe it is Rosie›s pleasure in people and life that inspires me to be grateful for every day I continue to live.

Jeanne
PS Rosie's father's rose reminding me of her:

The Rosie Rose

Dear Auntie Rowie,

Ever since I was a little girl, I always told my mom I want to be just like you. We are in Kybele, sunburnt after a day of going to markets and eating ice cream, sitting by the pool eating amazing food and laughing together. I remember you always went out to go enjoy the night life, after everyone went to sleep. You loved life and were always surrounded by people who loved you.

Dear Rowie, I still say I want to be just like you. You gave me my first bear, you gave me my forever nickname, you gave me the want to love life. You are the strongest, most beautiful soul. We are sitting at my favorite restaurant in the world called Paradise in Adrasan, eating chocolate ice cream and watching the ducks swim past. Now you're forever in paradise, Auntie Rowie and I will always miss you and love you, but I know you will forever be by my side.

I still want to be just like my Auntie Rowie; the most beautiful soul everyone was blessed to meet.

Your,
Frouie

Bud and Frou

Frouie and Rowie in Paradise, Adrasan

Frowie n Rowie at the Rixos in Antalya

Rosie ....
    I found myself standing behind the Imam as he began to sing the prayers.
    The beautiful melody resonating around and out across the mountains.
    I was struck by the way the men worked tirelessly, lovingly laying her to rest.
    The Imam's little cap crowning his head, beautiful green turquoise, brought her image clearly to me,
    I saw her in her mermaid outfit smiling.
    The beautiful loving laying to rest of our gorgeous friend was fit for a Princess.

The Rose Bud & Her Brilliant Adventures

Ella

Our mermaid

From Bella:

Rosie was an important influence in my young life. I adored her. We learned to push the boundaries. (As Charla interjected ... 'during our trips to Aldeburgh, all the boundaries were broken.....')

From Dad, at Rosie's Celebration of Life – October 5, 2018 -

'The day Rosie was born, she had a scrunched-up face with furious, flashing eyes. Una and I thought she slept with one eye open. She was very lively from a very young age. At about 18 months, she was diagnosed with a congenital hip disorder. A local chap Fred built a trolley for her, and she spent several months on her stomach. She would play with water for hours on her stomach in the backyard with no fuss. A promise of everything to come.

Rosie was artistically very gifted and attended the Central School of Art. This lasted only a short period of time. She then went to Aberwstwyth University where she studied English. She finished university and decided she wanted to become a teacher. Then she got her certification to teach English as a foreign language. She lived in France for a while and then returned to teach at an Inner-City school in London. She bought a flat in Stoke Newington close to many of her old friends. It was a very Turkish neighbourhood and she went into a travel agent one day and asked where she could go in Turkey that was lovely and unspoiled – also where she wouldn't be bothered. She went to Adrasan on holiday where she met Sue. She landed a job in Istanbul and started to seriously learn Turkish. She spent a while traveling back and forth to Turkey and had all sorts of adventures running the hotel Kybele. Her future husband Ali met her in front of the vet's office. He wanted to take the English course she was offering – at least that was his story and that was the beginning of the happiest period in Rosie's life.

"I remember it as if it were yesterday," chimed Ali.

Dad and Bud in Regent's Park Café.

The opening of the school Vizion in Kumluca with Katie was one of her greatest adventures. My girls all know how to organize people and work. She was a very good teacher indeed.

Increasingly she was very caring and enriched other people's lives, especially in the last 20 years of her life. She was a very loving daughter to me and made every effort to come and see me. She even came in the May before she died for my birthday. That was the last time we were all together.

Dad

Mourner's kaddish

When I die give what's left of me away
To children and old men that wait to die.
And if you need to cry,
Cry for your brother walking the street beside you.
And when you need me, put your arms around anyone
And give them what you need to give me.

I want to leave you something,
Something better than words or sounds.

Look for me in the people I've known or loved,
And if you cannot give me away,
At least let me live in your eyes and not in your mind.

You can love me best by letting hands touch hands,
And by letting go of children that need to be free.
Love doesn't die, people do.
So, when all that's left of me is love,
Give me away.

    Rosie, you inspire me not to sweat the small stuff, to make the best of every day, and to try to leave this world with something akin to the grace with which you did, my affairs in order and loved ones taken care of in every which way possible. If there is an afterlife, you will be filling it with love and laughter, the way you did this earthly life. No wonder you were so adored.

Kate
XXX

A Haiku for Rosie and Lucy
Lucy's sister Bud
Adventures among stars now
Always shining bright

XX
Carey

    Rest easy, my beautiful, brave friend. You have been and will continue to be such an inspiration to so many and have showed us all how to live life to the fullest. My life has been richer for your presence and I'm truly proud to have been able to call you my friend.
    Fly high, Rorabud. I will miss you forever, but you will always be with me in my heart – love you girl.
Sue

I miss her wise words, her friendship and companionship. We did a lot of random things together. Towards the end she said to me one day. 'You are a good friend, Ella.' It was nice she said it, she was also a good friend in every way to me in whatever way she could. I miss her organizing days out for us and our chats and her insights and our sharing time. She was part of my every day. But I do feel her around ...

Ella

Birgie, Sue and Bud on the Nihalim

We've had so much fun in the 14 years I've had the pleasure of knowing you. I remember the maid at Kybele fishing my underwear out of the pool at breakfast after my friends and I had gone skinny dipping the night before. All the nights we spent singing and laughing and playing 'The Moon is a Balloon' at Street Café. The bonfire parties we had on the beach and everything else besides. Right up to my last visit to Turkey in June when we shared 'High Tea on the Sea'. I will miss you and I'll never forget you.

Keri

She left us this morning, quietly and peacefully, but the impact of her indomitable spirit remains with us permanently. I'm so grateful for the time we had her here, grateful that I knew her. She belongs to the universe now.

Melissa

Our dear cousin Rosie made the world a sparkly and wonderful place. I have many memories from the last fifty years, but most of all, her smile and laughter in the face of pretty much anything that was thrown at her – a lesson for us all to live life to the max whatever the situation. We will always remember her with love 'til we meet again.

Caroline

My gorgeous brave Bud passed away peacefully this morning after her long battle against the bastard big C. Keep drinking fizz as you fly high over the Himalayas, my very, very special friend. I'm going to miss you more than you'll ever know.

- Charla

Lucy Mason Jensen

Bud and Charl

Deep peace of the running wave to you.
Deep peace of the flowing air to you.
Deep peace of the quiet earth to you.
Deep peace of the shining stars to you.
Deep peace of the infinite peace to you.
(A Celtic Blessing)

Ella

    Grief never ends, but it changes. It's a passage, not a place to stay. Grief is not a sign of weakness, nor a lack of faith. It is the price of love.

Unknown

    Grief, I've learned, is really just love. It's all the love you want to give but cannot. All that unspent love gathers up in the corners of your eyes, the lump in your throat, and in that hollow part of your chest. Grief is just love with no place to go.

Jamie Anderson

Here is the deepest secret nobody knows
(here is the root of the root and the bud of the bud
And the sky of the sky of a tree called life; which grows
Higher than soul can hope or mind can hide)
and this is the wonder that's keeping the stars apart
i carry your heart with me (i carry it in my heart)

e.e. cummings
(Also Big Sis, me.)

    In 2015 I lost the most wonderful person in my life, my mother. When I was told that her cancer had advanced and left her only 6 months to live, I quickly became angry. Was the anger aimed at the doctor? The hospital? The almighty? I had no idea, but I knew that I was pissed off.
    Just one week later I received a message from my brother, who shared that I should come to the hospital right away. My mom only had a few hours to live. Making the one-hour drive gave

me time to vent and cry and get even angrier. I barely had a chance to get my head around the 6 months to live and now I'm told it's a matter of hours. What bullshit!

Shortly after my mom died, I decided to see a therapist. The young lady was quite helpful and gave me a suggestion I was not expecting. She asked that I try to schedule my grieving. Say what? I first thought this was a silly idea, but did give it a try that Saturday morning. Alone in my kitchen, I played her favorite music, Gary Puckett and the Union Gap, and read some of the letters she had sent me over the years. I relived some wonderful memories, shed a few tears, and then got on with my day.

Darin

When I got the phone call in the Fall of 2004 that my mother was in the hospital with some serious medical issues and they didn't know if she was going to even make it long enough for me to make the hour drive to the hospital to tell her goodbye, I fell to my knees on my kitchen floor and sobbed. I was told it was dire and they didn't know what was wrong with her, but her kidneys were not functioning right. I pulled myself together and arrived at the hospital to find out that the doctors were still assessing her condition but, long story short, she had a rare blood cancer and would hang on for about six months, mostly in ICU, trying to fight what I know now was a losing battle. I grieved for my mother while she was still living, because I felt so sad for her that she was stuck in the hospital while I was able to carry on with my life through those days and months. I could leave the hospital and stop and get a sandwich and enjoy it while she was on a feeding tube. I found myself feeling guilty if I enjoyed my food. To see a once vibrant woman lying there and both of us trying to put on a brave face was heartbreaking and I know she felt that too even though she was unable to speak and relied on writing on a wipe board to communicate. When she finally left us in the Spring of 2005, I grieved again but this time, it was for those of us she left behind. She was at peace which gave me some comfort, but she would never see her grandkids grow up, never meet her great grandkids, and never get the only two things she asked me for when she was so sick: To go to the beach and have a Coca Cola in the sun. Grief and regret are powerful emotions and they come in waves and sometimes, at very strange times and you don't even know what triggers them. Sometimes fleeting and a tear or two rolls down your cheeks. Other times, a more significant and overwhelming feeling that sticks around a bit longer and takes half a box of tissue to deal with.

Dana

Those we love don't go away
They walk beside us every day
Unseen, unheard but always near
Still loved, still missed and very dear ...
Our lovely Rosie, my beloved friend.

Almila

Pink October in Antalya with Rosie, Almila and some of the pink ladies.

Today the world lost an incredible woman, when our beautiful Rosebud lost her long and courageous battle to cancer. Despite not having seen Rosie in person for over 25 years, the magic of FB bought us back in touch in recent years. Rosebud, you were there for all my 'firsts' in those important, formative years – first cigarette, first proper snog, first alcoholic drink. Many, many happy years of memories in Aldeburgh are ingrained on my memory forever. Photo of you with your trilby on – loving life as always. You will continue to shine.

Bella Wakes-Miller

Charla, Bud (in trilby) and other South Hampstead High girls

Thank you, my friends.

Thank you to all who have stood by us as we stared into the abyss of our loss since our amazing son Barney was tragically and needlessly killed when he was a passenger in a car driven by a drunk driver. Barn we miss you so.

We have been desolate at times and at others we have sought and found compassion in friendships and acts of love that we treasure dearly. For these many random acts of kindness we express our gratitude and thanks.

It is hard to describe feelings that change day to day, from hour to hour, from second to second. A beautiful bronze statue called "Emptiness" by Albert György for me speaks words I cannot find.

Grief sometimes feels like an enormous weight that I carry. Pinning me down at a cellular level. A weight I feel compelled to try and flip back to what the world was before loss. Impossible I know, such are the delusions of grief.

At night, falling through the blanket of grief I now lie awake bouncing between vivid grief and worrying over trivial issues. I surface trying to recall intimate details of love and a life lost compounding my stress feeding anxiety about the day ahead, the week ahead and the whole goddam future. I feel exhausted-beyond belief. My heart physically aches from the contortions of grief. My chest is tight. I gasp for air and wait for daylight that is often hours away. I know that dawn will bring another day of trudging through tiredness searching for meaningful purpose. Running has become a salvation to untangle the rusty and mixed-up chain of grief I carry behind me. More often, then further seems to work for now till my legs give up. My boys have recently had to walk some distance to see if this works for them too. If the depth of grief is equal to the volume of our love, then this abyss is bottomless, holistic and eternal. For me there are no quick fixes and solutions. There is no sanctuary for suffering in some new-fangled concept of 'mindfulness' or hollow empty religious platitude. Belief is when people stop asking questions and I for one still have plenty of questions and soul searching to do. With this in mind, I thank you all for standing by me and my family as we look forward to the future with open hearts and open minds. We will not put this behind us, we will move forward with the wonder of Barney, the love we have for each other, with you, my friends. As you are more than good enough.

From my heart, with love and gratitude

Duncan

Duncan Wakes-Miller

And it was Bella, suffering deeply from the loss of her son, who turned me towards a most memorable examination of grief in Megan Devine's analysis 'It's OK that you're NOT OK'—a book that I have thumbed through many times....."

And that's the truth about grief: loss gets integrated, not overcome. However long it takes, your heart and your mind will carve out a new life amid this weirdly devastated landscape. Little by little, pain and love will find ways to coexist."

"How do we become, not only people, but a whole wider culture, comfortable bearing the reality that there is pain that can't be fixed? How do we become people who know that grief is best answered with companionship, not correction?"

"Finding that middle ground is the real work of grief — my work, and yours. Each of us, each one of us, has to find our way into that middle ground. A place that doesn't ask us to deny our grief and doesn't doom us forever. A place that honours the full breadth of grief, which is really the full breadth of love."

"Loss stuns us into a place beyond any language. No matter how carefully I craft my words, I cannot reach where this lives in you. Language is a cover for that annihilated stillness, and a poor one at that."

"Unacknowledged and unheard pain doesn't go away. One of the reasons our culture is so messed up around grief is that we've tried to erase pain before it's had its say. We've got an emotional backlog sitting in our hearts."

In her work, Megan gives more than a nod to the teachings of Buddhism. "Love with open hands, with an open heart, knowing that what is given to you will die. It will change. Love anyway. You will witness incredible pain in this life. Love anyway. Find a way to live here, beside that knowledge. Include that knowledge. Love through that. Be willing to not turn away from the pain of this world — pain in yourself or in others."

Lucy

Lucy, I have learned (and continue to learn) so much from the old, beautiful and brilliant Mason women. Rosie will be missed around the world. Thank you for sharing your little sister and her big heart and personality with us.

Rika

It is kind of shocking when your world falls to pieces and everything and everyone around you carries on with life. How can the birds continue to sing? How can people carry on loving life? It is like you have become frozen in time and are now watching life like a movie. As the weeks and months roll by, life becomes more real again, but you will never forget that point in time when life stood still.

Zoe Clark-Coates

When D died of lung cancer, I was initially relieved that his pain and suffering and the inevitable death as it had become was ended and life could return albeit different. I went manic, it was a huge realization that life is so short. I had never been that close to death before, so I embraced just being alive and staying alive and healthy for the sake of the boys.

It's the small things you miss, and I would find myself crying at odd times like shopping in the supermarket.

Shortly after D died, I had a dream that I was leaving the earth flying up into the air, through the clouds, the amazing blue, higher and higher seeing the ground below getting smaller and smaller. I could have kept going and just disappeared but suddenly I heard children's voices down below playing and laughing, my children calling me back and I knew I had to go back and face the pain for them, to keep them safe and be their mother, they needed me.

To this day, exactly twenty years after D died, I can't talk about his death without tearing up, not so much for me as I have gone on to live a fulfilling life, remarried to a man I love, but for the boys who lost their father at such a young age. They were only 8 and 11, it is such a huge loss to grow up without a parent, that is truly irreplaceable.

My other grief is for my sister who died at the same age as D, only 56, leaving her only son who was 13. Her death was very different; she had frontal lobe dementia. The disease is truly awful, a slow disintegration of the person, and the terrible wreckage that it creates for the surrounding family and friends. It is a long period of grief, many years of losing the person you love until there is so little personality left that it is a relief when it is finally over. It's only then that you can relax and remember and celebrate the wonderful whole person she was eight years before she died.

I went pretty manic again for a while. It's my way of avoiding painful feelings, and her death was another reminder of how short a time we have to experience this amazing gift of life.

Caroline

It all started in the playground at South Hampstead High School for girls. Bud was the 'too cool for skool' kid with dyed auburn hair and make-up and I was the squeaky clean, regulation school socks, new girl from out of town. Although I was scared of her to begin with, I soon realized that if I stuck by Bud, the cool bits might rub off on me.

I think we bonded over sandwiches. And so, our lifelong obsession with food and our special friendship started. Rosie's mum, Una, used to make these unbelievable creations that combined marmite, cheese, peanut butter, salad and mayo between 2 slices of bread; a mouth-gasm, taste sensation. My mum used to give me lunch money and I would nip early in the morning to Mr Ferrari's, a local Islington Italian deli and buy fresh sesame rolls and slather them with cream cheese and cucumber. So while Rosie tucked into her lunch, I was busy selling sandwiches from the playground. Not only could I sell them, but I learnt I could do swapsies for some of Una's amazing sarnies.

Other early foodie memories from our teenage years:-
- ❖ Pilling our plate high at the salad bar at Garfunkles at Swiss Cottage. We would go on a double date with our boyfriends and see who could get the most on their plate.

- ❖ skipping school and going for hot chocolate and raisin toast at The Coffee Cup in Hampstead
- ❖ ordering a bowl of Chinese barbecued pork over rice from Green Cottage on Finchley Road – so cheap, but oh so cheerful
- ❖ making toast at Eton Ave to sober us up after a night dancing at the Camden Palace on a school night.

And then as we grew up and our taste buds and wallet contents improved, so did our joy for cooking, sharing recipes, planning meals and eating at special restaurants. Her bucket list wasn't huge or overly extravagant but one of the things she wanted to do was dine at a 2 Michelin star restaurant – and we chose Restaurant Sat Bains.

We went with her sister Mary and my husband John and booked the Chef's Table in the middle of all the action. It cost a bloody arm and a leg, but Rosie was treated like royalty that evening. I had mentioned to the chef why this was such a special meal, and he served each dish to us personally, explaining the thought behind the menu. And when Bud had beaten the odds and was still with us a year later, she asked to return to Sat Bains – I told her we couldn't, as they had only rolled out the red carpet as she was supposed to be dead by now!

We did all our growing up together me and Bud. Lost our virginity at the same time and even shared a couple of boyfriends (I always had them first!!) Bought our first flats a road apart from each other. Became career women and learnt to send them new-fangled emails. Even drifted apart for a few years during the 'selfish years.' But she was my ol' mucker – the person who managed to find the beauty in such a shitty situation. And who I loved and will always love. Who wasn't dying from cancer but had learnt to live with it! And boy did she live.

Charla

JP and the Bud

Joanne Cacciatore, PhD, provides an unparalleled examination of grief in her book 'Bearing the Unbearable.' This marvelous exploration of the topic resonated so deeply with me that I felt moved to share some excerpts in this forum :-

WHEN A PERSON BELOVED BY US DIES, our lives can become unbearable. And yet we are asked – by life, by death – to bear it, to suffer the insufferable, to endure the unendurable. When we love deeply, we mourn deeply; extraordinary grief is an expression of extraordinary love. Grief and love mirror each other; one is not possible without the other. When death robs us, our mourning, our loss, resonates through time. We mourn for tomorrow's moments, and next month's moments and next year's moments. Grief consists of countless particles, countless moments, each one of which can be mourned. And through them all, we always know in our very cells that some one is missing, that there is a place in our hearts that can never be filled.

Early grief feels wild, primitive, nonlinear and crazed. It commands our assent and our attention; it uses up all the oxygen in the room; it erupts unpredictably. Our minds replay grief-related content in habitual cycles. It feels inescapable and lasts for much longer than other people, the nonbereaved, think it should. Like an open, bleeding wound it begs our tending.

"I am here," grief says. "Be careful with me. Stop. Pause. Stay with me."

Grief violates convention: it is raw, primal, seditious, chaotic, writhing, and most certainly uncivilized. Yet grief is an affirmation of human passion, and only those who are apathetic, who stonewall love, who eschew intimacy can escape grief's pull.....

We need to find within us the courage to slowly stretch and strengthen our grief-bearing muscles so that one day, we are better able to cope with grief's weight and, perhaps, one day, to help another.....

Find those who are willing to join you and walk with you nonjudgmentally. Steer clear of those who claim to have a cure for your grief.

Surround yourself instead with those who admit they have no answers but who will enter into the realm of unknowing with you.......

Listen deeply and you will recognize other citizens of the country of sorrow.....

So, too, it is with waves of grief: surrender to the wave. I entrusted myself to both the calm and raging motions of grief. I was patient with its unpredictability, patient with the bitter taste it left in my mouth, and in exchange, it was kinder to me. We became cautious comrades — and I found my way back home...

Ritual serves to honor the contents of our hearts, both the love and pain. Every society has rituals associated with death and grief. They serve the function of connection maintenance — helping us feel closer to our loved one who has died. Emotional expression revives a sense of control, helps us feel meaning, and underpins communal structures within which we are better able to cope with our losses....

When we cannot hold in our arms our loved ones who've died, we hold them in our hearts. This is being with grief.

when we have been too long in the absence of their song, we turn towards their whispers. This is surrendering to grief.

When we cannot look into their eyes, we tender their vision of compassion where it's most needed. This is doing with grief.

In every moment without them, we do all we can for others. This is compassion.

Nothing is more mysteriously central to becoming fully human than this process...

I went through a whole cascade of emotions and experienced more mood changes throughout the course of just one day than you would think possible, after my Bud left us for the universe beyond. I was irritable, lonely, raw, confused, destructive, sad, absent-minded, thoughtless, self-absorbed, sickly, sleepless, furious .....all wound up tightly in my ball of loss. I attended group and individual grief therapy; I mercilessly bashed the eardrums of my friends and my animals. And, if anyone even dared go there with the 'she'd been ill for such a long time,' or 'she's at peace now' ... they are likely still running for the border.

But the one thing that helped me move away from Grief, my constant companion, that wrapped herself around me for too long, was to start writing about Rosie. Initially, I wrote letters to her, asking that she show herself to me, let me know that she heard me from wherever she was out in the universe. Then, I started to gather up my grief stories and put them in some sort of order. I'd dig through old boxes looking for letters and emails from her that I had saved and tried to piece together the fragments that I had somehow stashed away from her amazing life. I scrolled through the gazillion photos I had taken over the past several years. Then, by the time I finally started to write Bud's story, my edges had slowly and quietly softened. I would catch myself laughing when I could hear her voice again. It was delicious to have her back in the room with me again. Writing gave me a vital tool to start to rebuild some of my brokenness and give the life and love to her memory that it deserved. I would schedule my writing, as some schedule their grief and it became an important part of my journey on. It may be that I never finish her story; perhaps the door will stay open for more of her stories, because

I have loved spending all this extra time with her in places you would never imagine. It is, as I would say, a work in progress. Like all of us.

Lu

June 2018, Cirale. Our last day together. Likely her last trip to the beach.

The last paragraph of Megan Devine's 'It's OK that you're not ok' discusses how to help a grieving friend. It's not a job that many of us are good at. We can do better. When we know better, we can do better:-

Love.

Above all, show your love. Show up. Say something. Do something. Be willing to stand beside the gaping hole that has opened in your friend's life, without flinching or turning away. Be willing to not have any answer. Listen. Be there. Be present. Be a friend. Be love. Love is the thing that lasts.

Acknowledgments

So many thanks go out to all my people who helped me piece together the bits of Rosie's story – you know who you are – and those who felt moved to contribute. I hope you felt as comforted by your contribution as me.

Enormous nods of appreciation, and thanks, must also go out to the writers whose work I referenced in my book: -

Joanne Cacciatore, PhD – (Bearing the Unbearable) – thank you for your grief masterpiece (If you love, you will grieve – and nothing is more mysteriously central to becoming fully human.) Your book will always be on my shelf.

Megan Devine, (It's OK that you're not OK) – oh my goodness, another grief masterpiece. Thank you, Bella, for pushing it my way.

David Kessler, (Finding Meaning: the sixth stage of grief)

Stephen Grellet, (I shall not pass this way again)

LP Hartley, (The Go-Between)

Jamie Anderson, (Grief is just love)

ee cummings, (I carry your heart) – this brings me such solace I have it imprinted on my bedroom wall.

Please forgive me if I missed anyone; it was never intended.

Love,

Lucy

Printed in Great Britain
by Amazon